Joyce Marlow was born and bred in working life as an actress before turn published works include *The Peter Martyrs, Mr and Mrs Gladstone, Captain Boycott* and *Uncrowned Queen of Ireland: A Life of Katie O'Shea* and *Kessie, Sarah, Anne* – a trilogy of novels set around the First World War. A book on women's suffrage will be published by Virago Press. Married with two sons, she lives in the High Peak district of Derbyshire.

The Virago Book of Women and The Great War

1914-18

Edited by

JOYCE MARLOW

A *Virago* Book

Published by Virago Press 1999
First published by Virago Press 1998

This collection and introduction copyright
©Joyce Marlow 1998

Acknowledgements on pp 393–400 constitute
an extension of this copyright page

The moral right of the author has been asserted

A CIP catalogue record for this book is available from
the British Library

ISBN 1 86049 559 1

Typeset in Caslon by M Rules
Printed in Great Britain by Clays Ltd
St Ives plc

Virago Press
A Division of
Little, Brown and Company (UK)
Brettenham House
Lancaster Place
London WC2E 7EN

For Janet and Tony

Contents

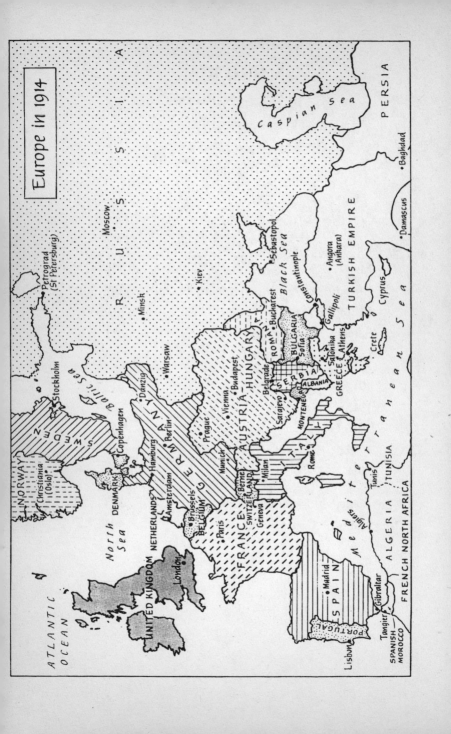

The Virago Book of
Women and
The Great War
1914–18

Introduction

Before the USA entered the conflict the American journalist Mabel Potter Daggett crossed the Atlantic to report on the female experience in war-torn Europe. The result was a book published under the imperishable title *Women Wanted: The Story Written in Blood Red Letters on the Horizon of the Great World War*. In it she said: 'I think we may write it down in history that on August 4, 1914, the door of the Doll's House opened – For the shot that was fired in Serbia summoned men to their most ancient occupation – and women to every other.' Since those lines were written, the material published about the First World War has been Amazonian in its breadth, depth and sheer volume but women's role in it has had a bumpy ride. As it was a generation of young men who were slaughtered in their millions in Flanders' and other shell-shocked fields, the mainstream has been written by and about them. If women are mentioned in these volumes they tend to figure as sweetly uncomprehending aunts, flighty flappers or bloodthirsty xenophobes, and to merit a few, not always complimentary, lines about their war work.

My early fascination with the Great War, as it was then known, was similarly male-dominated, fostered by my father who had served on the Western Front as a self-styled 'lance-private' of the Manchester Regiment. Having found an avid listener, he described his arrival in the lunar landscape of the Somme in mid-1916, how he once saw his commander-in-chief, Field Marshal Sir Douglas Haig, who 'looked very good on a horse', became 'lost' in Lincolnshire for much of 1917 (an area by then apparently awash with strays from every regiment in the British Army), returned to Flanders for the last months of bitter fighting on the Menin Road and celebrated his twenty-first birthday there in November 1918. My slightly younger mother rarely spoke of the war and the only women my father mentioned, albeit in glowing terms, were the nurses who tended him. It was not until the 1950s that I was given a copy of Vera Brittain's *Testament of Youth*, which stimulated an equal interest in my sex's involvement in what had by then become the First World War.

In her memoirs *A Woman at War* the army signaller Maude Onions remembered visiting a British war cemetery in France, where she stumbled over a broken piece of wood. 'It was the grave of a German soldier. Cautiously, afraid of being seen, I stooped and placed some flowers at the foot of the broken cross. Somewhere a woman was sorrowing.' It was to the valley of the shadow of death that millions were summoned. For every soldier killed, every sailor drowned, every airman shot down, at least one woman was left to grieve, and you could say this was their most ancient occupation. The experience of facing the future without a partner, of bringing up children alone, perforce made more women more independent and it altered the role-playing perceptions of many of the children.

Mabel Potter Daggett's comment about their being summoned to every other occupation is not far short of the mark. In 1917 a British government publication required *twenty-six* tightly printed foolscap pages to list 'Processes in which Women are successfully employed'. Apart from holding multifarious jobs in munition factories, the successfully employed women included brickmakers, tram and omnibus conductors and drivers, acetylene welders, letterpress-machine workers, newspaper subeditors,

2

chauffeuses, ticket inspectors, barrelmakers, carpenters, circular-saw feeders, railway porters, carriage cleaners, van drivers, optical-instrument makers, lift operators, hedgers and ditchers, stokers, coke barrowers, orchard gardeners, grooms, tanners and foresters. 'It's great to watch a grand old tree crash to the ground and to feel that you did it alone,' wrote a girl who joined the Women's Timber Corps. 'Life is just what I have always longed for.' There is no information about her apart from the name, Miss B. Bennett, but the prewar lot of working-class girls was limited, to say the least. Her life would probably have consisted of school, if she was lucky, until the age of fourteen followed by long hours in an ill-paid job, with maybe the occasional day trip to the seaside.

From financial necessity, more women were already 'gainfully employed' than is generally realised. The *War Cabinet Report on Women in Industry* shows that in 1914 the UK had a female population of 23.7 million, of whom 5.9 million were 'gainfully employed', though this included girls over the age of ten, 12.9 million were 'not occupied' (i.e. not out of the home) and 4.8 million were under the age of ten. The largest number of women, just over 2 million, worked in industry, mainly the textile and clothing trades, with the next highest figure, over 1.5 million, in domestic service. Without exception their wages were lower than men's and Mary Macarthur, known in her day as 'the Prime Minister of the Women's Trade Union Movement', declared: 'Women are badly paid and badly treated because they are not organised, and they are not organised because they are badly paid and badly treated.'

Middle- and upper-class women were mostly better treated, but many of their lives were circumscribed, too. Doing the London season, visiting country houses, 'lionising' the sights of Europe, may have been more interesting than blackleading grates, mopping floors or serving capricious customers, but it could be vapidly boring. Then, suddenly, unimaginable opportunities to make decisions, to stand on their own two feet, to travel

3

without a chaperon, were there to be seized by women of every class and creed. In July 1915 an affluent Englishwoman named Ethel M. Bilborough wrote in her diary:

> It seems to me that everyone who happens to be alive in such stirring epoch-making times, ought to write *something* of what is going on. Just think how interesting it would be to read years hence! when peace once more reigns supreme, and everything has settled down to its usual torpid routine of dullness (!) Terrible as it all is, I think I'd rather be living now than, say in early Victorian days! Now everyone is living and no mistake about it; there is no more playing at things, 'Life is real and life is earnest', and I doubt it will ever seem quite the same again as it did before the great European War.

Sharing the belief that life had become earnestly real, thousands of well-bred women volunteered as auxiliary nurses. In her auto-biography *The Silent Muse* the actress Tilla Durieux graphically describes the tasks they had to perform: 'The first time I attended an operation I nearly fainted when I was given a sawn off leg to put in a corner. It took all my strength to pull myself together, but I can still feel the weight of that leg in my hands today.'

Muriel St Clair Stobart had been out to South Africa during the Boer War and, partly as a result of that experience, in the 1912–13 Balkan War she formed the first of the women's convoy corps which gave succour to the sick and wounded before the often fatal journey to casualty clearing station or hospital.

Another British women's enterprise, the First Aid Nursing Yeomanry, self-defined as the 'First Anywheres' and soon popu-larly known as the 'Fannys', had its origins in the Sudan, when a wounded sergeant-major named Baker entertained a vision of a corps of lady riders galloping across the battlefield to scoop him to safety. In 1907 he put his dream into practice. The 1914 extract from Elsie Knocker's memoirs refers to this episode but the corps in fact quickly passed under female control. In 1912 they adopted a khaki uniform with split skirts that enabled them to ride astride, an equestrian position then considered suitable only for men, and by 1914 many Fannys were expert car drivers, if not owners. On the outbreak of war they immediately offered their services to their government but were as immediately turned down.

Patronising, sometimes contemptuous, rejection was the lot of other highly trained British women's units. Dr Elsie Inglis organised the Scottish Women's Hospitals which gave yeoman service in Belgium, Serbia, France, Salonika, Corsica, Russia and Romania, and became involved in two of the most terrible retreats of the war. On offering her services to the War Office in August 1914 Dr Inglis was famously dismissed with the words: 'My good lady, go home and sit still.' In his role as head of the British Red Cross, the renowned surgeon Sir Frederick Treves informed the redoubtable Muriel St Clair Stobart, of whose previous enterprises he must surely have heard, that there was no work fitted for women in the sphere of war.

Inevitably, as history is a continuum, my research included the prewar 'woman question'. The deeper I dug into crumbling newspaper clippings, out-of-print books and diaries long gathering dust, the more ridiculous seemed the claim, popular with some historians, that the pre-1914 feminist ferment was a waste of time and energy, the activists the rim of a dormant volcano that erupted solely due to the exigencies of the first industrialised total war, namely the need for women to replace the departed men. Had the minority not been preaching the gospel of equal rights and already shown what women could do, it seems to me unlikely that the majority would have been prepared to grasp the opportunities the Great War undoubtedly presented.

'Votes for Women' was the most clamorous, though by no means the only, prewar feminist cause. Twenty-six countries were affiliated to the International Woman Suffrage Alliance (IWSA) which produced a monthly newspaper entitled *Jus Suffragii*. That its editor, Mary Sheepshanks, managed to publish and distribute *Jus* from London throughout the war years, if not without difficulty as 1915 extracts show, seems to me little short of miraculous. It was while delving into copies of *Jus*, or *JS* as it was also known, that an interest in women of other countries was aroused and it struck me that hardly anything has been published about their similar yet contrasting wartime experiences. I have not attempted to cover all the belligerent nations but have concentrated on the women of Germany, France, Russia and latterly the USA, with brief extracts from a few others.

The nationalist, competitive element is another strand that has been ignored. In 1911 the South African author Olive Schreiner published *Women and Labour*, which became a feminist bible. In it, with considerable prescience, she wrote:

> If our European nations should continue in their present semi-civilised condition, which makes war possible, for a few generations longer, it is highly possible that as financiers, as managers of the commissariat department, as inspectors of provisions and clothing for the army, women will play a very leading part; and that the nation which is the first to employ its women may be placed at a vast advantage over its fellows in time of war.

In 1916, before setting off on her European assignment, Mabel Potter Daggett interviewed the German ambassador to the USA, Count Johann von Bernstorff, in New York. In *Women Wanted* she recalled the ambassador saying: '"In the ultimate analysis," he spoke slowly and impressively, "in the ultimate analysis," he repeated, "it is the nation with the best women that's going to win this war."' In the same year Chancellor Bethmann-Hollweg informed the Reichstag that Germany was failing to utilise its female workforce as effectively as Britain, and I have followed up the extent to which the major belligerent nations harnessed their women's efforts. From the start of the war Russia had female soldiers and later its women's 'Battalion of Death' but it may surprise some to learn that the only country that officially engaged women on large-scale active service was Britain.

The inclusion of women of other nations notwithstanding, the larger part of the material is British. This is not solely due to its being the work of my compatriots but has a validity in the context of First World War literature, the bulk of which was written by British authors. Indeed, latterday British revisionist historians, notably those intent on rehabilitating military reputations savaged by poets and novelists, have accused them of whinging about their Great War traumas in a manner, and to a degree, not indulged in by their European contemporaries. The whinging, or outrage, is unastonishing if one recalls that Britain had no standing army, which meant that her young men, unlike their European contemporaries, were not conscripted (not until 1916, anyway), and her citizens had grown accustomed to a small professional army fighting their battles in distant lands. The shock of wide-scale involvement in a horrific war largely taking place just across the Channel was consequently seismic. Literature is the major British art form, so it seems entirely predictable that citizens of what was then the United Kingdom of Great Britain and Ireland, male and female, should pick up their pens, or bang away on their typewriting machines, in greater numbers than their European counterparts.

The only female volume to have carved a niche in the British male canon of Great War literature is Vera Brittain's *Testament of Youth*. Although she herself became a dedicated, lifelong pacifist, the experiences recorded in her best-selling book were, like the men's, gained by her participation in the war.

I have devoted a section to the determinedly courageous band who shared the conviction of the English journalist Evelyn Sharp. When asked what she did in the war, she replied, 'I tried to stop the bloody thing!' However fervently some wish to believe that women are at heart pacifists, come the crunch, whatever their reservations, the majority have thus far in history supported their country's war efforts. It is, however, true to say that Vera Brittain was not the only woman who turned into an anti-war activist, appalled by the loss of life and horrific personal experiences.

In 1914 the British Empire was the largest physical empire the world had known, or is ever likely to know. Although it was the alleged arch-imperialist Rudyard Kipling who penned the line 'Lo, all our pomp of yesterday is one with Nineveh and Tyre', for the majority being a citizen of the Mother Country of the Empire on which the sun would never set was a cause for immense pride. The British Empire was merely the largest – Belgium, France, Germany, Holland, Italy, Portugal and Spain were all colonial powers – and within Europe itself tsarist Russia and Austria-Hungary ruled over dozens of subject peoples and the same was true of the Turkish Ottoman Empire in the Middle East.

The determination with which British women got themselves to the front lines and organised their hospital units derived in part from the example of the militant suffragettes with their slogan 'Deeds Not Words' but in my opinion it also stemmed from the confidence of belonging to a top-dog nation. Other factors were at work, too. Invaded France, Belgium and Serbia were so desperate for medical aid that the sex of those who offered it ceased to matter, though, as Dr Flora Murray noted in 1914, their officials were not always clear what they were getting.

By 1918, the UK total of 'gainfully employed' women had risen from 5.9 to 7.3 million. Once the men returned from the war they were thrown out of many trades but girls like Miss Bennett had a somewhat better chance of finding a better job, as prewar male preserves such as hairdressing, bank telling and secretarial work remained largely female. The really radical shifts were the 'processes' women had successfully undertaken, the consequent

8

boost to confidences, and the increasing belief that they were entitled to work if they wanted to. Having tasted comparative freedom, not to mention higher wages, 400,000 from the prewar 1.5 million girls failed to return to domestic service. The 'servant problem' patriotically faced by middle- and upper-class women in wartime became a peacetime cause for loud lament. Without going into further statistics, it's fair to say that similar sorts of increases in wartime female employment occurred in France, Germany and latterly the USA, though the postwar reactions differed.

In recent years a few books about the female experience in the First World War have been published and no lavishly illustrated coffee-table tome is now complete without a chapter on the Home Front, but full justice has still not, it seems to me, been done to the scope of women's efforts between 1914 and 1918, the multiplicity of their reasons for involvement, and the social and sexual revolution they effected. Before I too 'go west' – the British Tommies' euphemism for death, reflecting the setting of the sun – to pay my tribute to the women who grabbed their opportunities with both hands and thereby affected my life, I have chosen a year-by-year format, with the extracts grouped into sections. Apart from brief comments on the signing of the actual peace treaty in 1919, my cut-off point is Armistice Day, 11 November 1918.

On occasions I have been ruthless with my editorial pen and the em rules (long dashes) which indicate a cut may mean quite a large one, but I have left erratic spelling as it was originally written. In all cases I have striven to preserve the spirit, if not every word, penned by those whose names retain a resonance, those whose reputations have faded, and those unknown outside their immediate circle who, like Ethel M. Bilborough, felt they must record *something*.

Joyce Marlow, Derbyshire, 1998

Editor's Note

I have drawn on previous editors' work, notably *Women War Workers* edited by Gilbert Stone; *A History of the Scottish Women's Hospitals* edited by Eva Shaw McLaren; Sarah Macnaughtan's *My War Experiences in Two Continents* edited by her niece Mrs Lionel Salmon; *Deutsche Frauen Deutsche Treue* edited by Charlotte von Hadeln; and *Berliner Leben 1914–18* edited by Ruth and Dieter Glatzer. To avoid repetition and a confusion of subheadings I have not included the editors' names in the extracts. Full acknowledgements are at the end of the book but as neither of the German volumes has been published in English – the extracts from German newspapers are from *Berliner Leben* – I want to thank the translator, Dr Christiane Banerji. Translations from the French are mine but I should also like to thank Josette Charenton for double-checking my efforts.

Select Chronology

1914

28 June	Archduke Franz Ferdinand and his wife assassinated in Sarejevo.
28 July	Austria-Hungary declares war on Serbia.
1 August	Germany declares war on Russia
3 August	. . . and on France.
4 August	Invades Belgium. Britain declares war on Germany.
. . . August	Germans advance through Belgium and northern France.
	British Expeditionary Force retreats from Mons.
	Battle of Tannenburg: Germans halt Russian advance into East Prussia.
September	French government flees Paris for Bordeaux.
	Battle of the Marne halts German advance on Paris.
October	Fall of Antwerp. Only Ypres salient and small section Belgian coast left in Allied hands. First Battle of Ypres.
November–December	Serbs defeat Austrians and recapture Belgrade.
	Ottoman Empire (Turkey) enters war on Central Powers' side.

Campaign in German East Africa.

Onset of German submarine warfare. Naval battle of Falkland Islands.

Stalemate on the Western Front.

1915

March   Battles of Neuve Chapelle and Hill 60.

April–August   Second Battle of Ypres. First German poison-gas attacks.

Coalition government in UK. Lloyd George Minister of Munitions.

Italy enters war on Allies' side.

Sinking of the *Lusitania*. Execution of Nurse Cavell.

Socialist women's peace conference in Berne.

International women's peace conference in The Hague.

Dardanelles campaign. Allied troops land on Gallipoli peninsula.

Turks besiege Kut-el-Amara, Mesopotamia.

September–   Battle of Loos. French offensive in Champagne.

October   Germans launch attack on Serbia. Bulgaria enters war on Central Powers' side. Invades Serbia. Belgrade falls.

British and French troops land in Salonika, northern Greece, to aid Serbians.

November–   Serbian army retreats over Albanian mountains.

December   General (later Field Marshal) Sir Douglas Haig succeeds Sir John French as C-in-C British Expeditionary Force.

1916

January   Final withdrawal from the Dardanelles.

February–   Battle of Verdun, 'France is bleeding to death'.

December

April	Easter Rising in Dublin.
	Kut-el-Amara falls to Turks.
June	Russian General Brusilov's offensive initially successful in Ukraine.
	Naval battle of Jutland.
	Arab revolt against Turks in Hejaz – Lawrence of Arabia.
July–November	Battle of the Somme.
August	Romania enters war on Allies' side.
September	British/South African force captures Dar-es-Salaam, German East Africa.
November–December	Dobrudja retreat in Romania.
	Asquith resigns. Lloyd George prime minister.

1917

February–March	Riots in Petrograd. Tsar Nicholas II abdicates.
	Provisional government installed. Kerensky prime minister.
	British retake Kut-el-Amara and capture Baghdad.
	Women's Auxiliary Army Corps formed in Britain.
	Unrestricted submarine warfare.
April	USA enters the war.
	Arras (Vimy Ridge) and Chemins des Dames offensives.
June	House of Commons votes for (limited) women's suffrage.
July–November	Third Battle of Ypres, 'Passchendaele'.
October–November	Bolsheviks under Lenin seize Winter Palace and overthrow provisional government.
	New type of warfare: British tanks in action at Cambrai.
	Italians routed at Battle of Caporetta.

	'Tiger' Clemenceau prime minister of France.
December	General Allenby's troops enter Jerusalem.
	Germans retreat in East Africa.
	Bolsheviks negotiate armistice.

1918

January	Suffrage victory for British women.
	President Wilson's 14 Points for Peace.
March	Bolsheviks sign Treaty of Brest-Litovsk.
	Germans launch last offensive on Western Front.
May	US troops in action in France.
	General Foch C-in-C Allied Forces Western Front.
May	Romania signs armistice with Central Powers.
July	German offensive peters out. Allies counter-attack.
August	Second Battle of the Somme, 'Black Day of German Army'.
September	Allied success on Salonika Front. Bulgaria signs armistice.
October	German sailors mutiny at Kiel. Rioting spreads.
8 November	Kaiser Wilhelm II abdicates.
11 November	Armistice comes into effect. The Great War ends.

Abbreviations

Initials and Acronyms

FANY (Fanny) = First Aid Nursing Yeomanry
IWSA = International Woman Suffrage Alliance
NAWSA = National American Woman Suffrage Society
NUWSS = National Union of Women's Suffrage Societies
SWH = Scottish Women's Hospitals
WAAC = Women's Auxiliary Army Corps, which in 1918 became
QMAAC = Queen Mary's Auxiliary Army Corps
VAD = Voluntary Aid Detachment
WRAF = Women's Royal Air Force
WRNS or Wrens = Women's Royal Naval Service
WSPU = Women's Social and Political Union

Pre-decimalisation British Currency

1d = one penny   12 pennies = 1 shilling, written as 1/- or 1s
20 shillings = £1   £1. 1s = one guinea

Additional coinage:
Farthings = 4 to one penny, written as ¼d
Halfpennies (ha'pennies) = 2 to a penny, written as ½d

Threepenny bits = 3d
Sixpences = 6d
Two-shillings pieces, also known as florins = 2/- or 2s
Two-and-sixes or half-crowns = 2/6d
Crowns or 5/- pieces had disappeared before the editor was born

Bank Notes

10/- and £1 notes were introduced at the start of the Great War. Their introduction caused the same sort of outcry as the change back to 50p and £1 coins when the currency finally went decimal in 1972.

An item could be written as £5. 9. 6½d. = five pounds, nine shillings and sixpence ha'penny; 22/- = one pound two shillings; 45/- = two pounds five shillings. A favourite pricing was 19/11 or one penny short of £1.

For a not very useful comparison, at decimalisation in 1971, the old shilling = 5p: the old 10/- = 50p.

1914

When the Austrian Archduke Franz Ferdinand and his wife were assassinated in Sarejevo on 28 June 1914, a thrill of horror coursed round the world but, Balkan crises being common occurrences, it soon subsided. In that famously beautiful summer, holidays remained at the top of many agendas. In England political attention returned to Ulster, where the Protestant majority were threatening to rebel rather than become part of Catholic-dominated Home Rule Ireland, while France was engrossed in the most sensational murder trial in years, that of the former prime minister's wife who had shot the editor of *Le Figaro* at point-blank range.

The IWSA executive committee happened to be meeting in London. On 28 July its president, Mrs Carrie Chapman Catt, left for Liverpool en route for her native USA, unaware that the storm clouds were gathering fast. For on that day, exactly a month after the assassinations in the Bosnian capital, Austria-Hungary declared war on Serbia, which it accused of being implicated in them.

Within a week the leading European nations were at war. Quite why they went to war when they did has been the subject of endless analysis. For most people the suddenness was astonishing, the belief that it would all be over by Christmas widespread, with their side victorious, of course. Well before Christmas most of Belgium was in German hands and its citizens were among the refugees who, though always a part of war, were to be such a tragic feature of this conflict – and subsequent ones. The Germans were fighting against the Russians in the east, but their rapid advance on the Western Front had been halted. Thereafter they started to dig in and by Christmas a network of opposing trenches was snaking across northern France virtually from the Channel coast to the Swiss border. The stage was set for four years of unprecedented hell in which, from the start, women played a greater part than they had in any previous conflict.

'Europe Was Thirsting for War'

From *An English Wife in Berlin*,
the war diary of Evelyn, Princess Blücher

Diary of an English Governess

Budapest, 28 June 1914

We returned to our hotel for luncheon, to the accompaniment of gipsy music — Suddenly, half-way through the meal, the music stopped and a hush fell over the room. The head-waiter moved about, speaking in a low voice and, when he reached our table, it was to tell us that the Archduke Franz-Ferdinand (nephew of the Emperor Franz-Joseph) and his wife had been assassinated at Sarajevo — Within an hour or two of the tragedy becoming known Budapest had changed to a city of mourning. All entertainment was cancelled and black streamers and flags at half-mast appeared on public buildings. The few people in the streets moved quietly and spoke in hushed voices.

BEATRICE KELSEY

The Beginning of It All

War, war, war. For me the beginning of the war was a torchlight tattoo on Salisbury Plain. It was held on one of those breathless evenings in July when the peace of Europe was trembling in the balance, and when most of us had a heartache in case – *in case* England, at this time of internal crisis, did not rise to the supreme sacrifice.

It was just the night for a tattoo – dark and warm and still. Away across the plain a sea of mist was rolling, cutting us off from the outside world, and only a few pale stars lighted our stage from above.

The field was hung round with Chinese lanterns throwing weird lights and shadows over the mysterious forms of men and beasts that moved therein. It was fascinating to watch the stately entrance into the field, Lancers, Irish Rifles, Welsh Fusiliers, Grenadiers and many another gallant regiment, each marching into the field in turn to the swing of their own particular regimental tune until they were all drawn up in order.

There followed a very fine exhibition of riding and the usual torchlight tricks, and then the supreme moment came. The massed bands had thundered out the first verse of the Evening Hymn, the refrain was taken up by a single silver trumpet far away – a sweet thin almost unearthly note more to be felt than heard – and then the bands gathered up the whole melody and everybody sang the last verse together.

The Last Post followed, and then I think somehow we all knew.

VIOLET THURSTON

The Silent Muse

from *Berliner Leben 1914–18*

Berlin's streets resembled a teeming sea of people. Troops marched in endless columns with music playing, off to the front with flowers in the bayonets. Women clung sobbing to the soldiers' arms, dragging themselves as far as they could with them on the death march. *Deutschland über alles* rang from every throat. 'May God punish England' hoarse male voices were heard to shout. You could see women leaning across café tables, pressing their husbands' or sons' limp hands, which poked from the sleeves of their uniforms. They would not let go of the hand even for a moment, nor would they stop staring through their tears at the beloved, embarrassed face, perhaps for the very last time. Shyly, now and then, a soldier's finger would gently brush a women's trembling hand: Don't lose courage, eh? Don't go to pieces! We all have to go, don't we? The whole thing will be over before you know it.

The town became a boiling cauldron. Stones were thrown through the windows of the English Embassy and the glass splinters tinkled down on to the raging, screaming crowd below. Mounted police drove the masses down the Linden. People screamed because everyone else was screaming. They trampled so as not to be trampled upon themselves.

ASTA NIELSEN

Chronicle of Youth: Vera Brittain's War Diary 1913–1917

Tuesday August 4th

Late as it is & almost too excited to write as I am, I must make some effort to chronicle the stupendous events of this remarkable day. The situation is absolutely unparalleled in the history of the world. Never before has the war strength of each individual nation been of such great extent, even though all the nations of Europe, the dominant continent, have been armed before. It is estimated that when the war begins *14 millions* of men will be engaged in the conflict. Attack is possible by earth, water & air, & the destruction attainable by the modern war machines used by the armies is unthinkable & past imagination.

Autobiography

When the Speaker had finished reading the King's message all the members poured out of the House, and I went down to the Prime Minister's room.

Henry looked grave and gave me John Morley's letter of resignation, saying:

'I shall miss him very much; he is one of the most distinguished men living.'

For some time we did not speak. I left the window and stood behind his chair:

'So it is all up?' I said.

He answered without looking at me:

'Yes, it's all up.'

I sat down beside him with a feeling of numbness in my limbs and absently watched through the half-open door the backs of moving men. A secretary came in with Foreign Office boxes; he put them down and went out of the room.

Henry sat at his writing-table leaning back with a pen in his hand. . . What was he thinking of? . . . His sons? . . . My son was too young to fight; would they all have to fight? — I got up and leant my head against his: we could not speak for tears.

When I arrived in Downing Street I went to bed.

How did it — how could it have happened? What were we all like five days ago? We were talking about Ireland and civil war; Civil war! People were angry but not serious; and now the sound of real war waved like wireless round our heads and the whole world was listening.

I looked at the children asleep after dinner before joining Henry in the Cabinet room. Lord Crewe and Sir Edward Grey were already there and we sat smoking cigarettes in silence; some went out, others came in; nothing was said.

The clock on the mantelpiece hammered out the hour, and when the last beat of midnight struck it was as silent as dawn.

We were at War.

I left to go to bed, and, as I was pausing at the foot of the staircase, I saw Winston Churchill with a happy face striding towards the double doors of the Cabinet room.

MARGOT ASQUITH

My Commonplace Book

The Outbreak of War

Looking back on the very vivid memories of those weeks, I have no doubt the revulsion of feeling on learning of the Belgian invasion, which brought our Lancashire circle into wholehearted support of the war effort, reflected public opinion throughout Great Britain as well as in the 'corridors of power'. It was seen as a monstrous, wicked, unprovoked act of aggression against a small neutral country which we were honour bound to assist. The issue was as simple as that. Whether subsequent analyses of the remoter causes of the war uncovered more complex motives is another matter. Except for a small number of dedicated and obstinately consistent pacifists, in August and September 1914, the issue was as simple as that.

But though accepted as inevitable, the outbreak of the First World War was not accepted with pleasurable enthusiasm — On the day after the declaration, when mobilization was in full swing — I did a slow cross-country railway journey via

Birmingham and Westbury to Bridport. At every station there were crowds; but they were unhappy, bewildered, apprehensive crowds. I saw no flags waved.

MARY STOCKS

Diary of an English Governess

The Journey Home: Vienna–Harwich

Aug 2nd

One of the most miserable days! — Got to the Westbahnhof at 8.30 and booked 1st class to Charing Cross. They even registered the luggage. Train started at 10.30 p.m. Hundreds of reservists in it but I managed to get into a third class compartment. Between Linz and Passau reservists in the corridor started fighting. All the windows smashed; heads as well. We got to Passau 3 a.m. Aug 3rd and were turned out. That was the last I saw of my luggage until December 10th.

Her son who later typed out the diary commented that she was lucky to see it at all.

Mr and Mrs. Brodhead (Americans) were decent to me. Sat in waiting room till 10 o'clock and nearly got crushed to death in the scramble for the train which was going to Regensburg — All alone all day in the train. Changed into another one for Nuremberg at 6 p.m. and got there at 10 p.m. — I was parched with thirst having had nothing to drink for 24 hours — Then went in compartment to Wurtzburg. At 2.45 a.m. Aug 5th got another train (always troop trains, loaded with soldiers and their baggage) from Wurtzburg to Aschaffenburg. Quite alone packed in with the soldiers until daybreak. Search for spy at 5 a.m. He was found (Frenchman, under cover of Red X) and was led off to be shot. Also a girl who had locked herself in the waiting room, a Belgian.

Got to Aschaffenburg early on Wednesday morning Aug 5th — Left by another train for Frankfurt at 9 a.m. Saw on the station that England had declared war and was warned that I had until 10 o'clock that night to be out of the country. Found an Englishman (recognised by golf clubs) in my compartment. Got to Frankfurt at 12 o'clock, hopeless as to how to get on. Very hungry, having eaten only scraps since Monday night (Aug. 3rd).

She then joined a group of some 70 homeward-bound Britons.

Were allowed to leave Frankfurt and got to Mainz at 4.15. At 5 o'clock we were all marched to the commandant and examined. Were given a pass on the train and all travelled 4th class from Mainz to Bingenbrucke. There we were all hauled out by soldiers, to the jeers of the reservists. I had a narrow escape from a German bayonet, in trying to shout a message to Mr Brodhead who was on the train. We were told we should be kept in Bingen till the war was over. Cheerful prospect! At 10 o'clock we were marched off under guard to a little hotel and told to stay in our rooms there. We were guarded by sentries all night — Next morning we were all searched — Saw a man shot on the bridge. Also two motorists and began to realise our desperate plight. Got an order from the commandant to go to Cologne that night. Marched to the station under guard and put in the train. We were taken up the left bank of the Rhine – everywhere trains and all in total darkness. Thousands of men, siege guns etc. going to the front. We were packed in amongst the men and did not speak or move, for fear of violence. Got to Coblenz at 11 p.m.

Changed trains and got to Cologne at 5 a.m. on Friday Aug. 7th. There we were at once arrested and put under guard. We were made to carry our bags and taken over the famous bridge to a big barracks. The officer in charge (who spoke perfect English – had been at Oxford) was quite decent, compared to some of them. He handed us over to a soldier to be taken to the Polizei Präsidium. On the way this man told us he had lived in Sheffield for three years and was engaged to an English girl who had left Koln only the Sunday before. He asked us to send her news of him. (I afterwards wrote to her). We were kept waiting at the Polizei Präsidium for several hours and then searched minutely

25

and questioned and finally our soldier friend was instructed to take us to a Pension — We marched through the streets in pouring rain and finally found refuge — Other English and Belgians arrived from different places. Our passports were taken to the American consul to be visa'd, also to the Dutch consul to have permission to travel through Holland.

Monday Aug. 10th

We were told a Dutch boat had been chartered and we should be allowed to go up the Rhine into Holland — at 4 o'clock the next morning went on to the boat.

Aug. 11th

My 27th birthday! We left Koln at 5 a.m. thinking we were at last getting towards safety. Got to Dusseldorf at 8 a.m. and were held up for an hour by a dense river fog. Went on and at 10.30 were chased by a tug and told to return to Dusseldorf. We felt we were going to be taken back to Koln — After much talking and a guard coming on board, as well as the detectives who were conducting us into Holland, we were allowed to proceed — but at Wesel, after a delay of an hour, the military came on board and ordered all men between 18 and 40 to go ashore. We had only a few minutes to say good-bye to them —

The boat went on — but were obliged to anchor out in the river for the night. It was bitterly cold and very foggy — Next morning we went on. The detectives left us at the Dutch frontier and we got to Rotterdam at 2 p.m.

Left Rotterdam at 8 a.m. for the Hook. There we went on board a Great Eastern boat for Harwich. A glorious crossing with no unusual happenings — When we got past the Galloper lightship we put up the wireless and an aeroplane came out to meet us. We got to Harwich at 8 p.m.

Beatrice Kelsey

Captured at Sea

En route from South Africa to England

Union Castle Line S.S. 'Galician', Friday 14th August
Well, here we are captured by a German cruiser. It has been an experience, but I wish I knew what is going to be done to us. I dare say you will hear of the fate of the Galician long before this reaches you (if it ever does). I will hardly be able to tell you all that took place this afternoon, but it is something which none of us will ever forget. At 2.30 p.m. Gault (*her newly married husband*) and I were lying in our cabins preparatory to having a sleep, when one of the boys called to us 'Calwell, here's a German boat heading for us', & in two shakes we were on the deck.

We should never have called at the Islands, that was what we didn't want to do. But the Marconi fellow wired to Teneriffe that perhaps we could call there for coal, was the coast clear? The German boat picked up the message, and said yes, that they were the 'Carnarvon', so you see how beautifully we were trapped. When the German boat came in sight our Marconi man tried to send an S.O.S. for help to Teneriffe, of course the boat caught the message and said 'Follow us, or we sink your wireless, and we sink you.' Our silly old captain gave orders after that to send a wireless, but the first officer (a real hero) pulled him out by force. Our next message from the Germans was to take down our wireless. It was most exciting seeing them row from their boat to ours. The cinematograph was going all the time, the fellow got a number of jolly good films. The two German officers looked very smart as they walked on to the deck. They got all the papers, then the crew got orders to line up, then passengers. The officers (German) counted them all, called us all up by name. Gault and I went down to our cabins, packed a few things, in case there was any chance of our taking them with us —

Well! orders from the Germans now, are, that we are to be ready at dawn tomorrow, packed & all, so I'll not write any more.

I have a lot to see before then. Goodbye dears to you all and love from both of us,

Ada

ADA CALWELL

Journal of a Parisian Worker During the War

3 August

The station precincts are packed with soldiers, reservists, women; their eyes reddened, their lips smiling – tremulously, it's true – but everybody putting a brave face on things.

Sitting on the step of little door into the station a woman in mourning cries silently, her face hidden by a handkerchief.

No songs, no cries – the platform cordoned off. Large boards indicate the destination, and time and place of departure. Still another half-hour to go – better the farewells were cut short.

Tears fall, mouths tremble, Olivier and Marjolaine (*her cousin and his sister*) pale – we laugh, we embrace, we embrace again – we do not cry, we give last-minute advice, then abruptly we turn our backs as we cry out 'Au revoir!'

We walk back through the Jardin des Plantes, how peaceful it is, how lovely! Everything in bloom, a riot of colour – it's a sacrilege to unleash war, murder, as Prussia has done, when nature is so beautiful!

7 August

What a crowd at the Town Hall; boy scouts there to assist in keeping order, these valiant young men having been assigned to the Governor of Paris to use in the postal service, at town halls, and as couriers.

Curds are distributed — a troup of ragged, bare-footed children take them away. Two small kids using all their feeble strength cannot manage to lift a pitcher.

Eight days have passed since the general mobilisation. All the women are busy; some at the hospitals and with ambulances, others with the enquiries about the families of the mobilised; yet others in setting up sewing workshops, for household linen and clothes, and even the creation of orphanages. Everywhere, there is a ceaseless chase for work. How many women have said to me: 'If only I had work, I would ask for nothing more!' But so many factories and boutiques have closed.

30 August

It's just over two months since the Austrian Archduke heir-apparent and his wife fell to an assassin's bullets. And what a chapter of horrors! How much blood, death, destruction! Each day, we hear of new victims. In our district one poor woman who has six sons in uniform, has just learned that four are dead!

1 September

Our mothers lived through 1870 – shall we be less courageous? Though the Barbarians surround Paris, we must stay calm. Women must look after their homes, care for their children with greater vigilance and greater love. But how are we to rekindle the flame of their souls? Whose voice is strong enough to be heard? Which new Genevieve, which ardent Jeanne is going to emerge?

They say the Germans are at Crépy, that you can hear the sound of the cannon at Compiègne — that Russian troops have landed at Marseilles and are marching north — They say – they say — but we must arm ourselves with courage, we must steel ourselves against despair and remain for ever calm.

4 Sept

Where have our brave soldiers gone? Where are the Barbarians? The Government is at Bordeaux! The day before yesterday, from two in the evening until two in the afternoon, soldiers filed constantly along the boulevard Saint Michel.

The gates of Paris have been closed.

The battle continues – A mysterious whisper murmurs words of hope in all our ears.

LOUISE DELÉTANG

Women War Workers

The Women of Paris During the German Advance

The most serious questions of the hour were what to do with the unemployed and the refugees. In these, women played a big part and played it well. They organized rapidly and with efficiency, considering the conditions under which they had to work. There was a distinct blending of the classes in the united desire to do good. The aristocrat and the *bourgeoise*, the Roman Catholic and the Protestant, the free-thinker and the foreigner, all worked together to help those homeless women and children who poured into the city from the invaded district—

These two problems, refugees and unemployed, were the most pressing during the actual days of danger; but, as was quite natural, the spontaneous gesture of the women of France was toward the hospitals. Every one rushed into Red Cross uniforms, and the offices of the three societies which go to make up the French Red Cross were literally bombarded from morning to night with applications to serve. As somebody said whimsically: 'It was more confusing than the green-room of a theatre'—

It was all very charming, but it was not practical, and the military authorities soon began a vigorous combing out. An order was issued that no outdoor uniform was to be worn except on active service, and in the twinkling of an eye the streets lost their picturesque aspect and many of the women their ambition to become ministering angels. This gave the serious working women a chance to organize their forces, which they did not neglect, and the result was that Paris became a city of hospitals. Many of the big hotels, many private houses, well-known dress-making houses and shops turned part of their establishments into hospitals, and it was a little bewildering to go into a private house and find a well-known duchess in hospital blouse and *coiffe* directing the installation of a *lingerie*, or transforming her magnificent Louis XV salon into a hospital ward; or to enter a Rue de la Paix dressmaker's and find the *vendeuses* of other days attired in Red Cross uniforms awaiting wounded where, before, they had awaited customers to buy dresses—

Unnoticed, wearing no uniform, and without any pomp or circumstance, other groups of women set to work to unravel the difficult question of how the refugees were to be housed and fed permanently, and how the unemployed were to be given a chance to find work again—

Ouvroirs were opened all over Paris, and in the most unexpected places, from a drawing-room to an attic, a shop, or a newspaper office. In the big shops like the Printemps and the Bon Marché the shop assistants worked sewing-machines on the counters to make haversacks for the soldiers or sheets for the hospitals; and all down the Champs Elysées the big automobile shops were filled with working women making soldiers' shirts or children's frocks or something else that the men or the refugees needed.

MRS M. E. CLARKE

The Queen's Message to the Women of Great Britain: August 1914

In the firm belief that prevention of distress is better than its relief, and that employment is better than charity, I have inaugurated the Queen's 'Work for Women Fund.' Its object is to provide employment for as many as possible of the women of this country who have been thrown out of work by the war.

I appeal to the women of Great Britain to help their less fortunate sisters through this fund.

Mary R.

The Home Front

'Queen Mary's Sweat-Shops!'

The Fund was to be administered by a Central Committee for the Employment of Women — Mary Macarthur was made the Hon. Secretary, Susan Laurence, Margaret Bondfield, Dr. Marion Phillips of the Women's Labour League, and Mrs. Gasson of the Co-operative Union were members of the Committee. Their appointment received a wide and cordial welcome, in which I heartily joined. We hoped that these women would take the lead in protecting the status of women's labour — Alas, the Committee speedily covered itself with ignominy by setting up the sweated wage of 10s per week for adult women — Girls between 16 and 18 were to get 2d per hour, making a wage of 5s a week — These miserable rates were on no account to be exceeded, but they might be reduced at will—

'Queen Mary's Sweat-shops!' was the slogan I coined to attack their parsimonious standard, the influence of which was to depress even the existing most beggarly economic status of the women wage earner. Our members took up the phrase with avidity, and cried it in the ears of conventionally-minded patriots, and East End clothiers seeking cheap labour.

E. Sylvia Pankhurst

Then I went to the most amusing place called the National Service League offices, where a vast swarm of well-meaning and inefficient patriots are employed for fourteen hours a day in first classifying and then rejecting the applications of a still vaster swarm of still more well-meaning and inefficient patriots for posts which they are obviously incapable of filling – Baptist Ministers who volunteer as *vivandières* and so forth. I spent a very pleasant afternoon trying to put these people into classes. There were four classes, but the qualifications for each class were so peculiar that none of the 2000 applicants whom I examined were eligible for any one of the four. Next week the committee are going to alter the classification, and it is hoped that someone may scrape into one of the classes. It will be a proud day for England when this happens.

LADY DIANA COOPER NEÉ MANNERS

Vorwärts, 10 September 1914

Early yesterday morning, from 9 o'clock onwards, work was supposed to be offered at numbers 9–13 Rosenstrasse to women who have been made unemployed as a result of the war. Initially, workers were sought who were experienced in making men's shirts, men's trousers, men's jackets, bed clothes, towels and straw sacks.

The number of people applying for this work was unbelievable. From 6 o'clock in the morning onwards women looking for work queued in Rosentrasse — The army of women and girls grew from hour to hour and filled the wide pavement. Policemen kept the queue under control — Between quarter and half past eleven, as we drove through Rosenstrasse, we saw between 7 to 8000 people standing there.

Earlier Months of the War

Because the state of tense excitement in which we existed upset our judgment and made any event seem possible, and also because if people must go to war and continue to be at war they must be made to hate each other and to go on hating each other, war stories were a feature of our life. There are people who to this day believe that an army of Russians passed through Great Britain in 1914 on the way to the Western Front. Whatever the origin of this story may have been, the rumour spread like wild-fire, and testimony came from people all over the country, who said that they had seen, talked with or even touched Russian soldiers. One who troubled at the time to make notes regarding this rumour was told by a Mrs. — that the clergyman's wife of — had written to her telling her that she had seen and spoken to Russian troops at Berkhamsted station. Another friend said that his brother had seen train-loads of Russians at Eastleigh. Someone else had a son who had seen a train-load of Russians at Leith. They were seen on railway platforms 'stamping the snow off their boots' – they called hoarsely for Vodka at Carlisle and Berwick-on-Tweed and they jammed the penny-in-the-slot machine with a rouble at Durham.

MRS. C. S. PEEL

Der Weltspiegel, 1 November 1914

A True German Hygienic Miracle

German victory in the area of women's culture is relentless. Victory comes as a natural consequence of the rejection of all that is foreign. We are happy to report that a goal has been set to end the harmful effects of French corset fashions, which have made almost all German women ill. The one and only German article which achieves the development of true beauty without harming health, and which owes nothing to French models is the well-known Thalysia-Edelform. It is not tied, does not hinder breathing or freedom of movement, it is not cumbersome and is not as outrageously expensive as is the Paris corset. nor is it as shameless as the Paris corset, but gently changes even a figure which has become too voluptuous into a tender and German figure. The Thalysia-Edelform is, in a word, a true German hygienic miracle.

Recollections of 1914

Although sixteen years of age at the time, England had been at war three months before I knew. I was in domestic service on a farm near the River Humber and one day as I was attending to ducklings a shell whizzed over my head from the direction of the river. This was in November 1914 and I refused to believe a farm boy who told me England was at war. How could this be? — Why had I not known that England had declared war on August the fourth of that year?

Girls who worked as maids on those small farms were completely isolated. The farmers and their wives never talked with the girls except to tell them what to do next. They had no books and never saw a newspaper. They were on duty from five in the morning until ten at night & were not allowed to burn a candle at night.

OLIVE MAY TAYLOR

'I Tried to Stop the Bloody Thing'

Journalist Evelyn Sharp's response to the
question posed in the English poster,
'What did you do in the war, Daddy?' From her
autobiography *Unfinished Adventure*

Manchester Guardian, 1 August 1914

International Manifesto of Woman

We, the women of the world, view with apprehension and dismay
the present situation in Europe, which threatens to involve one
continent, if not the whole world, in the disasters and horrors of
war. In this terrible hour, when the fate of Europe depends on
decisions which women have no power to shape we, realising our
responsibilities as the mothers of the race, cannot stand passive
by. Powerless though we are politically, we call upon the
Governments and Powers of our several countries to avert the
threatened unparalleled disaster—

Whatever its result, the conflict will leave mankind the poorer,
will set back civilisation, and will be a powerful check to the
gradual amelioration in the condition of the masses of the people,
on which so much of the real welfare of nations depend.

We women of twenty-six countries, having bonded ourselves
together in the International Woman Suffrage Alliance with the
object of obtaining the political means of sharing with men the
power which shapes the fate of nations, appeal to you to leave
untried no method of conciliation or arbitration for arranging

international differences to avert deluging half the civilised world in blood.

Signed on behalf of the International Woman Suffrage Alliance
MILLICENT GARRETT FAWCETT
First Vice-President
CHRYSTAL MACMILLAN
Recording Secretary

To Women!

COMRADES WAR, HORRIBLE WAR is at our gates, and tomorrow perhaps your brothers and your husbands will be grappling with their comrades far beyond the frontiers!

WILL YOU PERMIT THIS MONSTROUS MASSACRE. No. All of you will stand as a living wall against menacing and murderous barbarism.

UNITE WITH THE PROLETARIAT OF THE WORLD who will rise up against the war and come to a meeting organised by the Women's Socialist Group, with a host of speakers, on Monday 3 August; at 9 o'clock in the evening; the Commune house, 49 rue de Bretagne (Paris).

LOUISE SAUMONEAU

Votes for Women, August 1914

International Meeting of Women in London

The great women's demonstration against war on August 4 had been called at a moment when peace seemed possible, but it was held in the very darkest hour that the world had ever known. And yet to many of those present the gathering was even more wonderful than the occasion that had called it forth: much more significant. They trusted that the war was the last great violent outburst of evil passions of greed and lust and hate which had shadowed the world since history began: they believed that the gathering was the earnest of the new splendid spirit that should brood over the face of the quietened waters and the devastated but expectant world: the spirit of woman's love and loyalty and sympathy for woman, and through her for humanity. Never before had such disaster threatened the world: never before had the conscious, organised articulate women of all classes and parties and of several nations met to make, on behalf of womanhood and childhood and the home, a protest against the time-honoured methods of brutal force by which men regardless of half the race have seen fit to settle their national disputes. It was a protest, passionate, sane and practical, of the civilised against the barbaric: of the spiritual against the material, and of the mother who takes thought for the future happiness of her children against the destructiveness of a brief, insensate rage.

Olive Schreiner was on the platform, better informed than any others as to the horrors of war, and hating it the more: Mrs Fawcett, Mrs Despard, Mrs Pethick Lawrence, Mrs George Cadbury, Madame Malmberg, the Finnish patriot, Madame Schwimmer, Hungarian representative on the International Suffrage Alliance, and many others.

I Have Been Young

Protest Meeting, Kingsway Hall, London, 4 August 1914

Mrs Fawcett presided at this meeting, partly I believe because, having agreed to do so, she would not seem to back out; but she had very grave doubts in her mind. One of the speakers, Mme. Aino Malmberg, a clever journalist and a powerful speaker, said bluntly that although she was against war, one good thing would certainly come out of this one; the liberation of her own country from the bloody tyranny of Tsardom. Now the Russians were 'our gallant allies,' and Mrs. Fawcett was so shocked by this reflection on them that she spoke to me with horror of 'that bloody-minded Finn.'

War provides everyone of us with new spectacles and we at once see the whole world in different colours. This was the first of many thousands of such transformations which I was to witness. For Mrs. Fawcett had doubtless formerly sympathized with humane British opinion about Russia's vile oppression of Finland.

HELENA SWANWICK

Common Cause, 7 August 1914

Let us show ourselves worthy of citizenship, whether our claim to it be recognised or not.

MILLICENT FAWCETT

Jus Suffragii, November 1914

The Effects of the War on American Women

—Soon after the outbreak of war one group organised a parade down Fifth Avenue to protest against a condition of society in which the forces of destruction could be appealed to in place of reason in settling differences between the nations. The parade was held in August, a month in which usually only those compelled by their circumstances remain in New York. Nevertheless some 3,000 women clad as mourners, marching to muffled drums down New York's main thoroughfare, was an impressive spectacle to many thousands of people thronged on the pavements. At the head of this procession was carried the standard of peace, followed by Mrs Henry Villard, whose hair has whitened in the cause of peace and Woman Suffrage.

No appeal was made to the driving power of any organisation of women. They marched as individuals spontaneously gathered to express a common sentiment.

Off to War

The Home Front

Meeting the Great Emergency

What liveliness and vivacity in London! Beautiful women in long white coats, flawlessly tailored, already were taking the part of chauffeurs. How speedily they had learnt to drive! It was truly amazing! One scarcely saw women driving before the War. How important, how joyously important they were, their gait more triumphantly instinct with pleasure than ever it was in the ballroom. To serve, to be needed, to feel themselves part of this world-embracing Cause, with all the nation beside one! Every woman who put her hand to the wheel was releasing a man for the trenches. Even if she had still a chauffeur in the background, for certain occasions, she was making a gesture – striking the right note – giving the men the cue for the trenches!

Already skirts were becoming shorter, elegant feet and ankles twinkled smartly under the petticoats. 'The women are wonderful!' It was Northcliffe, our old opponent, who said it, seeing their new emancipation – for war – for the slaughter.

As I saw them there was a cry within me: 'Stop all this! Stop this breaking of homes, these sad privations, this mangling of men, this making of widows!'

For women of means, undreamt-of activities, opportunities, positions, opened on the horizon. The War brought a vast unlocking of their energies. They threw themselves into its work pell-mell, and more adventurously than had been conceived of in any previous war.

E. Sylvia Pankhurst

Flanders and Other Fields

Once again I had to ask my foster-parents to look after Kenneth, for I was called to London for nursing service. London was in a ferment of activity, seething with schemes, some official, but many, in those far-off un-totalitarian days, splendidly freelance.

Committees proliferated, all intent on beating each other in the race to get to 'the Front,' and most of them, especially those involving many women, rejected by the War Office and the British Red Cross. Many ideas burned out in a blaze of talk, or died in a welter of vagueness. Others crumbled at the first touch of reality. One group which tried to enlist my sympathy if not services thought of sending out a detachment of women in khaki breeches to scour the battlefields on horseback to collect the wounded. This and similar schemes had that beautiful, crazy clarity which is the mark of armchair logic.

All the same, it was a heady atmosphere to move in, and it infected me with a strong desire to do something more than stay in London and wait for a bunch of men to tell me what to do. I heard of an ambulance corps which was going straight out to Belgium and I applied to join it. On the strength of being an expert driver and mechanic, as well as a nurse, I was accepted. Could this be what I had been preparing myself for?

This particular corps had already been rejected, I think, by the War Office and the British, French, and American Red Cross.

When the Belgian Red Cross accepted the offer of its services the British Red Cross thought better of it and weighed in with a few ambulances.

Perhaps the earlier rejections were not altogether surprising. The founder and leader of the corps, Dr Hector Munro, was an eccentric Scottish specialist, one of whose primary objects seemed to be leadership of a feminist crusade, for he was far keener on women's rights than most of the women he recruited. He was a likeable man and a brilliant impresario, but wonderfully vague in matters of detail, and in appearance the very essence of the absent-minded professor. His hair was liable to 'point' and his clothes to bulge in any and every direction.

There were two other doctors, three male stretcher-bearers, two chauffeurs, the inevitable padre (who wore an ill-fitting Tommy's uniform which made him look very comical), and the women. One of them, an eighteen-year-old Scots girl called Mairi Chisholm, I had met before, since she also was a keen motor-cyclist and was to have taken part in the famous motor-cycle trial planned for the summer of 1914. While waiting for things to develop we had both careered about London as despatch-riders for the newly formed Women's Emergency Corps. We fitted ourselves out at our own expense in big khaki overcoats, high lace-up leather boots, and riding-breeches. In fact, for at least a year we paid our own way, until funds were raised on our behalf in Britain. I had the remains of my legacy, and Mairi sold her precious motor-bike to raise some cash. We preferred to be financially independent. It gave us greater freedom of movement, and spared us some of the annoyances of red tape.

BARONESS DE T'SERCLAES
(Mrs Elsie Knocker)

Entertainment for the Troops

Of course one's heart was in war-work, and 'business as usual' made one groan in spirit; it seemed so absurd and selfish; and, besides, I had always longed that artists might have their proper recognition as a great arm of National Service. In our professional capacity we might be of as much use and as real a necessity as the Red Cross or St. John's Ambulance, for does not the soul of man need help as much as his body?—

In October I tried very hard to get the entertainment of troops put on national lines, and was interviewed several times on the scheme of 'every camp its own theatre', and the organising of the work by professional actors, but there was little interest shown —

We were still considered as 'useless as an actor, a billiard-marker, or a golf professional.' I do not know how the golf professional or the billiard-marker felt when he read this sentence in *Ordeal By Battle*. I expected they were in the Army, but I felt very sad and disheartened, and threw more energy than ever into the work of the Women's Emergency Corps.—

One never-to-be-forgotten day, when I had quite lost hope of the drama and music of the country being regarded as anything but useless, Lady Rodney called on behalf of the Women's Auxiliary Committee of the Y.M.C.A. She had just returned from France, and came from Her Highness Princess Helena Victoria, Chairman of the Committee, to ask if it was possible for a concert party to go to Havre.—

The conditions were: no advertisement, no making use of the war to aggrandise one's professional popularity, that every artist should be personally known to me, and that I should be able to guarantee their suitability to Her Highness and the Committee, and that every artist should become known to Her Highness, who became personally responsible for them and their conduct. They were to work with the Y.M.C.A., who would look after the billeting arrangements in France, and places, times, etc., for the concerts.

The experiment was tentative. There were grave doubts on the part of the Y.M.C.A. as to what unknown terrors they were letting loose upon themselves. Of course people are afraid of the unknown, and there is a great prejudice amongst a section of the nation against artists, especially actors. To them we are a class of terribly wicked people who drink champagne all day long, and lie on sofas, receiving bouquets from rows of admirers who patiently wait in queues to present these tokens of rather unsavoury regard. I think some expected us to land in France in tights, with peroxided hair, and altogether to be a difficult thing for a religious organisation to camouflage.

LENA ASHWELL

Women as Army Surgeons

The Women's Hospital Corps in Paris

Women who had been trained in medicine and in surgery knew instinctively that the time had come when great and novel demands would be made upon them, and that a hitherto unlooked-for occasion for service was at their feet. It was inconceivable that in a war of such magnitude women doctors should not join in the care of the sick and wounded, but it was obvious that prejudice would stand in their way. Their training and their sympathies fitted them for such work; they knew and could trust their own capacity; but they had yet to make their opportunity.

Amongst others, Dr. Louisa Garrett Anderson and Dr. Flora Murray were determined that medical women desiring to give their services to the nation should not be excluded from military work and from the great professional opportunities naturally arising from it. An opening, therefore, had to be found for them. As militant suffragists they had had dealings with the Home Office, and had gained an insight into the cherished prejudices and stereotyped outlook of officials. One government department is very like another, and to have approached the War Office at that time would only have meant to court a rebuff. But it was common knowledge that the French Army was inadequately supplied with surgeons and hospitals; and they turned their attention where the need was great.

On the 12th of August these two doctors called at the French Embassy and were received by one of the secretaries in an absolutely airless room. The atmosphere was enhanced by red damask wall hangings and upholstery, and by an aroma of stale cigar smoke. In somewhat rusty French they laid before him an offer to raise and equip a surgical unit for service in France. The secretary may have been rather mystified as to their intentions; for medical women were off his horizon. Very likely he never realised that they themselves intended to go to the aid of the French wounded; but he affirmed again and again the real need of France for medical and surgical aid, for stores of all kinds and for English nurses. He begged 'Mesdames' to call upon the President of the French Red Cross in London and discuss the matter—

On Tuesday the 14th of September 1914 the Women's Hospital Corps left Victoria for Paris—

A little apart, Mrs. Garrett Anderson, a dignified figure, old and rather bent, stood quietly observing the bustle and hand-shaking. One wondered of what she was thinking as she contemplated this development of the work she had begun. Her eyes were tender and wistful as she watched her daughter in uniform directing the party and calling the roll of the Corps. A friend beside her said:

'Are you not proud, Mrs Anderson?'

The light of battle – of old battles fought long ago – came into her face as she raised her head and surveyed the scene.

'Yes,' she answered. 'Twenty years younger, I would have taken them myself.'

FLORA MURRAY

A *Battlefield Visit*

I am a Parisian born and bred. In August 1914 I was aged thirty-four, had been married for fourteen years and had two children. My husband and I had worked hard to build up a business making mattresses. Like millions of Frenchmen he – and our male employees – went straight off to the war. Determined to keep the business going, I took on women to replace them and learned to drive our firm's five-tonne van.

During the terrible days of September 1914 I knew my husband was involved in the Battle of the Marne and became very concerned about him. Then I thought to myself: the Marne isn't far from Paris, is it? So I donned my smartest hat and dress and highest-heeled shoes, climbed in the van and drove northwards to the Marne. The nearer I got, the worse the destruction and desolation became. Alas, poor France!

Eventually I reached an HQ. When I espied a good-looking young Captain I climbed from the van, making sure he more than glimpsed my ankles and legs as I did so. I sashayed over to him, gave my husband's name, serial number and regiment and said: 'I want to see him, please.' I have never seen anybody look so utterly amazed as that young Captain. He said he couldn't understand how on earth I'd managed to get there and my request was an impossible one. I just stood there and said: 'I want to see my husband.'

Persistence – and maybe my legs – paid off. Eventually the Captain located his whereabouts and sent a soldier to fetch him. When my husband arrived he told the officer he'd long since given up being astonished by anything I did and he wasn't in the least surprised to see me. During the wait for his arrival, I had a most enjoyable dinner with the young Captain.

BLANCHE THIRIEAU

Letter from a British Nurse

Salles Militaries Hospice Unite
Saumur 22/10/14

Dear Mrs Cooke,

—Still the same round of operations, more or less successful. We are dreadfully hampered by not having an x ray here, and altho' the Chef has done all he can to insist, the Government are terribly slow, & in the delay, lives and limbs are being sacrificed. Nobody can ever imagine the fearful wounds these new large cannons of the Germans cause, and owing to the metals used they are very septic, so from the first are pretty hopeless – and it seems so cruel not to just give them something to let them sleep out—

There is a rumour in Saumur that the Japs are landed, & marching up from Marseilles, that Portugal & Italy will soon declare war on Germany – but such wild stories go about. It is a very pretty place – something like Shrewsbury – but then here are splendid chateaux. We are today going to the station in our lunch hour, as we hear a train of English wounded is passing thro.

The German prisoners are often to be seen doing scavengers jobs. They are all perfectly wretched. It would amuse you to see some of improvised utensils in the wards – I don't think the Hospital has more than 5 small basins for the 200 wounded! As to a bucket it is unheard of, and we use anything from teapots to dustbins. Hot water is as scarce as whisky, and one only gets about 1 pint daily, so the cleaning has to be done cold. There is no installed hot water system or lights of any sort. The water is heated on gas rings, and the wards by tiny oil lamps I am sure were used by Henri II who lies buried near here.

When the operations are after dark, it is a perilous procedure to get your case down a flight of stairs & thro 3 large wards, with a match! I have sworn at the men till I have got an oil lamp from the office, which is now placed on the stairs. I do so long for some reliable bearers. These are awful, & so rough. When they are tired, they dump the stretcher on the ground, regardless of place, and sit on the side. The orderlies are soldiers too mad or too bad to fight, so their capabilities are what you would expect. They never cease smoking, they shave not, neither do they wash, & their garments are anything to be found. We have just trained one he should not expectorate *on the floor*, but I know he does it the minute we leave the ward.

All these little things provide amusement but are most irritating at the end of a worrying day, however there is a war on and one must not grumble. Visitors to the Cardiff Hospital cannot get an idea what war is really — If I told you some things that come in here, you would be horrified and it's just as well that England has not seen yet these remains of what were bright young men brought in to die in a few dreadful hours—

This is such a depressing letter but it's all that here – so please write me a gay one. Much love to you & the children, kindest remembrances to Mr Cooke,

Ever Yours

SYBIL HARRY

Please excuse pencil.

Women War Workers

Nursing at the French Front

It is true that the nurse's bonnet, which looks so charming in England, where its meaning is recognized, is all out of focus in France and looks like a broken accent once it has crossed the Channel, and we have now modified it considerably. The costume, no doubt, helped the inhabitants of a village in the north of France to form their own conclusions with regard to the sisters. The suggestion that they must be suffragettes was handed all round the village. Suffragettes! The horror of it! Suffragettes were wild women who, when they could not get their own way, burnt your houses; women who had come to work in France because the British would not have them. From the cut of their bonnet, too, others had attached them to the Salvation Army – a movement, semi-hooligan and anti-Catholic as they regard it, whose wonderful work in East London is totally undervalued.

GRACE ELLISON
Directrice-Générale French Flag Nursing Corps

Deutsche Frauen Deutsche Treue

Type-Setting and Printing

My father owned a book-printing business and also published the district gazette in our home town in the former province of Posen. When the war broke out, our employees were called up, and it was impossible to find new employees, so I had to help out with the type-setting and the printing press. Sometimes I got into terrible difficulties when one or more carefully composed lines, or even a painstakingly type-set advertisement collapsed, or when my hands couldn't keep up with the printing press and I couldn't keep it stocked with sheets of paper. But things improved with time and my father was able to leave a lot of the work to me.

In addition to the practical work in the printing shop, all sorts of things had to be done in the office. The official telegrams and the reports from the Supreme Command had to be taken by telephone and posted up at the window every single day, including Sundays and holidays. The posters were always besieged, and some days the telephone never stopped ringing, with people calling to see whether the editor of the gazette knew this or that detail of how things were going at the front.

And of course in the evenings it was my bounden duty to work on my knitting and the force's parcels we sent to our soldiers at the front.

F.S.

Country Doctor

My husband left to join his Bavarian garrison, and on the second mobilisation day in August 1914, I returned from the town. It was only when an old farmer greeted me at the station with the words: 'I'll be coming to your surgery tomorrow' that I really grasped the immense responsibility that I would now have to bear, in addition to all the pain of parting and being separated from my husband. The health and lives of so many people had now been placed in my hands alone; I would have to be prepared to care for and think of others night and day. Would I have the strength and skill to cope?—

Driving through the countryside in my open car, with no protection from storms or rain (I had removed the roof to lessen the weight of the car, and thus save fuel), I sometimes felt heroic, as if I had made a great sacrifice. But all my pride evaporated when, dotted around the fields, I saw old and young women, kneeling on ground frozen by an early frost or sodden by the autumn rain, sliding from furrow to furrow, carefully searching out every last tiny potato. At times like that my own work seemed so easy, so comfortable!

—I am thinking of the child whose mother had to leave him alone while she went to work, whose clothes caught fire in the stove, whose handsome little face was horrifically disfigured for the rest of his life; and I remember the young woman who carried on working quietly and calmly for some time after news reached her of her husband's death, and who then went mad quite suddenly one morning, set fire to the barn which her work had filled, woke the old grandfather up, her clothes on fire, saying, 'Daddy, the barn's alight!' She met a miserable end and left her little boy an orphan.

DR BARTSCH

51

War: 'Little Curies'

Mme Curie had foreseen everything – that the war would be long and murderous, that the wounded would have to be operated upon more and more in the places where they were found, and that the surgeons and radiologists would have to be at hand in the front ambulances; that it was urgently necessary to organise the intensive manufacture of Röntgen apparatus – and, finally, that the radiological cars would be called upon to render invaluable service.

These cars, nicknamed 'little Curies' in the army zones, were equipped by Marie at the laboratory, one by one, regardless of the indifference or the latent hostility of the bureaucrats. Our timid woman had suddenly become an exacting and authoritative personage. She nagged at the lazy officials, demanded passes from them, visas and requisitions. They made difficulties, brandished the regulations at her. . . 'Civilians mustn't bother us!' . . . such was the spirit that animated many among them. But Marie hung on, argued and won.—

A telegram or a telephone call would notify Mme Curie that an ambulance laden with wounded demanded a radiological post in a hurry. Marie would immediately verify the equipment of her car and attach her apparatus and dynamo. While the military chauffeur took on petrol, she would go home and get her dark cloak, her little travelling hat, soft and round, which had lost both form and colour, and her baggage: a yellow leather bag, cracked and peeling. She climbed in beside the driver, on the seat exposed to the wind, and soon the stout car was rolling at full speed – namely, the 'twenty-miles-an-hour average,' which was its best – toward Amiens, Ypres, Verdun.

EVE CURIE

Belgium 1914

One evening we drove out to a turnip-field about half a mile outside Melle, where we were told that some wounded were lying — Tom and I loaded our ambulance to more than capacity, and I waited with the four men that were left while he made the journey to Ghent and back. There were three German sitting cases and one Frenchman with a badly mangled shoulder and arm.

The firing had died down, and it was very silent and getting dark. Suddenly a voice said: 'Schwester, sprechen Sie deutsch?' 'Ja', I replied, and the man told me to take a greatcoat from one of the German corpses and come and sit with them — it was weird sitting there chatting with the Germans (they showed me photographs of their families and asked about mine) and supporting the head of the unconscious Frenchman.

Back to Belgium

—We were to go to Furnes, which was the base for the Dixmunde sector, and bring in the wounded for treatment. We knew we were going into the thick of it, for the shelling was said to be of an intensity hitherto undreamed of. But I, for one, was glad.

—I had not time to ask questions or puzzle over the whys and wherefores. Every ambulance vehicle that could be mustered was needed for the Front, and there was such a shortage of drivers that I was pushed straight into a heavy Napier ambulance and ordered to move off in the direction of Dixmunde without delay. I had never driven anything like it before, but in the next few months I got used to driving strange vehicles at a moment's notice – including Daimlers, Wolseleys, Mercedes, Pipes, Sunbeams, and Fiats.

Fight for an Idea

—I wanted to set up a first-aid station (or Advanced Dressing Station, as it was called) where the wounded could rest and recuperate before being jolted over the roads to the operating-table. I had noticed how many of them died of superficial hurts, a broken arm, perhaps, or a gash—I knew why it happened. They were victims of shock – the greatest killer of them all—

At first it seemed that I would never even get a cellar to work in—

The Belgian Admiral Ronarc'h was present when Elsie Knocker pleaded for her idea.

He had never heard anything so absurd. Surely I knew that women were not allowed in the trenches? They had to be at least three miles behind the lines. If I chose to disobey orders I could expect no assistance, and that meant no rations and no medical supplies. The Admiral stated firmly, almost with relish, that because I was a woman (and, oh, how utterly disparaging those two words, *une femme*, can sound!) I could not possibly stand the strain of Front-line life —When he had finished I informed the Admiral as respectfully as I could manage that because I was a woman I could stand strain and hardship (I nearly asked him if he had ever heard of childbirth) — I was fortunate to meet a Belgian army doctor who fully agreed with my plans — He suggested that a village called Pervyse might be the spot, and we drove out to have a look at it—

'Our house' – for it was soon settled that Mairi Chisholm who had proved herself brave and steady as well as being an excellent driver, should accompany me – was a woeful sight. There was not a pane of glass left whole, the roof had fallen in, the walls were ominously cracked, and everything that was any good had been taken or looted. It was right at the edge of the village, nearest the tottering church and the trenches, and the stream of shells which the Germans lobbed across the water meant that we should have to sleep, cook, and nurse in the cellar. I could not wait to move in!

—We were unofficial visitors, there on approval and expected to leave in a few days with our tails between our legs. Those who didn't actually disapprove of us regarded us as a passing eccentricity. When our ambulances drove into Dixmunde the French marines had greeted us with shouts of 'Les folles anglaises' and though there were no such shouts at Pervyse, the thought was there — The trenches were only five yards away, and in those first days we took jug after jug of soup or hot chocolate to the men on watch. When they were relieved the men would come over to the Cellar House, as it became known, and queue up with their mugs — The soup and the chocolate made us known and welcome, but they were only a sideline—

Mme Curie who, with her daughter, was running an X-ray unit in Furnes, was most interested in our work, and did me the honour of visiting the Cellar House. She was only five feet tall, soft-spoken and gentle in manner. We had a long and most interesting technical talk about methods of treatment, and she agreed with me that the three greatest priorities of nursing were quiet, rest, and warmth.

Baroness de T'Serclaes (Mrs Elsie Knocker)

A Woman's Diary of the War

12 October 1914

This evening Dr. Hector Munro came in from the front with his oddly-dressed ladies, and at first one is inclined to call them masqueraders in their knickerbockers and puttees and caps, but I believe they have done excellent work. It is a queer side of war to see young, pretty English girls in khaki and thick boots, coming in from the trenches, where they have been picking up wounded men within a hundred yards of the enemy's lines, and carrying them away on stretchers. Wonderful little Walküres in knickerbockers, I lift my hat to you!

Sarah Macnaughtan

Antwerp October 1914

I stood on the road. There was no sound except the crackling of the flames of the houses on fire, and the screaming of the shells as they whizzed over my head. There was nothing living in sight down that long length of street. It was like a bad dream. But suddenly I saw tearing along towards me, at breakneck pace, three London motor buses – a dream-like touch of incongruity. But I ran out into the road and, risking being run down, spread out my arms to stop them. Would they heed? Thank God they did, and I asked the drivers, English Tommies, if they could help me and my nurses to the frontier. 'If you're quick as lightning,' they replied, 'but we have to get over the bridge of boats with our loads of ammunition, before it is blown up.'

I ran back to the staff, and in a few minutes we had collected our handbags which were waiting piled up on the road, and were all seated, sixteen of us, on the boxes of ammunition inside those motor buses which tore along the streets, dodging or bumping in and out of the great holes excavated by the shells. We laughed merrily at the thought of what fine fireworks we should be in the middle of, if a shell dropped our way. We were certainly, I believe, the last of the hospital staffs, and probably of the inhabitants, to leave the town and cross that bridge of boats.

A picture artist would have revelled in that night scene. It was seven o'clock, and behind us the town was in darkness save for the illumination caused by the burning houses. In front of us, gigantic flames from blazing oil-tanks along the river, gave the impression that the world was on fire, whilst over the swaying bridge-of-boats, streams of khaki-clad soldiers – the last hope of Antwerp – were hastily crossing, in orderly retreat, and disappearing into the darkness.

MURIEL ST CLAIR STOBART

56

My War Experiences in Two Continents

To-day I have been reading of the 'splendid retreat' of the Marines from Antwerp and their 'unprecedented reception' at Deal. Everyone appears to have been in a state of wild enthusiasm about them, and it seems almost like Mafeking over again.

What struck me most about these men was the way in which they blew their own trumpets in full retreat and while flying from the enemy. We travelled all day in the train with them, and had long conversations with them all. They were all saying, 'We will bring you the Kaiser's head, miss'; to which I replied, 'Well, you had better turn round and go the other way.' Some people like this 'English' spirit. I find the conceit of it most trying. Belgium is in the hands of the enemy, and we flee before him singing our own praises loudly as we do so. The Marines lost their kit, spent one night in Antwerp, and went back to England, where they had an amazing reception amid scenes of unprecedented enthusiasm! The Government will give them a fresh kit, and the public will cheer itself hoarse!

I could not help thinking, when I read the papers to-day, of our tired little body of nurses and doctors and orderlies going back quietly and unproclaimed to England to rest at Folkestone for three days and then to come out here again. They had been for eighteen hours under heavy shell fire without so much as a rifle to protect them, and with the immediate chance of a burning building falling about them. The nurses sat in the cellars tending wounded men, whom they refused to leave, and then hopped on to the outside of an ammunition bus 'to see the fun,' and came home to buy their little caps and aprons out of their own slender purses and start work again.

I shall believe in Britishers to the day of my death, and I hope I shall die before I cease to believe in them, but I do get some disillusions. At Antwerp not a man remained with us, and the worst of it was they made elaborate excuses for leaving. Even our sergeant, who helped during the night, took a comrade off in the morning and disappeared. Both were wounded, but not badly, and two young English Tommies, very slightly wounded, left us as soon as the firing began. We saw them afterwards at the bridge, and they looked pretty mean.

At Furnes Railway-Station

21 November

I am up to my eyes in soup! I have started my soup-kitchen at the station, and it gives me a lot to do. Bad luck to it, my cold and cough are pretty bad!

It is odd to wake in the morning in a frozen room, with every pane of glass green and thick with frost, and one does not dare to think of Mary and morning tea! When I can summon enough moral courage to put a foot out of bed I jump into my clothes at once; half dressed, I go to a little tap of cold water to wash, and then, and for ever, I forgive entirely those sections of society who do not tub. We brush our own boots here, and put on all the clothes we possess, and then descend to a breakfast of Quaker oat porridge with bread and margarine. I wouldn't have it different, really, till our men are out of the trenches; but I am hoping most fervently that I shan't break down, as I am so 'full with soup.'

Our kitchen at the railway-station is a little bit of a passage, which measures eight feet by eight feet. In it are two small stoves. One is a little round iron thing which burns, and the other is a sort of little 'kitchener' which doesn't! With this equipment, and various huge 'marmites,' we make coffee and soup for hundreds of men every day. The first convoy gets into the station about 9.30 a.m., all the men frozen, the black troops nearly dead with cold. As soon as the train arrives I carry out one of my boiling 'marmites' to the middle of the stone entrance and ladle out the soup, while a Belgian Sister takes round coffee and bread.

Sarah Macnaughtan

58

Viscount Feilding shows conspicuous gallantry, deserves his D.S.O. and gets it. His sister, Lady Dorothy, has likewise shown conspicuous gallantry, deserves her D.S.O. or some corresponding distinction, and does not get it. Surely it is the right moment for the invention of new honours for the sex that is never paid official compliments.

Daily Chronicle, 2 February 1915

Women at the Front

The finest part of it will never be known, for it was done in solitary places and in the dark when Special Correspondents are asleep in their hotels. There was no limelight on their field at Melle, or on that road between Dixmunde and Furnes, or among the blood and straw in the cellar at Pervyse.

MAY SINCLAIR

Fragment of Autobiography

Belgian Refugee Work

Dame Adelaide Livingstone (then Miss Stickney) was an American and therefore neutral. She went backwards and forwards to occupied Belgium escorting German women from London and bringing out refugees. After the fall of Antwerp, returning from one journey as usual via Holland, she brought an urgent request for help; thousands of refugees had fled into Holland from Belgium, and Dutch resources were strained to the utmost to provide food and shelter.

Crystall *(sic)* Macmillan took immediate action. From the

Belgian Ambassador she obtained a guarantee of £200 with which to buy food. She and I went to Lyon's head-quarters and then and there brought £200 worth of provisions. We saw the cases loaded on to lorries and sent off to the ship on which we were to take them to Flushing. There were hundreds of loaves of bread, cases of condensed milk, chocolate and other foods. We collected the things necessary for a couple of nights and joined the ship. We were the only passengers and the North Sea was as empty of shipping as our boat was of people. We had one qualm when we saw a periscope, but it turned out to be a British submarine.

Flushing was a tragic sight, swarming with refugees. The walls were covered with notices of missing persons, and hundreds of families were sheltering in huge railway sheds, with the arc lights full on and Dutch soldiers keeping guard. The weather was damp and bitterly cold, and in the big square tarpaulins were set up to give some shelter.

We had difficulty in finding beds for ourselves for the night, but finally the chef at one hotel let us have his private lodgings. We returned on a ship packed with refugees; and the next day I reported to the Foreign Office.

MARY SHEEPSHANKS

A *Stewardess's Diary*

Ferrying Belgian Refugees

Jan 6th 1915

Got up at 8 o'clock after a cold restless night & found we had left Parkestone Quay, bound for the Hook of Holland. 8.45 a.m. the ship ran aground just off Landguard, we had a nice breakfast of bacon & eggs, yet the time we had finished breakfast the ship had started off once more, we had a very fair trip, the weather being fine but as we had not been on board for some time we suffered from mal-de-mer, arrived Hook of Holland 4.30 p.m.

Got up at 7.30 a.m.—started work 9 o'clock getting ready for refugees—2.30 p.m. refugees began to arrive on the quay, from the Hague, & the order came that the Stewardesses were to go to help put labels on each refugee, but as there was a lot of business to go through they were unable to get on the ship until 7.30 p.m. then they were all given a good supper of Irish stew & potatoes, which they showed a good appetite for. They were a very good class of people and appeared very pleased at the idea of going to England. Retired to bed at 11.15

Got up at 6 o'clock, left Hook van Holland 7.15 a.m. the sea was rather rough so passengers & crew required nothing beyond dry biscuits & bitter coffee, everybody was sick during the morning, but about 1.30 p.m. some were able to eat a few sandwiches & as soon as got into Thames we were able to serve hot dinners, which every-one did full justice, we reached Tilbury 7.30 p.m, where we anchored, & passengers were taken to shore in small tenders, after getting rid of passengers we found plenty to do until supper time, retired to bed 11.30 p.m.

Miss Youngs made a further trip 11–13 January.

Had a busy day cleaning up getting ready for next refugees.

Left Tilbury 6.20 had a fair crossing, on nearing the Hook of Holland a pilot boat signaled for us to stop, as they had just sunk a mine they had found in our course, we were detained about one hour while they made a thorough search for others before we could proceed, arrived at Hook 5.30 p.m. went ashore in the evening & did a little shopping.

Had boat drill, and a very busy morning, rested in the afternoon
& evening.

Jan 17th

Sunday writing letters untill dinner time, refugees came on board
2.30 p.m. very rough lot this time, & about 536 of which there
were over 200 men, we fed them all with Hot Stew potatoes &
coffee, some were very gratefull, but several were very dissatis-
fied over the sleeping accommodation which we thought very
inconsiderate as they were using all the best parts of the ship
also cabins which ordinary passengers would have to pay 30/-
excess fare. However we got them all comfortably settled for the
nigh(t) about 10.30

Jan 18th

Left Hook of Holland 6.20, had a very rough crossing, until
dinner time it was quite impossible to give the refugees even a
drink of coffee, every-one was sick & lying about in all directions—

Miss Youngs crossed back to Holland on 20 January.

Jan 22nd

We were just leaving the Quay for Tilbury when the Captain
received a message that one of the Leith boats 'The Dunvar'
had been sunk by an enemy submarine U21 and it being considered rather dangerous for us to proceed with so many people
on board we remained at the Hook of Holland, the refugees
were very disappointed when they heard they would not be
able to go to England that day. The officers fixed up some
swings for the children, & also supplied them with ropes for
skipping, the grown up's amused themselves with cards & one
having a Concertina they were able to have some dancing &
singing—

Most of the refugees were astir very early & were served with breakfast at 7.15 a.m. they were still in hopes of going to England and were very disappointed when they heard they were going to Rotterdam we arrived there about 12.30 p.m. We serve(d) them with a nice hot dinner as we were proceeding up the river—

Jan 24th

—We left the ship about 10.45 a.m. & found our way around the principal throughfare of the town, this being the first time we have had the pleasure of going for a walk in the day-time since we left home on the 5th — After dinner some of us again took advantage of seeing more of the scenury of this quaint old Dutch town, the way the canals wind in and out of the main streets, & the way some of the Houses are built right down into the water appeared very striking, as did also the numbers of windmills for which Holland is noted—

Jan 26th

We left Rotterdam at daybreak, and had lovely weather on our journey home, we arrived alongside Parkeston Quay at 2.30 p.m. having been away just three weeks, & after waiting for orders we proceeded to our own home's wondering how long it will be before we shall return to Holland for more refugees.

Miss M. C. Youngs

Diary 1914

Belgian Refugees in England

Sept 24th

We decided to have two Belgian refugees & put them up in the rooms over the stable, should any Belgians be sent into Gloucestershire. We have whitewashed scrubbed & made the rooms most attractive. Today we heard that 50 refugees were arriving at Stroud at 3. We waited in the station till 5.30. Miss Dickenson who appeared to be in charge, told us to carry off any that would suit us.

The refugees when they did arrive stepped off in a forlorn & apathetic manner, clutching bundles & baskets & numberless babies. All seemed to be huge families, the smallest lot being 6. These we commandeered. Father stout & had been rather dapper, Mother tall, stout & had been fashionable, 2 daughters also stout, red cheeked & yellow haired. Little boy of 12 not so stout. Baby very stout pale straw coloured hair & a most bewitching smile.

We got them all into a car which was waiting to help distribute them & brought them along. While they had supper in the kitchen we flew around & made up extra beds, putting the two girls in Joan's room. It was 8.30 by the time every thing was arranged so as they seem dead beat we let them go to bed.

Sept 26th

Their name is Yeughels & their story as follows. They lived just under the church tower in Malines. When the bombardment began fearing it would fall on them they lived for 3 days in the cellars & then fled. For two nights they slept in a greenhouse. Then they went on to Antwerp & came to England in a refugee boat. The father was a traveller in wines wall papers & corn, a most peculiar mixture!

Nov 20

Belgians getting on pretty well though they are a bit exacting about their food & raiment. Mrs refused a charming little red coat because 'red does not suit fair babies'. The baby is a dear and has already begun to talk English. He says 'Mees West, pudding, what is dat? Chickens etc.' Other peoples Belgians are not so amiable. Those in Woodchester do their own catering & run up huge bills, buying only the best joints, & quantities of butter &

eggs—Most people agree that they are fat, lazy, greedy, amiable
& inclined to take all the benefits heaped on them as a matter of
course.

Miss G. M. West

Women of the War

Commandant Damer Dawson

The employment of women for police service, in vogue for some
time on the Continent and in the United States of America, has
been developed in this country only by the outbreak of the war—
  —The influx of Belgian refugees in August 1914 became the
starting-point of the movement. While aiding forlorn exiles in
London byways in the small hours of the night, it was borne in
upon Miss Damer Dawson how much work in the streets could
be done by an organised band of trained women, armed with
authority. The idea took root in her mind and grew with her work.
She was soon joined by Miss M. S. Allen and Miss Goldringham,
and from that period the Women Police Service may be said to
have originated.

Barbara McLaren

The Forbidden Zone

Belgium

Mud: and a thin rain coming down to make more mud.

  Mud: with scraps of iron lying in it and the straggling fragment
of a nation, lolling, hanging about in the mud on the edge of disaster.

  It is quiet here. The rain and the mud muffle the voice of the
war that is growling beyond the horizon. But if you listen you can

hear cataracts of iron pouring down channels in the sodden land, and you feel the earth trembling.

Back there is France, just behind the windmill. To the north, the coast; a coast without a port, futile. On our right? That's the road to Ypres. The less said about that road the better: no one goes down it for choice – it's British now. Ahead of us, then? No, you can't get out that way. No, there's no frontier, just a bleeding edge, trenches. That's where the enemy took his last bite, fastened his iron teeth, and stuffed to bursting, stopped devouring Belgium, left this strip, these useless fields, these crumpled dwellings.

Cities? None. Towns? No whole ones. Yes, there are half a dozen villages. But there is plenty of mud, and a thin silent rain falling to make more mud – mud with things lying in it, wheels, broken motors, parts of houses, graves.

This is what is left of Belgium. Come, I'll show you. Here are trees drooping along a canal, ploughed fields, roads leading into sand dunes, roofless houses. There's a farm, an old woman with a crooked back feeding chickens, a convoy of motor lorries round a barn; they squat like elephants. And here is a village crouching in the mud: the cobblestone street is slippery and smeared with refuse, and there is a yellow cat sitting in a window. This is the headquarters of the Belgian Army. You see those men, lolling in the doorways – uncouth, dishevelled, dirty? They are soldiers. You can read on their heavy jowls, in their stupified, patient, hopeless eyes, how boring it is to be a hero.

The king is here. His office is in the school-room down the street, a little way past the church, just beyond the dung heap. If we wait we may see him. Let's stand with these people in the rain and wait.

A band is going to play to the army. Yes, I told you, this is the army – these stolid men standing aimlessly in the drizzle, and these who come stumbling along the slippery ditches, and those leaning in degraded doorways. They fought their way out of Liege and Namur, followed the king here; they are what is left of plucky little Belgium's heroic army.

And the song of the nation that comes from the horns in the front of the wine shop, the song that sounds like the bleating of sheep, can it help them? Can it deceive them? Can it whisk from their faces the stale despair, the unutterable boredom, and brighten their disappointed eyes? They are so few, and they have nothing to do but stand in the rain waiting. When the band stops they will disappear into the estaminet to warm their stomachs with wine and cuddle the round-cheeked girls. What else can they do? The French are on one side of them, the British on the other, and the enemy in front. They cannot go back; to go back is to retreat, and they have been retreating ever since they can remember. They can retreat no farther. This village is where they stop. At one end of it is a pigsty, at the other end is a grave-yard, and all about are flats of mud. Can the noise, the rhythmical beating of the drum, the piping, the hoarse shrieking, help these men, make them believe, make them glad to be heroes? They have nowhere to go now and nothing to do. There is nothing but mud all about, and a soft fine rain coming down to make more mud – mud with a broken fragment of a nation lolling in it, hanging about waiting in it behind the shelter of a disaster that has been accomplished.

Come away, for God's sake – come away. Let's go back to Dunkerque. The king? Didn't you see him? He came out of the school-house some time ago and drove away toward the sand-dunes – a big fair man in uniform. You didn't notice? Never mind. Come away.

MARY BORDEN

Field Hospital and Flying Column

The Bombardment of Lodz: November 1914

At 5 a.m. there came a lull. The tragic procession ceased for a while, and we went to lie down. At seven o'clock we were called again – another batch of wounded was being brought in.

The shelling had begun again, and was terrific; crash, crash, over our heads the whole time. A clock-tower close to the hospital was demolished and windows broken everywhere. The shells were bursting everywhere in the street, and civilians were being brought in to us severely wounded. A little child was carried in with half its head blown open, and then an old Jewish woman with both legs blown off, and a terrible wound in her chest, who only lived an hour or two. Apparently she suffered no pain, but was most dreadfully agitated, poor old dear, at having lost her wig in the transit. They began bringing in so many that we had to stop civilians being brought in at all, as it was more than we could do to cope with the wounded soldiers that were being brought in all the time.

At midday we went to a hotel for a meal. There was very, very little food left in Lodz, but they brought what they could. Coming back to the hospital we tried everywhere to get some bread, but there was none to be had anywhere – all the provision shops were quite empty, and the inhabitants looked miserable and starved, the Jewish population particularly so, though they were probably not among the poorest.

On our way back a shell burst quite close to us in the street, but no one was hurt. These shells make a most horrible scream before bursting, like an animal in pain. Ordinarily I am the most dreadful coward in the world about loud noises. I even hate a sham thunderstorm in a theatre – but here somehow the shells were so part of the whole thing that one did not realize that all this was happening to *us*, one felt rather like a disinterested spectator at a far-off dream. It was probably partly due to want of sleep; one's hands did the work, but one's mind was mercifully numbed. Mercifully, for it was more like hell than anything I can imagine. The never-ending processions of groaning men being brought in on those horrible blood-soaked stretchers, suffering unimagined tortures, the filth, the cold, the stench, the hunger, the vermin, and the squalor of it all, added to one's utter helplessness to do more than very little to relieve their misery, was almost enough to make even Satan weep.

VIOLET THURSTON

A *History of the Scottish Women's Hospitals*

These first few days at Royaumont I shall always look back on as an experience worth having. In surroundings of mediæval grandeur – amid vaulted corridors, Gothic refectories, and cloisters – we proceeded to camp out with what we carried. The Abbey, in all its magnificence, was ours; but during those first few days it did not offer us very much beyond magnificence and shelter. It had not been lived in for years, and its water-supply had been cut off when the nuns left it for Belgium. Hence we carried water in buckets up imposing staircases and along equally imposing corridors. Our only available stove – a mighty erection in the kitchen that had not been lit for a decade – was naturally short-tempered at first, and the supply of hot water was limited indeed. So, in consequence, was our first washing at times very limited indeed. Our equipment, after the fashion of baggage in these times of war, was in no great hurry to arrive; until it did arrive we did without sheets and blankets, wrapped ourselves in rugs and overcoats at night, and did not do much undressing. We borrowed teacups from the village ironmonger, and passed the one knife round at meals for every one to take a chop with it. We were as short of lamps as we were of knives – shorter; and we wandered about our majestic pile with candle-ends stuck in bottles; little twinkling candle-ends, that struggled with the shadows under the groined roofs — We are getting electric light in now, and already I find it in my heart to regret these bottled candles with their Rembrandtesque effects — A few days ago our equipment condescended to arrive, and now we have knives all round, and blankets and towels. More important still, there are rows of beds in the wards, and we are waiting the formal visit of inspection of the French Military Authority.

CICELY HAMILTON

Life on an Ambulance Train in France

1914–1917

It is a life of uncertainty. A Sister receives orders she is to join a certain Train – where is the Train? No one knows – Where, when and how can she join it? No one knows. Who arranges where and when an individual Ambulance Train shall run? No one knows who is the Deux ex Machina—(I say individual advisedly – for the train on which one lives becomes as much an individual companion or friend as one's horse or Motor Car.)—

To the waiting Sister the longed for intelligence comes at last, and an order to be at such and such a place at a certain time. Probably the time is night, or early dark and cold morning. Personal belongings are reduced to a minimum; a car or an ambulance drops the train seeker at the nearest point to the Garage, and in darkness a perilous foot journey intervenes, among and across railway lines, moving trains, shunting trucks, points and signal wires, clutching Suit Case and Hold-all, before the Train is boarded.

The Staff Coach is usually in the middle of the Train and is occupied by the Medical Officers and Nursing Sisters.

It has a Corridor and the compartments are transformed into Bed-Sitting Rooms and Mess Rooms.

Away from this centre, at either end, runs the long, long Train – a shining, vibrant, living creature of sinuous grace. It is a very patient and long-suffering creature, for it has many and various Drivers – some French, some English, some who understand its Brakes and ways, some who do not, and like a well or badly driven horse, so it responds. But it has no vice and when bumped and jerked and broken, it still holds its load safely. Thus it winds its way, up hill and down, through woods and vales and towns: along single lines or threading, bumping, grating its mysterious track among labyrinths of metals, into great junctions. Dashing at high speed 'Empty' to a far advanced Casualty Clearing Station

(C.C.S.) to gather a 'Crisis Load'; or returning at ten miles an hour, bearing within it the shattered remnants of those, who so proudly and bravely sallied forth against the foe, on the Battlefield a few short hours before. Sometimes under shell fire, sometimes under raiding or fighting aeroplanes it serenely 'carries on.'

On arriving at the 'Rail Head' where the Casualty Clearing Stations lie, the work for the staff begins.

The patients are brought to the Train in Ambulances or on little trollies run on light rails. They lie on stretchers and are passed into the coaches or 'wards' of the Train and are then transferred to the beds. The Sisters receive them and examine their Medical Cards, decide what Diet they should have and arrange their shattered limbs, by means of bandages, pillows, sand bags etc, to travel with as little suffering as possible.

Mud, blood and sweat clothe them still, and the tormenting parasites accompany them unless they have been detained for a period at the C.C.S. until fit to undertake the journey, in which case they have been cleansed and clothed afresh.

No tongue can tell what these patients have been through, and none, who have not at least seen them in their Battle-field array, can form any conception of it—

The space is very confined. 'Stretcher cases' fill up the floors of the Wards, in addition to the occupied beds which are arranged in tiers like the bunks in a ship's cabin. Water is heavy and difficult to carry, therefore must be used economically – sterilizing or boiling of water for fomentations, tea or bovril, has to be done on a Primus Stove, in the midst of the crush and in spite of the swaying, jerking train, helpless patients to be fed in almost inaccessible positions, carrel tubes charged, splints adjusted, dressings attended to by sisters in acrobatic and perilous positions. But whatever is done is so necessary and so joyously and gratefully received, that the handicaps, limitations and crass imperfections of the nursing, per se, are compensated—

It usually takes about two hours to load and two to unload an

Ambulance Train and the journeys (loaded) last anything between six and thirty-six hours. The average length of time is probably twelve hours for a journey loaded.

The Ambulance Train comes 4th in the Traffic Schedule, and is often held back for troops, Ammunition and Supply Trains which have precedence. A loaded Ambulance Train has a speed limit also. But long though such journeys are for sick and wounded, the patients are so much more comfortable than they have been for many long weary days and nights on active service, that they sleep and rest, thankful to have done their bit, and to be getting away from the horror of it all for a while—

On reaching its destination the loaded Train becomes again like a beehive in swarm.

In the early morning hours, dark and cold and wet, the unloading usually takes place.

Ambulances, stretchers and Stretcher Bearers appear like a waiting Shadow Crowd, as the Train glides into her berth, but soon, under a few dim lights, the shadows spring to life. Ambulances hum, Bearers shout and moving lights and vague forms thread a maze-like dance, which to the uninitiated, must look weird and dangerous in the extreme. The Engine is taken off and the Train seems dead, though every door is flung wide open and a constant stream of stretcher borne, blanket wrapped figures passes out from the hands of the Train Orderlies, to those of the Platform Stretcher Bearers—

Once in the Ambulance, the Train Staff has no more jurisdiction over the patients. Slowly and carefully they are driven away; the Train Staff knows not whither. The orders as to which Hospital each loaded Ambulance is bound for are given by an officer at the station exit.

The Train is now 'Empty', except for its permanent dwellers. These return to their various quarters and labours—

The Engine Driver, French or English, is the best authority as to the destination of an Ambulance Train and even he is not to be relied upon, as he may only drive to a certain point and then hand over to another authority and driver, French or English –

Also the hour at which an Ambulance Train starts, is as uncertain as the weather.

Information may be given to the Officer Commanding that the Engine will not 'come on' for a couple of hours at least. The O.C. thereupon, having due regard for the health and necessities of his staff, allows certain members, Sisters and others, to go out: but it is quite possible that, during their absence, long before the stated hour, those left on the Train will feel the familiar little thud and vibration, which means 'Engine on – we're off!' and regardless of the feelings or inconvenience of anyone, 'off' we are, and 'on' the absentees are not.

These are exciting moments.

By means, however, of telephone, cars and messengers, the missing members are usually retrieved before the Train has crawled, bumped, laboured and shrieked its long length over points, paused at Signal boxes and got up speed.

Two hours only is the regulation leave of absence from the Train and often it is impracticable to take that.

Sisters are not allowed 'out' singly except at the Base towns and one Sister must always remain on the Train.—

The scenery through which the train runs is most varied. Flourishing towns and fair rich country in the peace areas, give place to desolation, chaos and ruin, as the track of the Armies is followed up. Traces of German occupation and ruination give way to British occupation and re-construction, followed by re-possession by French. Shattered villages with ruins, barely marking out former streets, in seas of mud, thronged with Khaki clad troops, living in cellars or roofless, almost wall-less rooms; among them the few French women and old men, who braved all, rather than leave their wrecked homes, with their tiny displays of goods to tempt the Tommy: the forlorn and homeless cats, the booming of big guns, the rattle of machine guns, the hum of aeroplanes, the cram and crush and crowd of the high roads: troops marching or riding in old London buses, cavalry, motor lorries and cars, bicycles, German prisoners; as the Army presses on, a forlorn and haunted emptiness, till safety being assured, the inhabitants begin to creep back again: the awful aspect of shell destroyed land under winter snow and mud, retreats before the miracle of Spring when Nature throws a veil of beauty over the hideous desolation and ruin, making the remembrance of what *was* impossible before what *is*.

This account of A.T. work would be incomplete without reference to the special difficulties attached to the work on 'French' trains that have been adapted to this use, as against Khaki or English Trains, built for the purpose.

The Khaki trains have a corridor passing down their whole length and many special arrangements facilitating the work.

The adapted French train is merely an ordinary non-corridor passenger train. Thus each ward or coach becomes self-contained and isolated from others. Two orderlies are in charge of each coach and the M.O.s and sisters visit their appointed number in turn. This necessitates constant jumping up and down when the train is standing, in rain, wind or snow, unspeakable mud, daylight or pitch black night, or 'foot boarding' from coach to coach.

The lights of the train are closely veiled. If an air raid takes place over and around it, all lights are extinguished and like a long dark snake it squats on the lines, waiting till the danger is passed.

Thus the difficulties, fatigue and danger of the work on a 'French' train are considerably added to by its construction – so also are the interest and the 'thrill.'

MISS BICKMORE

Animals at War

Letter to the Daily Mirror, 11 August 1914

For the Horses

I chanced to be at Waterloo Station when several fine horses were patiently waiting to be taken off to war, and the thought struck me how infinitely sad it is to contemplate the terrible pain that these poor creatures may be called upon to bear when left to die slowly, and in torment, on the battlefield.

Can no one suggest means whereby these suffering animals could be mercifully put out of their misery at the end of an encounter? Of course, the men come first, for whom our hearts are aching with sympathy, but have we none to spare for the friend of man, the noble cavalry horse, who has to suffer untold agony caused by shrapnel and other hideous inventions of the civilised world?

ETHEL M. BILBOROUGH

Belgium 1914

On the way back to Ghent to open a centre for women and children – for our unit did not allow the 'military only' rule to stifle mercy – I noticed a small cart drawn by a big dog. In the cart was a baby, and the mother was walking behind holding a child of two or three years. With the baby in the cart was a pitiful bundle of possessions.

As we drew alongside I saw that the dog was limping along on three legs. The woman told me that her husband had been killed, and as I spoke to her the dog took a few moments to lie between the shafts and lick his badly gashed leg. I bent down to look at his wound, and in his eyes saw the pathetic appeal: 'Please help me; I am in such pain'. I knew the dog could not carry on, so I bandaged his wound — and we bundled the mother, children, and dog into the back (*of the ambulance*), and saw them safe and provided for in the city.

BARONESS DE T'SERCLAES, (Mrs Elsie Knocker)

Journal

Belgium, 1914

My heart bled at the pathetic sight of the many dogs & cats that refused to leave the piles of what had been their homes. Many of these were mad with starvation & snarled when we approached them. It seemed so terrible that these faithful dumb pets of scattered families should also have to suffer in such an awful way. The next day I returned, borrowed a rifle from a soldier, & another soldier & myself went round shooting these miserable howling & starving things.

We had very nearly finished our gruesome job, when we had to stop suddenly as the Germans began to answer our rifle shots from a wood beyond. I saw a small kitten, frightened by our firing, rush out of the remains of a house, & I was just about to shoot it when it ran towards me & sat down at my feet.

I hate cats, but the poor wee thing looked so pathetic as it looked up at me with its little mouth open, that I stooped & picked it up, & it was then I saw that it had but three feet, one of its back ones having been shot off & the stump was bleeding. I carried it to the hospital & dressed its wound, & that night it went back to Antwerp with us as the smallest & youngest 'blessé' & the mascot of our hospital.

GERTRUDE HOLLAND

Modern Troubadours

The first of the concerts we gave in the open air was at Forges les Eaux, so called because of the iron spring that was discovered about 400 years ago. It had been a watering-place with a Casino and Hotel des Bains ever since — Forges les Eaux was the horses' hospital, a wonderful example of human organisation. The horses had their operating theatre, sterilising apparatus, chloroform nose-bags, surgical instruments and pills a fearful sight those pills, rather like cartridges in size and colour – doses and tonics, just like their human brothers.

LENA ASHWELL

Dîk: A Dog of Belgium

They called him bomb-proof Dîk, because the noise of battle never moved him.

Even when he was training for his career as a Red Cross dog in Antwerp he did not start to run, as was the way with other dogs when the trainers made strange, unearthly sounds issue from

77

various corners, in order to accustom his pupils to the roar of the cannon and the explosion of bombs—

It was when the firing had ceased, after battle, that Dîk's duties began. Then he went forth with the Red Cross to search for the wounded. Wearing his uniform of white blanket with a red cross stitched on either side, Dîk would stand stiffly at 'attention' before his commanding officer, and at the short, sharp word *'Cherchez!'* he would bound away, filling the desolate wood and field with a penetrating, yet gentle 'woof-woof' in order that the wounded might know, from afar, that a comforter approached.

For comforter, indeed, was Dîk. His blanket pockets were laden with all the requisites of first-aid – a bottle of brandy and water, a bottle of hygienic liquid for the cleansing and easing of wounds; food tabloids in a little pocket by themselves, and in still another, bandages and medicated cotton wool. Close to the prostrate men in the blue uniform with the red stripes Dîk would go, 'standing by' while those who could help themselves would put their hands in his pockets and take out the bottles and tabloids — *(but)* some were so badly wounded that they were helpless.

Dîk understood all this in a moment, and so he did not 'stand by', but with just a reassuring bark he would turn and bring back with the utmost despatch the men who carried the stretchers. He had learned to know, too, when no help could be rendered to the stiff, stark figures, which lay upon ground, and so he went on understanding that the wounded must be helped first and that afterwards the dead would be buried. There were times when Dîk stood a lonely mourner while one of his human comrades was hastily lowered to a quickly dug grave—

ELIZABETH BANKS

Glossy Golden War Dogs

On the roads there was the usual medley of the races of the world, added to, as we drew near the town, by Canadian nurses in streaming white veils and uniforms of brilliant blue and also – for surely the most delightful of created beings may rank as a race of the world – by the glossy golden war dogs, who also have their training camp near here, and take their walks abroad, waving their plumey tails and jumping up on their masters, like any leisured dog at home. But – to my sorrow – I was not sent to look at war dogs, and so had to pass by and leave the wagging plumes behind.

F. Tennyson Jesse

1915

To offset the generally discouraging war news, newspapers increasingly focused attention on their splendid women, particularly those who had taken over men's jobs.

Despite the propaganda, the replacement of male by female labour was anything but rapid. In Britain 14 per cent of 'gainfully employed' women had been thrown out of work and it was not until the spring of 1915 that prewar levels began to be restored. Similar figures were true of other belligerent nations, though Germany and France were faster off the replacement mark. In Britain the 'shell scandal' (the lack of shells during the Second Battle of Ypres) led to the formation of a coalition government and to David Lloyd George's appointment as Minister of Munitions. It was 'the Welsh Wizard' who negotiated with deeply suspicious men's trade unions about 'dilution', the code word for female labour. The arguments about what had and had not been agreed with regard to pay and conditions simmered throughout the war – and from time to time erupted – but Britain had the clearest agreement of any warring country.

This was the year in which pacifist women did their utmost to bring the hostilities to an end. The logistics of holding peace conferences in war-battered Europe were difficult, to say the least. The first group to overcome them were Socialist women who met in neutral Switzerland. Their efforts were virtually ignored by the world's press. The British government's reaction to the news of an International Women's Congress in neutral Holland was swift. It closed the North Sea to all ships in British waters. In contrast to the Berne Congress, the one held in The Hague received an avalanche of publicity, most of it hostile. Although they continued to campaign throughout the war, the women pacifists never again garnered such attention.

It was in 1915 that the Germans executed Edith Cavell and sank the *Lusitania*. Even if Nurse Cavell was guilty of assisting British soldiers to escape from the Brussels hospital of which she had remained matron, and the *Lusitania* carried war material as well as its civilian passengers, the Germans showed ill judgement in perpetrating both actions.

Italy entered the war on the Allies' side, Bulgaria on the Central Powers'. In the spring the Allies launched the disastrous Dardanelles campaign against the Turks (and the name Gallipoli was burned into Australian and New Zealand folk memory.) The Serbs had held the Austrian invaders at bay but in the autumn a joint German and Bulgarian attack squeezed their army like a nut in a nut-cracker. A rearguard of the Scottish Women's Hospital including their leader, Dr Elsie Inglis, stayed with their seriously wounded Serbs. They were captured but eventually released. Most of the British women from the various units which had gone out to give desperately needed medical aid, retreated with the Serbian army across the Albanian mountains in the most appalling winter conditions. With the exception of a SWH nurse who died from injuries sustained when her lorry slithered over a cliff, all the British women survived.

'We Demand the Right to Serve'

A banner carried in the women's demonstration,
London, July 1915

Daily Sketch, 27 January 1915

Women in War: Mrs Pankhurst's Plan

In Paris just now there are many interesting Englishwomen, some
of them followers of the Red Cross, others on the trail of adventure at the edges of the war, but none of them more interesting
than a lady who is spending a quiet holiday in her daughter's flat,
a good stone's-throw from the Arc de Triomphe, in the Avenue de
la Grande Armée.

I went to talk to her in a bookish, newspaperish sitting-room,
comfortable in the English way, and with only a bright green
cushion and a purple one among the sofa-furnishings to give the
least clue to any stranger who wished to make deductions as to
the identity of its owner—

But it *was* Mrs. Pankhurst who began to talk, in the quiet way
which always surprises those who meet for the first time one of
the most resolute women in history, of a war-scheme which is at
present occupying most of her interest.

'I'm not nursing soldiers,' she told me. 'There are so many
others to do that. We have always worked in a national way, and
now we feel that our duty is still on national lines, so we are doing

everything we can to help recruiting, and make it possible for more and more men to go to fight.

'Annie Kenney has described the situation by saying that the Women's Social and Political Union has been the Downing-street of the women's movement, and that it is no more to be expected that our organisers should now necessarily take to knitting and nursing than that Mr. Asquith should set his Ministers to making Army boots or uniforms.

'Here in Paris I have been much interested in the women who are working as conductors on the trams. They do the work so well and cheerfully and look quite trim and business-like in their caps and woollen tippets—

POTENTIAL SOLDIERS HELD UP.
'It seems to me that the scheme would be practical on the London tramways, too – and, of course, we don't want it to stop at tramways. Before I left London I was able to compliment a girl who was cheerfully and cleverly working a lift in a London store, and thus in a sense, making possible another soldier. Why cannot women be allowed to release the men behind the counters, too?

'There are hundreds of women typists who could be drafted into war service while clerks and cashiers were defending the country. I think that women in banks could do a great deal of the work which is now holding up potential soldiers.

WASTED ENERGY.
'I feel sure that all women would welcome an industrial reserve scheme of this kind. Sex has nothing to do with patriotism or with the spirit of service. Women are just as eager to work for the nation as men are.'

EDITH SHACKLETON

Memoir

Munition Worker: London

Born in 1895, the eldest of six children, I grew up in Kentish Town which was then a 'respectable' working class district. At the age of fourteen I went into service. When the war broke out I was working for a nice American lady in Golders Green (some of my previous employers had been dragons). A hospital for wounded soldiers soon opened nearby and from the fruit in the garden we made hundreds of jars of crab-apple jelly for them!

As soon as I heard about the call for women to register for war work – that was early in 1915 – I shot down to Camden Town Labour Exchange. When nothing happened I found myself a job at a factory in the Grays Inn Road. It was only a small place, with white-washed walls and stone floors, and we called it the 'cow-shed'. The factory made fuses for shells and apart from the tool-makers and the foremen all the staff were female. It was a 24-hour operation with three 8-hour shifts working on a six-week cycle. We women were paid 5½d per hour but the men tool–makers got 2/6d. If our work was up to scratch, every six weeks, when we changed shifts, we received a bonus.

I started work on the machines which honed the fuses into shape. We had caps to cover our hair, and to stop the hot brass hitting our necks we turned our collars up, but otherwise we had no protection. There were minor accidents, of course, but I don't remember any serious ones. After a while I was promoted to be an 'examiner' which meant I had to check each fuse with a gauge to make sure it was dead level. On the night shifts, when the body is at its lowest ebb, we were allowed to sing! A group of us became so enthusiastic that we formed a choir and sang at charity concerts and to entertain wounded soldiers.

The Royal Free Hospital was then just down the road and we organised a 'comforts fund'. On pay-day everybody, well nearly everybody, put something into the kitty. By then they'd stopped moving the long convoys of ambulances by day for everybody to see and they came up at night from Charing Cross Station to the Royal Free. When we were on the night shift, during our break my friends and I used to go into the Grays Inn Road and wait for the convoys to pass. They moved very slowly and a lot of the ambulances had open backs so we ran alongside them, chatting to the less seriously wounded and giving them the chocolates and cigarettes we'd bought. Sometimes we saw somebody we knew and were able to tell their mum or their wife they were wounded but safe in England, which was nice.

ALICE CONNOR NÉE KEDGE

Berliner Leben 1914–1918

Munition Worker: Berlin

On 1 April 1915 I stood with my sister at half past five in the morning in front of the gates of the Spandau Munitions Works. The day before a doctor had examined us to see if we could be used as workers. Today we were to start. Soon a sergeant came with the friendly words: 'Right, women, it's down to work!' He shouted at a colleague who had rather a large behind: 'You'll soon be rid of your fat arse! Here work rules, it's full steam ahead!'

He was right. Women and girls were worked like animals. Alongside steam, dirt, unspeakable vulgarity and barbaric slave driving ruled. There were no such things as safety guards, or wherever there were small measures, they were rendered illusory by the speed of the work. In the first week alone three women lost fingers of their right hands in the casing of the engines — but the pace of the work was not slowed, nor was a guard attached.

The so-called 'union representative' had only one concern; to keep in touch with the supervisor and military officials so that he did not have to go to the Front. The working day: from six to six with half an hour for lunch and a quarter of an hour for breakfast.

A week of day shifts or a week of night shifts — And we stood for twelve hours and made grenades: instruments of death.

And there were the emotional traumas which the women suffered. Every day they came with swollen eyes, having heard the news that their husbands or sons had been wounded or killed—

One event shocked me deeply — There was a very young blonde woman in our row who had married just before the war broke out. If she didn't get a letter she would be ill and miserable that day. And one day – we were all traipsing exhausted back to our machines after breakfast when a terrible screaming echoed round the room. The blonde girl was huddled on the floor! She had received the letter: 'Fallen on the battlefield of honour.'

ANONYMOUS

Daily Graphic, 14 March 1916

The original Railway Free Buffet was opened on February 4th 1915, by Miss Margaret Boulton and Miss Marietta Feuerheerd, with whom originated the idea of the free buffets which have proved such a help and comfort to our soldiers and sailors. Thousands of men are served each week with hot tea, coffee, cocoa, bovril, sandwiches and cake—A writing table is also provided and constantly used. Cigarettes, socks, comforters and mittens are distributed freely.

Ladies Worth Fighting For

'May I have another cup of tea?' asks 'Tommy Atkins' at Victoria Station Buffet.

'Certainly, two if you would like them,' is the immediate reply.

'Thank you very much. You ladies are worth fighting for. You don't know what we think of you in the trenches.'

*By the end of the war 7,973,825 soldiers had been fed at station buf-
fets. Canadian Highlanders paid this tribute to London Bridge
Station:*

> *The ladies are very good to us here*
> *We do not require any more beer*
> *They make us so happy and send us away*
> *Shouting Hip, Hip, Hip Hooray!*

A War Diary

Visiting an Internment Ship

2 February 1915

On Saturday I had a long day going to Southend to the prison
ships. Two hours' train and hanging about on the pier for a boat
and under two hours on the 'Royal Edward' and 'Ivernia.' So I
saw very little except the officers, who seemed kindly nice people
on the whole. The general look of the ships – fine liners – as
pleasant as confinement can be, and the special young German I
went to see, Hermann Umfrid, son of Pastor Umfrid of Stuttgart,
who had written to L. to ask his good offices for his only son. The
young man looked a nice fellow – 22. Theological student for
the Ministry; volunteered, sent out to front after eight days' training, and captured at Ypres about two months ago. He knows little
English and I no German, so we talked through my companion,
Mrs. Bridgwater, a wonderful little woman, who is one of our
camp visitors (Emergency Committee) and evidently a welcome
one to prisoners and officials, for they all smile pleasantly at her,
and she seems to know nearly everyone. Well, Umfrid says he is
well and looked so, and quite satisfied – has everything he wants.
There are 1,400 on one boat and 1,600 on the other. The
Adjutant, Capt. McCullough, we have found a most kind, wise
man, and he and Mrs. B. were busy together arranging for the

marriages of several civil prisoners who had informal, but stable, relations with mothers, or about to become mothers, of their children. They had confided to Mrs. B. their trouble about leaving these young women wholly unprovided for with a baby coming, and wished to legalise the union, which in most cases has been permitted. Capt. McCullough was going on shore with half a dozen of his prisoners this week, to see them married. A curious job!

LADY COURTNEY OF PENWITH

Intelligence Work for the Empire

Dear Mums,

I am very nearly brilliant! What do you think of me at the War Office saving the Empire. Yes *really*! I went there on Sat to pass my test in French German Dutch Flemish & being full of swank I put 'Matabele and Zulu' on my paper! (Simply for doggo as I never thought it would be of *any* use to me again!)

But first – The German agents in Hamburg and Tembu-land are writing to each other in Kaffir re. assassination of Native Commissioners on receipt of smuggled arms & the details of the gun-running scheme were given – dates and all! Other important matters too re shipping thereof. Now you see, there are Englishmen in plenty who can speak & even write in Kafir *(sic)* but for instance 'guzaza gwambile nje' means absolutely nothing to them as not knowing *German* they fail to perceive that it is the *German* way of spelling 'Kusasai Kwenpili' & no one cd find the former in any dictionary & thought it 'obscure dialect' & gave it up. But M.D.B. the sleuth hound with the aid of Kropfs German-Zulu Dic. got the whole message down to a dot & you wd have blushed to hear the things said about your daughter — There was not a soul in the W.O. who cd do it & all squeaked in the test room when they saw 'Zulu' on my paper—

It really is a snip & I may have saved hundreds of white lives or

prevented the landing of thousands of guns ammunition &
assegai heads in Tembuland & district. Tally ho. One to me!

MURIEL DAYRELL-BROWNING

Intelligence Work for MI5

Out of the blue I received a letter from the clerical department of
M.I.5. No previous training or secretarial experience was necessary. The important thing was that we should have some further
education and should be a responsible type who could be trusted
to hold her tongue. Candidates for these posts were selected by
private recommendation and there was never any advertisement.

The department of M.I.5 to which I was sent was situated at 16
Charles Street, Haymarket. There were of course qualified typists
and secretaries but there was also a team of untrained women
who were search clerks. There was one very large room known as
the Registry in which there was an enormous card index which
grew daily. It stretched round the room like a snake. To this index
came cards with the names of spies, suspects, accomplices and
places often with actual addresses, and all kinds of information –
these had to be carefully inserted into the right places. Every
day there arrived from the different sub-departments files about
people suspected of being in league with the enemy. It was our
duty to look these up in the card index and try to connect the
information in the files. Sometimes through quite a chance reference to a place or person one would hit on an exciting trail and
unravel a piece of useful case-history. Many other times nothing
of value could be found and it gave one a pang to put N.T. (no
trace) and initial it and return the document to the original
department wondering 'Have I missed something?'—

One day I was sent for by one of the officers and asked if I
could re-organise and tabulate what was known as the 'Museum'.
This was a collection of all kinds of spy paraphernalia – books
with inter-leaves stuck together with messages inserted, invisible

inks, codes, and various means of transmitting information all intercepted or taken from captured spies. I gathered that I was asked to do this, not from any academic interest but for the entertainment and distraction of various V.I.P.'s who came calling, and to whom the hierarchy did not want to divulge anything of great importance. So every now and then I was called from the card index to show off the Museum to Brigadier or Air Marshal so and so. This I did, I hope, with an appearance of efficiency and it certainly seemed to intrigue them with a kind of school-boy interest.

MRS D.B.G. LINE NÉE DIMMOCK

Sussex Daily News, 1 May 1915

'Copperettes'

London has not yet grown accustomed to its policewomen. I saw one today at the corner of Whitehall, and she appeared very conscious of the attention she was attracting. There is nothing very distinctive about the neat blue costume that the women wear, and their hats rather suggest that they have just returned from a morning ride in the Row. It is only when you notice the WP on their shoulders that you recognize the work on which they are occupied. Physically the women are not of the type you would expect, and they seem little fitted to face the hurly-burly of a street row. Most of them are slight and fragile in build, and their hands are of the small, delicate type generally associated with the artistic temperament. If the women police act with tact and discretion, there is useful work for them to do in the West End of London, but the average Cockney seems at present to resent their presence in the streets. The suffragettes are to blame for this in large measure, for in the public mind the 'Copperettes', as the girls are called, have come to be associated, quite erroneously no doubt, with the women who used to break windows, and shout, 'Votes for women' in Parliament Square.

Women's War Work at Home:
Women's Emergency Corps

It should not be forgotten that women were foremost in the field, that women interpreters and women helpers met those tragic crowds at Charing Cross and Cannon Street stations. The Corps has still an interpreting depot and a Belgian clothing store. You will find them, oddly planted, in a chapel in Carton-Street. At the west end, under the gallery, the piles of garments are sorted and distributed; what was once the south aisle is given over to the Colonial Section, where garments sent from Australia and New Zealand arrive in great chests, to be dealt with by ladies who have come over to help the Mother Country. They will show you 'baby's kits' from Toowomba, Queensland, and other remote regions. There is something infinitely pathetic about bags full of little frocks and nightgowns and woolly vests that have travelled so far to the chapel in Carton-street.

MAY SINCLAIR

Deutsche Frauen Deutsche Treue

'It Wasn't Easy'

Our farm comprised 44 Morgen of land. When mobilisation came in August 1914 we were midway through the harvest. On the sixth mobilisation day my husband reported for duty and I had to bring in the grain alone with my fourteen-year-old sister. We could only use one of our two young horses, because the other had not been broken in yet. For months we had to do all the work in the stables and in the fields alone. Then we had a stable lad for a time; but he too was called up in January 1915. That year we also had to give up our best horse for war service.

When the time came for bringing in the fodder in summer we had to find another horse. Luckily, after many difficulties, my husband managed to get leave and was able to see to it himself. He bought a Russian horse. But what a creature that was! Whenever we tried to harness it, it would dance around on its hind legs. We had to exercise with it every day for a long time before we could finally use it for work. Later we got another fourteen-year-old boy to help us. But in the main I had to do all the work alone: looking after the horses and the animals, all the work in the fields, the threshing and clearing away, etc. It wasn't easy!

In 1916 I was given a Russian prisoner of war to help me. Now at least I didn't have to do the hard work myself. But he wasn't always easy to get along with. He could speak very good German, but often pretended he couldn't understand, and he was always cursing the 'damned Germans'. I kept him anyway; at least he was good at his work. I didn't want to have to start all over again with another one – who knows what I would have got instead.

In the evenings when I had put my little ones to bed – the youngest wasn't born until 1915 – I would write to my husband, telling him any good things I had to report and comforting him, so that he didn't have to worry about us at all.

Elise Löhnig

Recollections

I was born in a Suffolk village and my father was employed by a Duke of a large estate. We lived in a cottage overlooking the gardens—Those were happy days, with no cares or worries and life was good, but at about the time I was to leave school the 1914 war began. My two older brothers joined up as did my younger brother, despite the fact that he was under age.

At the time I left school, my sister (who at that time was living in London) decided she would come home to live and that she would join the Land Army. This was in the Spring of 1915. I too thought I would 'do my bit' on the land. We were issued with a green armlet but I think we had to buy all our clothes. I know we had short thick skirts, thick black boots and, for the wet weather, black leggings.

We started on the Dairy Farm of the Estate. It meant early rising and hard and dirty work, cleaning muck off the cows before they were milked, milking by machinery, stripping the cows after the machine had been taken off and cleaning out the cow houses after milking. We had to get the fodder ready and carry out the hundred and one tasks that make up dairy farming.

We enjoyed walking to work those Spring mornings, which were particularly lovely that year, and everything was bursting into life. At that time war seemed far away from our village, but almost overnight the Mansion was turned into a Red Cross Hospital and the wounded began to arrive. Soon we were to be familiar with the 'Hospital Blues' worn by the wounded. As the boys began to recover and were able to get about again, we got to know them – Canadians, Australians, New Zealanders, Scottish, Irish and, of course, English. After all these years I still remember them. In my autograph book, one of the Scotsmen wrote the following:-

'If I ever join in wedlock,
And the chances are but few,
I will wed you Edith Airey,
Or a girl the same as you.
And when this war is over,
And vanquished are our foes,
I will come back to Easton
And wed my English rose.
Then through life's dark journey,
We everything will share.
The thistle and the English rose
Will make a happy pair'.

EDITH AIREY

Work on a Farm

Extracts from a letter from Miss Dorothy Chalmers, who is working on a farm near Nantwich:

I have been here a fortnight to-day, and got my uniform the day before I came: I would not get it until I was really working! I am learning all kinds of outdoor work, and can milk, feed calves, and pigs, and poultry, and drive the milk float. This is such a lovely old-fashioned farmhouse, black and white, with funny little windows and a beautiful garden. I get up at four o'clock every morning, and enter into the joys(?) of milking, with the cows' tails tied to prevent them swishing into my eyes. Then I scrub out milk tankards – this is hard, especially if any milk has been left in the bottom – and I nearly fell into one the other day. We do have fun, though the most part is really heavy, dirty work.

I was knocked over by a calf this morning, and my hand is pretty badly hurt, but the experience did not equal that of being chased by the old sow, as I was the other day; she took a dislike to me as I was carrying a huge sack of potatoes up the field. Of course I ran as fast as I could, but she kept up with me until I backed through a hedge, tearing my dress on a piece of barbed wire. My revenge was complete, though. Yesterday, we went (the farmer and his wife and I) to the market and sold the offensive animal for £9.10.0.

My farmer is also the village blacksmith, and I am learning to shoe a horse and blow the bellows; the sparks fly from the anvil and make holes in your clothes – not to mention yourself.

Some people tell me that I shall not be able to go on with my farm work in the winter, because it will make my hands so bad. But I intend to stick to it. Our men don't stop fighting in the cold weather, and neither shall I. My only brother is in the trenches – so you know how I feel about it!

Experiences of a Would-be Helper

Does anyone propose to tell me that a woman musician is not sufficiently capable of taking the place of a man whose work consists of three or four hours daily playing in a café? Then I saw a way in which I could do my share. I could and I would therefore make a try for a post in some orchestra and thereby release one man for service. I made up my mind to make a tour of several picture houses to find out how many managers were willing to take lady musicians. I may state that I am a fully experienced solo and orchestral violinist – have held musical directorships of some of the largest cinema theatres in London and have many excellent references. My experiences are as follows (I refer to the different cinemas as A, B, etc.):

A. – 'It was not a question of capability, possibly my references were irreproachable, they simply did not take ladies.'

B. – 'Would let me know.' I afterwards found that I was not even allowed a trial here because – they did not want ladies.

C. – 'Did not engage lady musicians.'

D. – 'Would keep my address handy in case of change.' The manager here reorganised the orchestra a fortnight later – a male trio again; the former one took up another engagement in Hoylake!

E. – 'Never engaged ladies on any consideration.'

F. – Here I saw the managing director, who said ladies had no tone. I offered to play a matinee with piano only (and free of all charge) and guaranteed as satisfactory results as could be got from most trios – at least as strong a tone as any man. My offer was not even deemed worth the courtesy of a reply.

G. – 'Would keep my card,' and, after about four months, still keeps it.

The Nation's Need for Economy

—Germany realised at the outset of the war the necessity of economy. White bread was forbidden, flour was augmented by a percentage of potatoes, an allowance of bread allotted to each individual, and the people were instructed in the duty of cultivating the land to the utmost, keeping livestock even in small dwellings, and in thrifty cookery. All superfluities were abandoned. Women willingly gave up their jewellery in exchange for iron rings and children brought copper articles to school for the use of the Government. No sacrifice seemed too great to enable these people to wage effective warfare.

We too are making sacrifices, and we shall be called upon for greater efforts if we are to win. As a nation we are unthrifty. The French women will make a tasty and nourishing meal from scraps, which we throw into the ashpit or pig bucket. Pea-pod soup, for instance, made of the pods of young peas, and a few crusts of bread with a little seasoning, parsley, thyme, celery or mixed vegetables, costs almost nothing. We must copy our French friends and practice economy in a hundred ways, and so help our country as surely as the brave boys who go to fight. The nation must be fed as wholesomely and as effectively as possible, so we must study food values, give up luxuries, and save as much money as we can.—

'How are we to save, give us details,' cries the busy housewife. Firstly, the housewife must do her own shopping, and choose her own fish, bacon, or vegetables. She must buy less expensive food stuffs, and reduce meat which is the most expensive of all food to a minimum. She must carry home her own parcels, and so release the man or boy who delivers parcels for more important work. Only this week a lady entered a grocer's shop where I was buying goods, and ordered half a pound of biscuits, and required to have them sent two miles. This is an uncommon incident, for ladies no longer disdain to carry baskets, one meets them daily carrying fruit and comforts to the hospitals, and what they can do for the soldiers, they can surely do for their own households. The days when a man called daily for orders and a quick delivery of goods was ensured are over for the present. This is an expensive method of shopping, for the wages of the men and the upkeep of the delivery vans have to be added to the price of the articles purchased—

Households accustomed to two servants can dispense with one, and the housewife and the daughters can do the cooking themselves. It will doubtless be the daintier and more appetising. The ladies can also attend to the garden and greenhouse themselves and release the gardener or boy for work more needed by the state. Children must be encouraged to clean their own boots, bicycles, and keep their clothes and drawers in order. Many girls and women can do more for their country by staying at home and attending to household economies and duties, and releasing their servants for the more strenuous labours required by the state, than if they offered their services for work for which they were physically unfitted.

CATHERINE I. DODD

'Sparrows Twittering in a Tempest'

Mr Asquith's description of women pacifists

Berliner Leben 1914–1918

The First Demonstration: Berlin 1915

There were only a few policemen there, and they were taken by surprise, to the extent that the thousand people were able to stand for more than half an hour unmolested in front of Portal V of the Reichstag, through which the Reichstag representatives entered the building. One after another they came, the 'representatives of the people'. 'We want peace! Give us back our husbands! Give us back our fathers and brothers!' These words rang out to the bourgeois Reichstag representatives—

And then came Karl, our Karl. Excited calls receive him. Everyone wants to shake his hand. Soon he is wrapped in a crowd of people. Again and again hats and caps are tossed into the air: 'Up with Karl Liebknecht, down with the war!'

A larger police contingent moved towards us. We retreated in a closed line down the Linden — We crossed the Alexanderplatz individually. In Landsbergerstrasse we decided to gather again. We walked together to the cemetery of those who fell in the 1848 revolution — There were only two wreaths but they said a lot —

18 March – the anniversary of your deaths

4 August – the anniversary of our deaths

ANONYMOUS

Socialist Women's Congress: Berne, April 1915

But in Berne we met unexpected difficulties. We were certainly pleased to have not only German but also French and English women delegates meet for a common purpose while the cannon thundered on all fronts. Women were the first to demonstrate that the spirit of internationalism could not be killed entirely. The French delegate, Louise Saumoneau, was not sent by her party but joined us on her own responsibility. It was her courageous campaign against the war which later caused her country to jail her for a long period.

I had a long discussion with the two official British delegates, Margaret Bondfield (in later years the Minister of Labour in the MacDonald cabinet) and Marion Phillips, the very intelligent leader of the women's trade union movement in Great Britain. They insisted that Britain had gone to war in order to defend little Belgium, whose neutrality had been violated by the Germans. Although I had protested most vigorously against this violation, I doubted the generosity of a British government which had tolerated so many injustices in the world and which, itself, had committed some of them. It seemed to me more probable that Britain had entered the war for the sake of her own interests—

Nikolai Lenin, pulling wires behind the scenes, created some difficulties at Berne. The majority group in the conference demanded international action of the women in all countries to put an immediate end to the war and to reach a peace without annexations or conquests. This was the main issue on which we had gathered. But the Russian women, directed by Lenin from another room of the Berne Volkshaus, introduced a completely different resolution. It called for immediate splits in our respective parties – definite breaks with the majority Socialists, who supported the war. All of us were opposed to forcing splits.

TONI SENDER

How German Women Met English Women

Can the women of Europe stop the war?

That was the question which lay before us as we sat in conference the other day at Berne, Switzerland, we four British delegates, with delegates from the chief belligerent and neutral Powers, who had come almost at the risk of their lives to exchange a few words with each other.—As we compared notes together I was struck with the remarkable similarity of conditions that existed between the two countries.

There were the same cases of unemployment in the peace factories, and double and treble overtime in the war factories. Bread and vegetables were dear, and housewives were told to economise just as with us; wives losing husbands, mothers losing sons, and so forth, except that in Germany everybody seemed to be hit one way or another.

In some points, however, the two countries differed.

The soldier's wife is not half so well provided for as in England; she has not a pound a week, but only about five shillings, save where the municipalities increase the Government allowances; while if a woman is able to earn her own living or possesses a private income, even this small sum is knocked off.

The women of Germany particularly noted our generosity to unmarried women who were mothers; in Germany they get nothing.

The officialism of the Fatherland, too, is getting more and more stringent; the bread allowance is getting less and less, and anything like criticism is looked upon as treason – all of which, of course, will make the proposed co-operation of our German sisters more difficult, and it is for this reason that we have continually refrained from publishing their names, so as not to make their lot harder once they get back.

DR MARION PHILLIPS

International Congress of Women,
The Hague, Holland, April, 1915
Call to the Women of all Nations

From many countries appeals have come asking us to call together an International Women's Congress to discuss what the women of the world can do and ought to do in the dreadful times in which we are now living.

We women of the Netherlands, living in a neutral country, accessible to the women of all other nations, therefore take upon ourselves the responsibility of calling together such an International Congress of Women. We feel strongly that at a time when there is so much hatred among nations, we women must show that we can retain our solidarity and that we are able to maintain a mutual friendship.

Women are waiting to be called together. The world is looking to them for their contribution towards the solution of the great problems of today.

Women, whatever your nationality, whatever your party, your presence will be of great importance.

The greater the number of those who take part in the Congress, the stronger will be the impression its proceedings will make.

Your presence will testify that you, too, wish to record your protest against this horrible war, and that you desire to assist in preventing a recurrence of it in the future.

Let our call to you not be in vain.

Daily Graphic, 24 April 1915

The Hague Congress

Mrs Pankhurst said: 'What we criticise is the holding of the Congress at all. We are perfectly satisfied, and we have information which supports that belief, that the whole thing has been engineered by agents of Germany. Well-meaning, honourable woman have proved to be no match for German agents. I am very glad that the cancelling of the service has made it impossible for Englishwomen to attend, and I think as time goes on they themselves will be very glad that a fortunate accident has spared them an irretrievable mistake. The presence of Englishwomen would be entirely misunderstood by our Allies and neutral countries — I am glad to say no one officially connected with the W.S.P.U. or prominent in it has had anything to do with the Congress.'

Maria Vérone 'the famous French barrister' said: 'What! A part of our territory still occupied by the enemy, as well as the great part of Belgium, and we are to meet face to face the women of all nations – and consequently German women – to make known our conditions of peace. What do they take us for? The game is a very obvious one, is it not? We were betrayed before the war, and we refuse to be betrayed while the war is in progress. Yes, I, a Socialist, Pacifist, and Suffragist, say it straight out. We were betrayed by the German Socialists and by the German Pacifists. Once is enough.'

Daily Express, 26 April 1915

Peace Cranquettes

A dismal group of Peacettes are waiting at Tilbury for a boat to take them to Holland for their international chirrup with the German fraus — They were a sad but determined group yesterday as they watched the dark leaden river with the cold rain falling on it, and waited hour after hour for the boat that never came — There is a little regret in some suffragist circles over the splitting of the ranks but, apart from this, leading women in London expressed their keen pleasure yesterday at the boatless dismay of the would-be Dutch trippers. Some of the 'most important' of the Peace Cranquettes have actually gone to Tilbury in order to jump on board any boat proposing to take them across should the embargo be lifted.

The Clarion, 14 May 1915

The Peace Congress

The Hague

The Women's Peace Congress has assembled and dispersed. The women from Germany, Austria, and Hungary have met the women from America, and missed those from Great Britain. A thousand women were said to be present. Of these eighty were from the United States and were Americans 'of *all* nationalities.' France was unrepresented, and by an oversight (?) the letter of protest sent to the Congress in reply to an invitation to French women to attend was not read—

Of Englishwomen only four were present officially, and one or two by chance. Miss Kate Courtney (Manchester) and Miss Chrystal Macmillan (Edinburgh) were on the platform all through the Congress, and the former worked specially hard in interpreting many of the speeches into English. Mrs. Pethick Lawrence spoke two or three times and was second to none in oratory. Attired in a dress of rich Eastern design, she made a striking figure in the rostrum. Her voice rang out loud and clear, but she said nothing. This, indeed, was the characteristic of the Congress. It was words, words, words! Miss Rosicka Schwinner (sic), in most impassioned and spiritualistic phrases, worked on the emotions of the audience, all her speeches culminating at a point where, in the middle of an impressive oration, she suddenly called upon the people present to stand for a few moments and silently to pray for the souls of those dead on the field of battle. The Congress stood and prayed, and the solemn effect of the moment might have bitten into the memory of everybody had not a cynical young American journalist whispered at the Press table, 'Oh, that's Rosicka's old trick. She has worked that dodge on every one of her audiences in America. It makes them remember her as something out of the ordinary.'—

Every woman who paid her fee of 10s. and became a member of the Congress had a right to speak, but she was bound by specially-framed rules *not* to speak on the war. It was 'Hamlet' with the Duke left out. And so the Congress fell flat flat and stale—perhaps unprofitable. Women who had travelled a long way to be present complained privately of the barrenness and futility of the whole thing. They had hoped that some practical scheme would have been placed before them upon which they could have started to work at once. But the morning, afternoon, and evening of the first day came and went and nothing was brought forward. The second and third days were the same, and the Congress closed with kindly expressions and hopes for peace—some day. I forget, something *was* done: it was decided officially to send flowers to the wounded lying in the hospitals in each of the belligerent countries.

AMY LILLINGTON

Diary 1905–1924

22 June [41 Grosvenor Road]
Jane Addams, with whom we stayed at Hull House, Chicago, on our first world tour, dined with us last night. Since we knew her seventeen years ago she has become a world celebrity – the most famous woman of the U.S.A., representing the best aspects of

the feminist movement and the most distinguished elements in the social reform movement. Some say that she has been too much in the limelight of late, and that she is no longer either so sane or so subtle in her public utterances. But to us she seemed the same gentle, dignified, sympathetic woman, though like the rest of us she has lost in brilliancy and personal charm – the inevitable result of age, personal notoriety and much business. Her late mission to the governments of the world, as the leading representative of the neutral women at the Hague Conference of Women, has brought her into still greater prominence. She and one or two other women of neutral countries were charged with the 'Peace Mission' to the governments of Germany, Austria, Hungary, Italy, France, Belgium and England. She had found Sir Edward Grey politely encouraging, expressing his own personal pacific sentiments, but saying nothing about his government —

Jane Addams herself thinks it inconceivable that the U.S.A. should come into the war and she clearly sees little or no difference between British and German policy, either before or during the war – at least that is the impression she leaves on our minds.

BEATRICE WEBB

Peace and Bread in Time of War

Resolutions of the Hague Conference

A series of resolutions was very carefully drawn as a result of the three days' deliberations. A committee, consisting of two women from each country, called 'The Women's Committee for Permanent Peace,' was organized and established headquarters at Amsterdam.

At its last session, the Congress voted that its resolutions, especially the one of a Conference of Neutrals, should be carried by a delegation of women from the neutral countries to the Premier and Minister of Foreign Affairs of each of the belligerent countries, and by a delegation of women from the belligerent countries to the same officials in the neutral nations. As a result fourteen countries were visited in May and June, 1915, by delegates from the Congress—

At this time an unexpected development gave the conference of neutrals only too much publicity and produced a season of great hilarity for the newspaper men of two continents. Madame Rosika Schwimmer, who still remained in the United States, had lectured in Detroit where she had been introduced to Mr. Henry Ford—During a long interview which Madame Schwimmer held with Mr. Ford and his wife, he expressed his willingness to finance the plan of a neutral conference and promised to meet her in New York in regard to it—

The difficulties, however, began when Mr. Ford asked his business agent to show us the papers which chartered the Norwegian boat 'Oscar 11' for her next trans-Atlantic voyage—I was at once alarmed—we needed Mr. Ford's help primarily in organizing a conference but not in transporting the people. Mr. Ford's response was to the effect that the more publicity the better and that the sailing ship itself would make known the conference more effectively than any other method could possibly do. After that affairs moved rapidly—We had not expected any actual cooperation from the newspapers, but making all allowances for that, the enterprise seemed to be exhibiting unfortunate aspects.

JANE ADDAMS

'Ships of Fools'

Carrie Chapman Catt to Millicent Garrett Fawcett

November 29th

Since dictating the foregoing some new things of interest have happened. Henry Ford has chartered a Scandinavian ship and is proposing to take a delegation of pacifists to Christiana, Stockholm, Copenhagen and the Hague. He proposes to pick up delegations at the three Scandinavian capitals. I was invited to go as were many men and women of much greater importance, but I doubt if a single one of real nation-wide influence has accepted. It is generally regarded as the wildest possible example of a 'fool and his money.' Rosika claims that she persuaded him to do this and she tells me (also corroborated by Miss Addams) that he has given $200,000 to the International or perhaps National Woman's Peace Party. Money is flying right and left. Rosika is happier than at any time of her life. She is doing much of the spending. Certainly it does read like a fairy story. Rosika thinks she has accomplished wonders here. In fact, she has messed everything she has attempted and has unconsciously thwarted her own aims. I have not told her so, and shall not because she wouldn't believe me.

Adela Stanton Coit to Millicent Garrett Fawcett

Dec. 27, '15

Rosika seems to be 'bossing' the show! Poor Mr Ford! He has now found out what he was let in for & taken the wise step of running away! I would give anything to have an authentic report of the happening on board the 'Ship of Fools'.

The Standard, 8 July 1915

Austrian Women's Cry for Peace

The peace demonstration before the Hofburg was timed to take place in the afternoon, when the Emperor is always in his apartments overlooking the inner courtyard of the palace. Without any preliminary warning, this extensive courtyard was invaded by a throng of women belonging to the working classes of Vienna.

They poured through the archway facing west and through the archway leading from the Kohler-Strasse, and in huge numbers they swept in from the adjoining Volksgarten, a popular public park. Before anyone in authority knew what was happening this immense oblong courtyard of the Imperial palace was packed so closely with women that it was impossible even for a single individual to find a path among them. They were jammed tightly on every available square inch of ground, and there was an overflow of them at all the approaches. Many of them were dressed in deep mourning for the husbands and sons lost at the front in this terrible war, against which they had assembled to demonstrate. No sooner was the palace courtyard full than all the women began a heartrending wail: 'We want peace. We want our men to return. We want bread and work. We want peace.'

Finally, a most effective method of soothing and conciliating the women was adopted. A window opening on to a balcony overlooking the courtyard was thrown open, and the Emperor Francis Joseph stepped out into full view of the multitude. The Emperor will be 85 years of age in August, and he looks his age; his figure is bent, and he has the appearance of being feeble and worn. He was wearing, as usual, his general's uniform, with sword suspended from his belt, yet he looked weak and helpless rather than imperial and commanding.

There was an instantaneous hush; the women looked at the balcony, and refrained from any hostile demonstration against the Emperor, who raised his hand and began to speak to them. His words were inaudible to the greater part of the crowd, but those who were immediately under the balcony were afterwards able to report the gist of the Imperial appeal to the women to go home quietly and to go on enduring for Austria—

He added that a little more patience was needed before peace could be concluded, but that this would not be long delayed, and that it would be peace with honour, bringing renewed prosperity and security to the whole country. When the Emperor, who had remained alone on the balcony while delivering his speech, had

109

finished, the women dispersed. There was no more noise; there were a few isolated cries of 'We want peace!' but the crowd went home quietly and without disorder. They were all sad rather than rebellious.

Labour Leader, 29 April 1915

Towards a Permanent Peace

If women desire peace, their desire is at least as respectable as men's desire for war. Of course, we are told that men do not desire war; they, too, it seems, desire peace. What childishness is this? Who makes the wars then? Governments? Governments all consist of men, and who puts the Governments into power, and who keeps them there? If, indeed, men desire peace, they have proved themselves singularly incompetent to attain their desires. Wars are made by the inertia of the masses of men, who will not think and organise and insist upon directing the policy of the nation, and the inertia of women, who will not think and organise and insist on getting their freedom from men. If we honestly desire peace, we must 'make peace' with all the passion and courage with which we 'make war'. Some of that passion and courage women can supply.

HELENA SWANWICK

The Great Adventure

You cannot kill a wrong idea except with a right idea. This warfare is the most heroic of all, and heroism will always move mankind. It is the heroism of war, not its cruelty, that leads all the world after it. Whose heart is not stirred, whose breath does not come faster, when the soldiers pass us in the street? Look at their faces, and realise how much they are prepared to sacrifice. Everyone of them faces death, and there are things worse than death, and they go gaily to face all these things. Is it not heroic? Well, I tell you that there is a mightier heroism still – the heroism not of the battle, but the cross; the adventure not of war, but of peace. For which is the braver man when all is said – the man who believes in armaments, or the man who stakes everything on an idea? Who is the great adventurer – he who goes against the enemy with swords and guns, or he who goes with naked hands? Who is the mighty hunter – he who seeks the quarry with stones and slings, or he who, with St. Francis, goes to tame a wolf with nothing but the gospel? We peace people have made of peace a dull, drab, sordid, selfish thing. We have made it that ambiguous, dreary thing – 'neutrality.' But Peace is the great adventure, the glorious romance. And only when the world conceives it so, will the world be drawn after it again. 'I, when I am lifted up, will draw all men unto Me.'

A. MAUDE ROYDEN

Jus Suffragii

Manchester Guardian, 25 January 1915

A remarkable achievement of the suffragists since the war has been to keep going the work of the International Women's *(sic)* Suffrage Alliance and its official Journal 'Jus Suffragii'. Many people had doubts whether it was wise or even possible to bring out a journal which could be read with pleasure by the women whose countries were at war with each other, but the little paper has managed to record from its headquarters in London news of what women are doing in Germany, Austria, Belgium, France, Russia, Great Britain and Ireland with so much tact that grateful letters of thanks are now reaching the offices of the Alliance from the women of the belligerent as well as of the neutral countries.

From the Office of the President
L'Union Française Pour Le Suffrage des Femmes

Paris, the 18 September 1915

Dear Mrs Fawcett,

   —Mrs Catt, at the distance she is in a neutral country, cannot possibly understand the effect produced in France by the pacifism of Jus, nor the difficulties it causes us; Jus is moreover on the wrong track internationally. On this subject some people are demanding that we quit the Alliance. There is no question of that, but it is essential that Jus *which is the organ of the Alliance, remains uniquely a suffragist journal throughout the war* as our rules exact one aim only: the suffrage.

MARGUERITE DE WITT SCHLUMBERGER

To Mrs Fawcett

December 17th., 1915.

Dear Mrs. Fawcett.

I must say I wish the militarist-suffragists would show their appreciation of 'Jus Suffragii' in the same practical way that the pacifists have done, namely, by getting subscribers to it. It is noteworthy that I never received one single complaint or one single withdrawal from the paper during the ten months in which the 'pacifist' articles appeared, whereas now that they have stopped I get withdrawals by every post, and that whereas we had innumerable letters expressing appreciation I did not receive one remonstrating, whereas now that there is a change in the paper I do not get one single letter of appreciation, on the contrary I receive a number of letters of regret. I really feel worried from the practical point of view as to the falling off in subscribers. Putting pacifism aside, it is of course a plan adopted by most papers to take up some subject that will rouse fresh interest and attract fresh subscribers, and that the pacifist articles succeeded in doing for us – whether rightly or wrongly I will not now discuss, but it is difficult to see what practical steps to take to increase the circulation and to fill the places of those who have refused to renew their subscriptions.

MARY SHEEPSHANKS

Notes on the Policy of Jus

In the present critical position of affairs, when any reference to political conditions may hurt national susceptibilities, it must be clearly stated that the International Woman Suffrage Alliance maintains a strictly neutral attitude, and is only responsible for its official announcements. Reports from affiliated societies are inserted on the responsibility of the society contributing them. Other articles are published as being of general interest to our readers and responsibility for them rests solely with their signatories.

Jus Suffragii, August 1917

I am writing at the request of the Executive Committee of the Irishwomen's Suffrage Federation to ask you to be good enough to explain why Ireland is consistently omitted from the list of countries given each month in 'J.S.' Readers of your valued paper are thus driven to suppose that Ireland is either a part of Great Britain or that she is non-existent. I hope that by publishing this letter you will show me the opportunity of assuring them that neither of these suppositions is correct.

O, damn the shibboleth of sex!
God knows we've equal personality.
Why should men face the dark while women stay
To live and laugh and meet the sun each day.

From the poem 'Drafts' written during the war
by Norah Bomford

Nurse at the Russian Front

The Initiation Ceremony

Before each jewelled icon the *lampada* glowed with a ruby light.
On the altar the high brass candlesticks held steadily-shining candles; near them stood a silver chalice containing holy water, with
the Book of Books alongside; a silver plate, heaped with red
crosses, had been placed in the centre of the Holy Table. In front
of the congregation, standing side by side, were sixteen young
women, the first draft of nurses from a class of nearly two hundred. They were wearing the light grey dress, white apron and
long white head-veil of the hospital nurse. A priest, in full canonicals, entered and slowly made his way towards the altar. Soon his
rich, resonant voice was heard reciting the beautiful Slavonic
prayers of the Greek Orthodox liturgy. Heads were reverently
bowed; a murmur of voices rose and fell. The censer was swung
lightly to and fro, emitting trembling breaths of fine grey, fragrant
smoke.

Finally there was silence. The golden-robed priest rose from
his knees and faced the congregation, crucifix in hand. At a sign

from him, the nurses moved slowly, in relays, to kneel at the altar. The priest then pronounced God's blessing on the red crosses and on their recipients and, taking the crosses in his hand, moved towards the kneeling nurses. Bending down, he asked each one her name; the answers came, softly but distinctly: 'Vera', 'Tatiana', 'Nadezhda' . . .

Now he was standing before me. 'Your name?' 'Florence,' I answered. The priest paused and whispered to his deacon-acolyte. A book was brought and consulted, then he consulted me: 'Of the *pravoslavny* [Orthodox] Church?' 'No,' I whispered, 'of the Church of England.' Again the whispered consultation, again the book was referred to. I felt myself growing cold with fear. But he was back again and resumed the prescribed ritual, his tongue slightly twisting at the pronunciation of the foreign name: 'To thee, Floronz, child of God, servant of the Most High, is given this token of faith, of home, of charity. With faith shalt thou follow Christ the Master, with hope shalt thou look towards Christ for thy salvation, with charity shalt thou fulfil thy duties. Thou shalt tend the sick, the wounded, the needy; with words of comfort shalt thou cheer them.' I held the red cross to my breast and pressed my lips to the crucifix with a heart full of gratitude to God, for He had accepted me.

FLORENCE FARMBOROUGH

Birmingham Post, 3 March 1915

Women's Active Part in Battle

The number and the exact position of Russian women at the front are obscure matters, but there is no doubt that enough women to make half a battalion have in different ways got into the army. A lady named Treskoff, who is interested in the matter, puts the number at 400. An attempt was privately made to induce the Minister of War, General Sukhomlinoff, to give the women fighters formal recognition. This failed. Women, as before the war, are in theory excluded from the army. Their existence as combatants is de facto recognised and winked at. They get into the army by personating reservists who are dead or sick. I have read that 10,000 women have made the attempt. The majority were found out at once, and sent back. If their appearance is masculine enough to pass muster at a cursory glance, they have still to face medical examination. This is effected again by personation. A man in the plot undergoes examination, and when examination is over his place is taken by the would-be woman warrior. Of the women who succeed so far many give themselves away within the first days and weeks, and of these some are at once sent back. But some are apparently allowed to stay. If the disclosure is made after months, and if fighting has been gone through, the fact that the women have survived privations and done nothing unsoldierly is a test of their physical and moral fitness. Such women are seldom sent back. They are 'officially' men, but every one knows their sex, and even after newspapers print tales of their exploits they remain with the colours—

The women warriors are mostly of good family; or they belong to the urban classes. The peasant 'baba' woman has not the sensibility which makes a Jeanne d'Arc.

Modern Troubadors

The first concert was at No. 15 in the Harfleur Valley. The valley was a sea of mud, with tents and a few huts, and as a pathway through this sea of stickiness there were duckboards to walk on. If you fell over, you were done in, for the mud was ankle deep, and very often knee deep. We wore top-boots. The winter had been very cold and abnormally damp, and the cold and rain and mud without made a very great contrast to the fog of smoke and the heat within the huts and tents. There was a

117

great concert in the new Cinema Hut, which we, the Concert Party, opened in great style. The Base Commandant and the officers of the Base were all present. The wooden hut was packed to suffocation. No one would ever believe now that human beings could take up so little room. The men had been waiting for hours and smoking incessantly, and the fog of smoke and the heat within the hut was a tremendous contrast to the cold, rain, and mud without. The acetylene lights were very new and very glaring, and quite suddenly they all went out. We were all sitting on the platform, as we always did, partly because there was nowhere else to go, and partly to save time. The concerts had to be fairly short – two hours at the most – and there was no time to spare for entrances and exits. When the lights went out there was a rush for candles, and a row of candles was lit in front of us and along the side of the hut. No one can imagine how hot rows of candles can be. The heat of the candles, the smoke, the enthusiasm, the terrific roar of response to our small efforts were quite incredible.

Ivor Novello, who was one of the party, had just written 'Keep the Home Fires burning,' and when he sang it, the men seemed to drink it in at once and instantly sang the chorus, and as we drove away at the end of the concert, in the dark and rain and mud, from all parts of the camp one could hear the refrain of the chorus.

LENA ASHWELL

from Women of the War

We gave *The School for Scandal* in a wood, with half our audience on the grass, the other half dangerously overcrowding the branches of the nearest trees. *Macbeth* was given in a great hangar, with Army blankets for the walls of the banqueting-hall, and a sugar-box for the throne. *Macbeth* was an enormous success. Its reception was wonderful. We gave it to vast audiences; they listened breathlessly in absolute silence, and then cheered and cheered and cheered — There were never such audiences in the world before – so keen, so appreciative, so grateful.

LENA ASHWELL

Modern Troubadors

The most pathetic sight almost is to see the patients who have been severely wounded by lyddite explosion; their poor faces, stripped of all the skin, are swathed in cotton-wool and bandages until their heads appear out of all proportion to their bodies. In the midst of the mass of bandages are cunningly arranged funnels which lead to the patient's eyes and enable him to have a some-what constricted idea of what is passing in the outside world. His hands, too, may be swathed in bandages until they are larger than boxing gloves, but that does not prevent him from 'showing his appreciation in the usual way.' The pathetic way in which those two eerie funnels attempt to follow your every movement show that, despite the terrible handicap of smothering bandages, he is not missing anything he can help. It is only natural that hospital patients should enjoy most what they can appreciate with the least effort, and it can be therefore readily understood that the ballad-singers, and above all the instrumentalists, should be most popular in the hospitals. The last movement of the Mendelssohn Concerto and the Intermezzo of the *Cavalleria Rusticana*, Handel's 'Largo,' were always much loved in hospital. When the nursing sister would have kept a Serious Cases Ward sacred and undisturbed, the men asked that some music might come in to them. Literally, music is what they crave for, even when they are dying. On one occasion there was a man in very great pain; his tense face strained and infinitely weary, he was waiting for the music to start. When the violinist passed him he said, 'Give us something nippy, Miss.' She went up to the top of the room and played the gayest tune she knew, but when she looked for his face at the end of it, she saw that he had passed on to the Great Unknown while she was playing.

LENA ASHWELL

Fanny Went to War

The First Gas Attack: Spring 1915

Out of the queer green haze that hung over everything came an unending stream of Tommies, stumbling, staggering, gasping, all a livid green colour. One just reached our gatepost before he crumpled up. Five men supporting each other staggered along with a wounded comrade. The grass on each side of the *pavé* was thronged with those who could go no farther. It was the first gas attack.

We dashed to the kitchen and prepared large quantities of salt and water to help them vomit the poison. A heavy green liquid resulted, and we thanked God that they seemed relieved. No two men were affected in the same way, constitution playing an important part in resisting the gas of that time—None of them had respirators and they had been taken unawares in their sleep.

We noticed that those wearing the South African medal had clung to their rifles and equipment, but the young boys had left the trenches without theirs.

'Gawd, it's a woman,' breathed one, finding himself in a manger with Hutchinson bending over him.

'Smoked out like—rats, we were, by them—'Uns.'—

Ammunition columns began to come up and unload with feverish haste, and the shells were carried by hand through the yard to the guns; we improvised respirators with cotton-wool and weak carbolic solution for those going forward. Motor ambulances began to arrive, became entangled with ammunition wagons, disentangled themselves and finally each went their ways. We covered the men with blankets and placed them on hay in a shed

120

to await collection. Hutchinson went inside the kitchen to prepare breakfast for our battery.

It was only then that I noticed that her face was blue and swollen and her eyes appeared to be twice their natural size. My own were giving me considerable pain and I supposed that I looked the same. 'Tear' shells were falling everywhere, and looking towards the front from where this hell had come, I saw the sun rising, blood-red above the gas, in one of the most perfect skies I have ever seen—

As a result of the report given to G.H.Q., an urgent letter reached us at Lamarck, two days after our return, from the A.P.M. at Cassel, asking us for details of the respirators issued us by the Belgians and the chemicals they contained, whether we considered them effective at any distance from gas, if we could procure and send him a pattern and other technical points, as the British authorities were anxious to remedy the absence of protection against gas in the future. We felt exceedingly proud and important and our reply went back by despatch-rider. Perhaps this was the most useful result of our sojourn with the 7th Belgian Regiment, attached 5th British Division, during that gas attack on May 24th, 1915, at the Second Battle of Ypres.

I dedicate this account to my brave and reliable companion, Hutchinson, and to the officers and men with whom we served.

ACCOUNT BY I. M. LEWIS
PAT BEAUCHAMP

My War Experiences in Two Continents

February 1915

The communal life is a mistake. I wonder if Christ got bored with it.

April 1915

The Canadians and English who poured in from Ypres were

terribly damaged, and the asphyxiating gas seems to have been simply diabolical. It was awful to see human beings so mangled, and I never get one bit accustomed to it. The streets were full of British soldiers, and the hospitals swarmed with wounded. I went to visit the Casino one. The bright sun streamed through lowered blinds on hundreds of beds, and on stretchers lying between them. Many Canadians were there, and rows of British. God! how they were knocked about! The vast rooms echoed to the cries of pain. The men were vowing they could never face shells and hand grenades any more. They were so newly wounded, poor boys; but they come up smiling when their country calls again.

But it *isn't right*. This damage to human life is horrible. It is madness to slaughter these thousands of young men. Almost at last, in a rage, one feels inclined to cry out against the sheer imbecility of it. Why bring lives into the world and shell them out of it with jagged pieces of iron, and knives thrust through their quivering flesh? The pain of it is all too much. I am *sick* with seeing suffering.—

Well, I got back to my work at Adinkerke in the midst of the fighting, and reached it just as the sun was setting. What a scene at the station, where I stopped before reaching home to leave the chairs and things I had bought for the hospital there! They were bringing in civilians wounded at Ypres and Poperinghe, which place also has been shelled (and yet we say we are advancing!), and there were natives also from Nieuport.

One whole ambulance was filled with wounded children. I think King Herod himself might have been sorry for them. Wee things in splints, or with their curly heads bandaged; tiny mites, looking with wonder at their hands swathed in linen; babies with their tender flesh torn, and older children crying with terror. There were two tiny things seated opposite each other on a big stretcher playing with dolls, and a little Christmas-card sort of baby in a red hood had had its mother and father killed beside it. Another little mite belonged to no one at all. Who could tell whether its parents had been killed or not? I am afraid many of them will never find their relations again. In the general scrimmage everyone gets lost. If this isn't frightfulness enough, God in heaven help us!

May 1915

—There were six Germans at the station to-day, two wounded and four prisoners. Individually I always like them, and it is useless to say I don't. They are all polite and grateful, and I thought to-day, when the prisoners were surrounded by a gaping crowd, that they bore themselves very well. After all, one can't expect a whole nation of mad dogs. A Scotchman said, 'The ones opposite us (*i.e.*, in the trenches) were a very respectable lot of men.'

The German prisoners' letters contain news that battalions of British suffragettes have arrived at the front, and they warn officers not to be captured by these!

SARAH MACNAUGHTAN

Women as Army Surgeons

The Women's Hospital Corps in Paris
Encounters with 'Brass-Hats'

'Has Sloggett been to see you?' asked one Brass-hat, referring to the Director of Medical Services for the British Armies in France.

'No, he has not been here.'

'I wonder at that. Great man with the ladies, Sloggett.'

'I expect we are not his kind of ladies,' rejoined the doctor drily, to the great appreciation of her hearer.

An R.A.M.C. general in a responsible position called one day when the senior medical officers were out. He was received by another member of the medical staff, and assuming the semi-jocular, semi-familiar attitude which professional women dislike so much in their colleagues, permitted himself to say:

'I don't know anything about lady doctors. Do you bite?'

FLORA MURRAY

Fanny Went to War

Prepared for All Immersions

A mild sensation was caused one day by a collision on the Boulogne road, a French car skidding into one of our ambulances, luckily empty, and pushing it over into the ditch.

Heasman and Lowson were both requested to appear at the subsequent Court of Enquiry. Sergeant Lawrence of the R.A.M.C., who had been on the ambulance, was bursting with importance and joy in anticipation of the proceedings. He was one of the chief witnesses, and apart from anything else, a Court of Enquiry meant an extra day's pay for him, though why I never understood.

As they drove off with Boss as chaperone, a salvo of old shoes was thrown after them by the light-hearted F.A.N.Y.s. They returned with colours flying, for had not Lowson saved the situation by producing a tape-measure three minutes after the accident with which she measured the space that the Frenchman swore was wide enough for his car to pass in, proving thereby that this was a physical impossibility?

'How,' asked the colonel who was conducting the enquiry, 'can you declare with so much certainty that the space was three feet eight inches?'

'I measured it,' said Lowson promptly.

'May I ask with what?' he rasped.

'A tape-measure I had in my pocket,' replied she, smiling affably. (Sensation.)

The Court of Enquiry went down like a pack of cards before

that tape-measure. Such a thing was unprecedented; from then onwards the reputation of the 'lady drivers' being prepared for all 'immersions', as someone put it, was established finally and irrevocably.

PAT BEAUCHAMP

Fanny Went to War

'James' the Motor Bath

James was seven years old when he came to me, sound in wind and limb but self-opinionated. His limousine body had been replaced by a bulky caravan-like object – the 'Incubus' – containing ten canvas baths, a cold-water tank, a disinfecting cupboard and two huge Primus-stoves. He was a 1907 Daimler, chain-driven and especially selected for his strong chassis. He had both low and high-tension ignition, a governor and a curious bicycle-pump stowed away under the steering-box, the function of which was to produce pressure for the oil and petrol systems. Other of his peculiarities were: two gear-levers, a hand-brake which moved in a vertical line, and the absence of an accelerator.

The Incubus was, if possible, still more intricate. Built of wood, it had a tent rolled up on either side under the eaves, and a hot-water tap protruding from each flank. When stationary and prepared for work, these tents were let down to form 'lean-to's', in which were placed the baths – five in each tent – and a length of hose was fixed to each tap. A supply pipe, similar to that of a steam wagon, was placed in the selected source of water, and it then became the painful duty of one of James' satellites – he always had two – to pump the tank full. Meanwhile the second satellite was fully but not agreeably occupied in starting the Primuses. Paraffin was always provided by the 'bathees', and was frequently very dirty, with the result that the unfortunate person who had the care of the lamps spent most of the day flat on her face, coaxing them with sops of petrol-soaked waste.

James' first expedition was to Houthem, where he was attached to the Belgian aerodrome. His arrival was celebrated by the Boches with a splendid air-raid, to which the mitrailleuse in our back-yard responded with much spirit.—

On James' next job for the British, he had the honour of Boss's (Lieutenant Franklin) assistance. We left Lamarck in the early hours as usual, and were at our destination, searching for a suitable water supply, by eight o'clock. Our hosts had selected a site in the middle of a bridge – they had not then seen James. As we did not want to hold up all traffic, we got James down into the field beside the stream, though with difficulty. The officer in charge of bathing operations was a modest young man and asked if we should 'be going for a walk' in the meantime. We pointed out James' inner workings and he agreed that we should have quite enough to do to keep us out of mischief and had better remain on duty.

The troops were splendid and kept up a constant stream of bathers, and it soon became evident that we should not finish that day, so a billet was arranged for us and we were invited to dinner in the mess. As we had not come prepared to stay, it was a slight struggle for us to get sufficiently clean and I turned my collar inside out as a last desperate expedient. We had a good quarter of a mile of thick mud to traverse and on our arrival felt that we looked anything but our best.

The C.O. was a most alarming man. He looked as if he had stepped straight out of Savile Row. After the soup, he sent a wretched subaltern to change his collar. I was so terrified lest he should observe mine that I remember nothing more.

Next day I distinguished myself by swearing at a visiting general who opened the door just as I was coaxing the lamp, but he bore no grudge and helped Lieutenant Franklin with the pump obligingly.

By nightfall we had bathed over 600 men and prepared to

depart. This was easier said than done, for James had sunk in the mud and had to be towed out with horses. After breaking three sets of chains and side-slipping into the farm midden, we once more reached the road and set off for Calais and a wash—

In 1916, James joined the British convoy and thereafter was not much used until in November, 1917, he was lent to a Belgian battery at Oostkirke, whereupon he began to play up; he punctured both back tyres, broke the jack, and in Poperinghe gave up the ghost in a narrow street, completely blocking the traffic. Every conceivable kind of vehicle piled up behind him and at last we were pushed into the square. It was his bicycle-pump, and the rest of the journey was accomplished with Marian Gamwell lying on the wing, pumping for dear life, our 'pass' between her teeth—Eventually James was sold as a motor-boat engine.

PAT BEAUCHAMP

Deutsche Frauen Deutsche Treue

From the Platform to Points Duty

On 1 December 1914 I started train duty. At first I was employed with three other women as a ticket inspector on the platform. This was easy work, once we had got used to working at night. We had to check and clip the tickets and provide passengers with simple information on arrivals and departures, and on train connections and so on.

After half a year I was put on train duty on a trial basis. At that time this was tried out with only three women in the whole of Germany. Later, a large number of female train conductors were employed on passenger and goods trains.

Of course this work was more difficult than our duties at the platform barrier. But we managed it, and once we had passed our exam, we were given a uniform and joined the ranks of the train conductors.

Before departure we had to check that everything was all right with the train. We had to make sure it had the right signs, help the passengers when they got on, check their tickets and give them information on connections, arrival times etc. Once underway, we called out the names of the individual stations, opened and closed the doors, and finally, when we were sure that everything was in order, we gave the signal to the train driver to leave. When darkness fell we had to light up the train. First, two large rear lamps were put up in the last carriage, and then a tail light was hung at the bottom left. Then it was the turn of the compartments.

I travelled from Göttingen on the lines to Hanover, Kassel, Bebra and Bodenfelde. On this last line cattle trucks were coupled on to the train. Shunting was the hardest duty for us women. Once, while switching the points, I stumbled and fell. Luckily I fell between the tracks and the train rode over me without injuring me. The locomotive driver had missed the stop signal and it is only due to the presence of mind of my train guard that I was not hurt.

Frau Hölscher

Deutsche Frauen Deutsche Treue

A Sixteen-Year-Old Handywoman

When the war broke out my father had a repairs, glazing and house painting business in Ostbevern, Westphalia. My older brother, who had helped him, was called up immediately; our journeymen were also soon conscripted, and before the year was over my second brother was also sent to the front.

In February 1915 my father died suddenly and my mother and I were left alone. What would happen now? Again and again our old customers came and asked my mother if there was anyone who could carry out the repairs they needed, for all the other craftsmen in the town had long since gone. We needed money too. I began to wonder whether I could continue the business. As a child I had always adored watching in the workshop and was blissfully happy when I was allowed to mix the paint or help fix a pane of glass with putty, or when I was given a paintbrush. I had also helped my father more and more during the last year of his life. But my mother said it would be impossible. Then one day a gardener's wife, who was also continuing her husband's business alone, came to us, wringing her hands and complaining that she couldn't find anyone to glaze her broken hothouse roof. Half-jokingly she asked me if I could do it. I decided on the spot: 'Yes, of course I can do that,' I said. The woman had faith in me and so I received my first commission. I fell from the roof while I was doing the work, but didn't suffer any injuries and soon the new panes were sitting firmly and cleanly in the frame. Of course, the news soon spread around the town and I received more and more orders. Wearing my brother's blue work clothes, which my mother had altered to fit me, I cycled in all weathers, a pannier on my back. Often it took hours to get to my place of work. I fixed windows, painted doors and window frames, whitewashed ceilings and stables. If a coffin had to be painted or a corpse laid out I had to pitch in. That was quite difficult for a sixteen-year-old girl.

EMMA WINTERBERG

Deutsche Frauen Deutsche Treue

A Mending Room and Laundry on Enemy Territory

In April 1915 I was asked to go to France to set up and manage a sewing and mending room, which was to be attached to a laundry.

In mobile warfare our soldiers had been forced to throw away at least some of their laundry. We could now put an end to this unacceptable situation.

And so, on a dull April morning, we left Düsseldorf and headed for the war, filled with apprehension as to the work and other experiences this new chapter in our lives would bring us.

Our place of work was in the factory town of Wattrelos, which is linked to Roubaix by an electric railway. It used to be a wool laundry and had large work-rooms and living quarters, which also served as our accommodation.

Our sewing room was a rough factory room with no windows, a glass roof and a brick floor: boiling hot in summer (up to 32 degrees) and ice-cold in winter.

When we entered the room for the first time, we found three frightened French girls sewing there. They had clearly been very scared when they heard we were coming. But once they realised that they were going to be treated in a friendly and fair manner, as human beings and not as 'enemies', they soon relaxed.

The laundry, uniforms, blankets and so on were brought from the hospitals or formations. They were taken in by the orderlies who ran the laundry. They were disinfected (in spite of which we sometimes still found live lice in them) and then washed in large laundries by French women, dried in drying rooms and then they were brought to us in the sewing room. We inspected everything, numbered the individual batches, and distributed the work among the girls. The items left us mended and ironed. We started on a small scale, but once the laundry became widely known following an army order, we were sometimes unable to cope with the work. Later, washing came in by the company-load.

Apart from the regular laundry, we had to deal with one-off batches, such as: 500 sets of underwear, blankets and waistcoats; 600 pairs of wristlets; and a few hundred pairs of socks, which then had to be sorted more or less into pairs.

After a while our four sewing girls couldn't manage the work alone any more, despite the fact that we all helped them. But I have to say that in all that time I never had any problems with any of the French women workers; on the contrary, they were all obliging and always touchingly concerned for me.

FRAU ELSE THIEL

From a Field Hospital on the Eastern Front

April 1915

After an eventful journey in almost every vehicle you can think of, I presented myself to the captain of the medical corps. There were some other nurses with me too.

'You look healthy and strong', the captain said to me. 'You can work in the plague hospital – unless of course you are too scared to go?' Of course I said, 'No, sir!'

But this plague hospital is worse than anything I could ever have imagined. It is situated in an abandoned villa. There are some bedsteads with straw sacks, but that's about it. Blankets are in short supply and some of the patients are just lying where they were brought in. On my corridor I have typhus, dysentery, scarlet fever and erysipelas. Upstairs there are mainly typhus patients. We have a single thermometer for all the different patients, and I have just one white coat, because until now I have always only worn aprons. I've been given a couple of Russian prisoners to help me, but I can't talk to them, and they're useless. The kitchen is nothing to write home about either: the soup is stirred with a tennis racket.

Our quarters are fifteen minutes away in the village. We have to wade through the mud to get there. In the room where five of us are supposed to sleep there are two beds with mattresses and a pile of coal in the middle of the floor. Of course, we take it in turns to sleep on a bed, since you can't exactly get comfortable on the hard floorboards, using the heap of coal as a pillow. We can't lock the door, and all night long it is pulled open by soldiers looking for a place to sleep. 'Sorry! Occupied!' we shout, and exhausted, the poor souls stagger on.

ANONYMOUS

The Dardanelles 1915

Tuesday June 15th

Arrived Suez 6.10 a.m. 76 nurses got off here – 40 for Heliopolis, 36 for Alexandria — Waited until 1 p.m. for a train to Alexandria — terribly hot day — at each station natives rushed up to sell rock & water melons & oranges & turkish delight & nougat. Irrigation almost all the way & a strip of land on either side of the train cultivated, mostly rice fields & corn, donkeys & camels all along.

July 16th

Arrived at Mudros Bay at 1 p.m. Beautiful entrance. Many battleships & cruisers. 'Lord Nelson' & 'King George' among them. The twin ship to the 'Luisitania' 'Mouritania' also 'Aquatania' biggest boats afloat. Four hospital ships counting our own in harbour.

Sat July 24th

Came on board R.M. S Ionion. We were brought over in a barge from 'Galeka'. It belongs to the Allan Line and usually runs between London & Montreal. It has been bringing troops backwards & forwards & is now waiting orders. The Galeka went out on Sunday morn 25th laden with wounded from Dardanelles going back to Alexandria.

Sunday 25th

Had a very peaceful day. The Captain from a neighbouring boat came over & entertained us for the afternoon. A good deal of firing going on all day, either from the land, or the men o'war — A very hot day. We sat up on the top deck, & watched the war boats signalling each other. It was beautiful up there in the moonlight (full moon)

Lovely day. Left at 10 a.m. in a sailing boat — sailed round. Back to lunch at 2 p.m. thoroughly enjoyed it. Capt. G came over for bridge in the p.m. Saw big submarine pass us – one of the latest, had sunk some Turkish boat. Big troop ship went out, cheering & cooeeing – mostly Australians.

July 31st

Very hot morning. We were to have gone for a sail at 9 a.m. but no wind, played bridge instead. Went over to 'Tunisian' for lunch — Got home at 7.30. Played bridge & ate chocs.

Aug 1 Sunday

Ironed own & others' clothes. Went for a run in Lieut. Seaton's motor boat. Heard that No. 3 Gen. Hos. is anchored very near us. Are expecting to get to see some of them & hear the news.

Aug 6th Friday

—News arrived for us to go to Cape Hellos to sail at 6 p.m. escorted by 'Doris'. They say a big action is going on now. Sailed at 6 for Imbros. Arrived at daylight. Up all night. Many hospital ships passed us during the night. Heard firing & saw flashes from Aschi Babar.

Aug 7th Sat

Worked to get place ready for wounded which arrived in p.m. 1380 of them, mostly stretcher cases & very bad. Some brought on dead. Had 20 deaths during voyage. Saw aeroplane very close to us, one French one, also submarines & T.P.Ds. Heard firing all day. Could see smoke distinctly — We spent all afternoon & night dressing wounds. We left 8 p.m. Men in every corner of the ship. Wards frightfully hot. A good many Australians amongst men. M.Os operated nearly all night.

Aug 8th Sunday

Arrived Mudros again in a.m. Stayed all day for no purpose. Very hot. Men very ill. Sailed in the evening. Worked hard all night. Beautiful sight going out from Mudros.

Aug 10th Tues

Arrived at Alex at 1 p.m. Unloaded 3/4 of men to various hosps. Was on duty for rest of men who got off at 9 a.m. on Weds.

Sunday 15th

Expect to sail at 6 p.m. — Word came that troop-ship had been sunk on way from Alex. to Mudros. 1100 troops on board — it was torpedoed. No other particulars. Very comfortable on this boat. She is a P & O & very cool cabins. Heard that nearly 1000 perished on 'Royal Edward'. Slept nearly all day.

Mon Aug 16th

Passed Rhodes Is. To have a memorial service for those on board Royal Edward — Ship stopped at the spot where the disaster occurred & the burial service was read. Very impressive. Dead March was played. We saw a great deal of wreckage as we passed the region.

Miss E. Campbell

Journal of a Parisian Worker During the War

Aerial Monsters and Amputees

22 March 1915

Undoubtedly an aeroplane — French or Boche? — Two minutes later the horns and bugles restart loud and clear 'Take shelter', while the firemen shout furiously: 'Get inside. It's a Zeppelin!'

And since then the city has been plunged into darkness! Searchlights cross the cloudy sky — We settle ourselves into the back room – furthest away from the windows – maman, my sister and Marjolaine work while I read to them about William

Short-Nose in the songs of the Aliscans. No sound of cannons nor bombs – Eventually, tired out, maman, Marjolaine, then my sister go to bed – Shall I follow their example? I go to look out of the windows – Everything is dark in the street. Nothing to be seen through the slatted shutters. From the windows looking into the courtyard I watch the beams of light; the sky is clear; the stars shine brightly.

Have they lost the Zeppelin? Or hidden in the darkness has it gone to bring devastation further afield?

Paris has not suffered much from the first visit of the aerial monsters but the suburbs, particularly Asnières and Levallois, have been damaged.

21 August

'I should like to visit the hospital for the amputees at Neuilly-sur-Marne,' the Countess of R. said to me when I went to deliver the dresses she had ordered 'will you come with me?'

Far from refusing I accepted willingly – because for a long time I have had a secret wish to approach the badly wounded. I wanted so much to let them know how much we owe them, we whose homes and lives they have saved — if only I were rich, if only I had the time!

I am not rich, but I do have some time! — On this lovely Sunday, with the air fresh from yesterday's torrential rain, I have accompanied the countess to Neuilly. By underground train, tram across the Bois de Vincennes — and here we are at the White House.

With its central pavilion in the style of Louis XIII, a huge basket of scarlet geraniums in the middle of a vividly green lawn, separate pavilions in red brick and millstone surrounded by grass, this establishment was a lunatic asylum for women and it looks rather pleasant.

The lunatics have been evacuated. Sent to various hospitals in southern France. The nurses have returned, it's they who care for the convalescents—

The countess hands out cigarettes and packets of tobacco while talking gently to the amputees – As for me, I feel intimidated, like a little girl in front of this army of legless, armless, handless men, I feel so helpless that I dare not tell them what I really think, and then while we are leaving the hospital, crossing the road where the convalescents come in for supper, I bow my head as we pass close to them.

30 August

Another journey to the White House with the Countess of R—

Kindly, with a beautiful brown moustache, a clear gentle expression, the chief medical officer explains to the countess why the amputees have to wait so long for their artificial limbs. These have to be articulated, light and well-made, but the shortage of man-power keeps the men waiting so long. To help them to get about more easily, they are given American crutches, but this apparatus harms and deforms the stump. Currently there are seven hundred amputees; since the designation of the White House, fourteen hundred have passed through it. Already it is said twelve thousand men have been mutilated! What a price in suffering we shall pay as our ransom!

LOUISE DELÉTANG

Heroines of the World-War

Emilienne Moreau

'Head Quarters, First Army,
'British Expeditionary Force,
'October 7, 1915.

'I have the pleasure to inform you that the assistance you rendered to the medical officer attached to the 9th Battalion Black Watch at Loos on September 25 and 26, 1915, and also the courageous way in which you assisted to attack the enemy, have been brought to the notice of the General Officer Commanding the First (British) Army.

'General Sir Douglas Haig has directed me to write to you, and to express his sincere admiration of the patriotism and courage shown by you on the above occasion, and to say that he had much pleasure in bringing your conduct to the favourable notice of the French military authorities.

'I am,

'P. E. J. HOBBS,
'Major-General, Deputy Adjutant,
and Quartermaster-General, First Army.'

The outcome was that, in a memorable ceremony at Versailles, Emilienne Moreau was decorated with the Croix de Guerre by General De Sailly. Amidst valiant soldiers wounded in battle, she was lined up and had the War Cross fastened to her bodice.

E. W. WALTERS

'Extraordinary Stupidity on Behalf of the German Government'

From Mrs C. S. Peel's *How We Lived Then*

Edith Cavell: Pioneer and Patriot

Her Execution: Pastor Le Seur's account

'When we arrived at the Tir National,—a company at full strength (250 men) was drawn up in accordance with the regulations under the command of an officer. The Military Prosecutor, Herr Stöber, his secretary, Captain Behrens, commandant of St Gilles, and a medical man, Dr Benn, were also there—

'The sentences were now read in German and in French, and then we two ministers of religion were permitted to say a last word to the condemned. I thought I had to make what I said as brief as possible. So I took Miss Cavell's hand and repeated, of course in English, the Grace of the Anglican Church. She pressed my hand in return, and answered in these words: "Ask Mr Gahan to tell my loved ones later on that I believe my soul is safe, and that I am glad to die for my country."'

'Then I led her to the pole,—to which she was lightly bound, and a bandage tied over her eyes which, as the soldier who put it on told me later, were full of tears. A few seconds now passed which appeared like an eternity because the Catholic priest spoke longer with M. Baucq. Then one sharp command was given, two salvoes rang out at the same moment from two parties of eight men at six paces, and both the condemned sank to the ground without a sound. My eyes were fixed exclusively on Miss Cavell, and what I saw was terrible. With a face streaming with blood – one shot had gone through her forehead – she had sunk down forward, but three times seemed to raise herself up without a sound. I ran forward with the medical man but he was right when he stated these were merely reflex movements as bullet holes, as large as a fist in her back, proved that she was killed immediately. The doctor certified death and a few minutes later two plain wooden coffins were lowered into graves.'

A.E. CLARK-KENNEDY

M. Baucq, a Belgian, had been involved in the underground escape route and similarly condemned to death by the German military court.

The Home Front

That month came news of the execution of Nurse Cavell; her last words made one's heart thrill: 'I realise that patriotism is not enough. I must have no hatred or bitterness towards anyone.'

She had grasped a tremendous truth, and had risen nobly above resentment for her execution. Could her words have reached the Higher Command responsible for her death, one felt that her life must have been spared; yet maybe the notion was moonshine, for war is ruthless. The war-mongers here acclaimed her as a heroine, but spurned the truth she voiced in her last message. In the flood-tide of their lust for victory, they used her martyrdom to fan the flames of the hatred she had overcome.

The pacifists praised her in lower key; some even refused to admit her worth, hearing her so lauded by the war party.

In the future her story will become a great source of legend, because it typifies an important passage in social evolution. Herself of the fairest flower of patriotism, she understood that it

had had its day, and must give place to its loftier successor –
Internationalism.

E. Sylvia Pankhurst

This Was My World

Edith Cavell's Funeral Procession, London, May 1919

Nurse Cavell's funeral. It passed up Victoria Street in the still
misty sunlight, and we got out on to our balcony to watch. Just
above it, on a level with our window, two white butterflies were
fluttering. Queer.

Viscountess Rhondda

This Was My World

May 7th, 1915

On Saturday, May 1st (the day on which the *Lusitania* was to sail),
in order that there might be no mistake as to German intentions,
the German Embassy at Washington issued a warning to passengers couched in general terms, which was printed in the New
York morning papers directly under the notice of the sailing of the
Lusitania. The first-class passengers, who were not due on board
till about ten o'clock, had still time after reading the warning,
unmistakable in form and position, to cancel their passage if they
chose. For the third-class passengers it came too late. As a matter
of fact, I believe that no British and scarcely any American passengers acted on the warning, but we were most of us very fully
conscious of the risk we were running. A number of people wrote
farewell letters to their home folk and posted them in New York
to follow on another vessel.

There were some two thousand people aboard altogether,

counting passengers and crew. Curiously enough, there were a large number of children on the passenger list. We noticed this with much surprise. I think that the explanation lay in the fact that a number of the families of Canadians serving in the war were coming over to join them—

We were due to arrive in Liverpool on Saturday, May 8th, and we had all imagined that the attempts would be made in the Irish Sea during our last night. We were wrong. On the Friday afternoon, at about two o'clock, we were off the south-west coast of Ireland, the Old Head of Kinsale was visible in the distance; my father and I had just come out of the dining-room after lunching and were strolling into the lift on 'D' deck.—There was a dull, thud-like, not very loud but unmistakable explosion. It seemed to come from a little below us and about the middle of the vessel on the port side, that was the side towards the land. I turned and came out of the lift; somehow, the stairs seemed safer. My father walked over to look out of a porthole. I did not wait. I had days before made up my mind that if anything happened one's instinct would be to make straight for the boat deck (it is a horrible feeling to stay under cover even for a few moments in a boat that may be sinking), but that one must control that and go first to one's cabin to fetch one's lifebelt and then on to the boat deck. As I ran up the stairs, the boat was already heeling over. As I ran, I thought, 'I wonder I'm not more frightened,' and then, 'I'm beginning to get frightened, but I mustn't let myself.'

My cabin was on 'B' deck some way down a passage. On my way I met a stewardess; by this time the boat had heeled over very much, and as we each ran along holding the rail on the lower side of the passage we collided, and wasted a minute or so making polite apologies to each other.

I collected my lifebelt, the 'Boddy' belt provided by the Cunard Company. On my way back I ran into my father's cabin and took out one of his belts, fearing that he might be occupied with his papers and forget to fetch one for himself. Then I went up on to 'A' deck (the boat deck). Here there was, of course, a choice of sides. I chose the starboard side, feeling that it would somehow be safer to be as far away from the submarine as possible. The side further from the submarine was also the higher out of the water, as the boat had listed over towards the side on which she had been hit and the deck was now slanting at a considerable angle; and to be as high as possible out of the water felt safer too.

—Just after I reached the deck a stream of steerage passengers came rushing up from below and fought their way into the boat nearest us, which was being lowered. They were white-faced and terrified; I think they were shrieking; there was no kind of order – the strongest got there first, the weak were pushed aside. Here and there a man had his arm round a woman's waist and bore her along with him; but there were no children to be seen; no children could have lived in that throng. They rushed a boat before it was ready for them. A ship's officer made some feeble attempt to prevent them, but there was no real attempt at order or discipline.—Two seamen began to lower the boat, which was full to overflowing, but no one was in command of them. One man lowered his end quickly, the other lowered his end slowly; the boat was in an almost perpendicular position when it reached the water. Half the people fell out, but the boat did not capsize, and I think most of them scrambled back afterwards. I do not know. We turned away and did not look. It was not safe to look at horrible things just then. Curious that it never for a moment struck any of us as possible to attempt to get into the boat ourselves. Even at that moment death would have seemed better than to make part of that terror-infected crowd. I remember regretfully thinking something of this sort.

That was the last boat I saw lowered. It became impossible to lower any more from our side owing to the list on the ship—

The list on the ship soon got worse again, and, indeed, became very bad. Presently Dr. F— said he thought we had better jump into the sea. (We had thought of doing so before, but word had been passed round from the captain that it was better to stay where we were.) Dr. F— and Miss C— moved towards the edge of the deck where the boat had been and there was no railing. I followed them, feeling frightened at the idea of jumping so far (it was, I believe, some sixty feet normally from 'A' deck to the sea), and telling myself how ridiculous I was to have physical fear of the jump when we stood in such grave danger as we did. I think others must have had the same fear, for a little crowd stood hesitating on the brink and kept me back. And then, suddenly, I saw that the water had come over on to the deck. We were not, as I had thought, sixty feet above the sea; we were already under the sea. I saw the water green just about up to my knees. I do not remember its coming up further; that must all have happened in a second. The ship sank and I was sucked right down with her.

The next thing I can remember was being deep down under the water. It was very dark, nearly black. I fought to come up. I was terrified of being caught on some part of the ship and kept down. That was the worst moment of terror, the only moment of acute terror, that I knew. My wrist did catch on a rope. I was scarcely aware of it at the time, but I have the mark on me to this day. At first I swallowed a lot of water; then I remembered that I had read that one should not swallow water, so I shut my mouth. Something bothered me in my right hand and prevented me striking out with it; I discovered that it was the lifebelt I had been holding for my father.

As I reached the surface I grasped a bit of board, quite thin, a few inches wide and perhaps two or three feet long. I thought this was keeping me afloat. I was wrong. My most excellent lifebelt was doing that.—

When I came to the surface I found that I formed part of a large, round, floating island composed of people and débris of all sorts, lying so close together that at first there was not very much water noticeable in between. People, boats, hencoops, chairs, rafts, boards and goodness knows what besides, all floating cheek by jowl—

Many people were praying aloud in a curious, unemotional monotone; others were shouting for help in much the same slow, impersonal chant: 'Bo-at . . . bo-at . . . bo-at . . .' I shouted for a minute or two, but it was obvious that there was no chance of any boat responding, so I soon desisted. One or two boats were visible, but they were a long way away from where I was, and clearly had all they could do to pick up the people close beside them. So far as I could see, they did not appear to be moving much. By and by my legs got bitterly cold, and I decided to try to swim to a boat so as to get them out of the cold water, but it was a big effort swimming (I could normally swim a hundred yards or so, but I was not an expert swimmer). I only swam a few strokes and almost immediately gave up the attempt, because I did not see how I could get along without letting go of my piece of board, which nothing would have induced me to abandon.

There was no acute feeling of fear whilst one was floating in the water. I can remember feeling thankful that I had not been drowned underneath, but had reached the surface safely, and thinking that even if the worst happened there could be nothing unbearable to go through now that my head was above the water. The lifebelt held one up in a comfortable sitting position, with one's head lying rather back, as if one were in a hammock. One was a little dazed and rather stupid and vague. I doubt whether any of the people in the water were acutely frightened or in any consciously unbearable agony of mind. When Death is as close as he was then, the sharp agony of fear is not there; the thing is too overwhelming and stunning for that. One has the sense of something taking care of one – I don't mean in the sense of protecting one from death; rather of death itself being a benignant power. At moments I wondered whether the whole thing was perhaps a nightmare from which I should wake, and once – half laughing, I think – I wondered, looking round on the sun and pale blue sky and calm sea, whether I had reached heaven without knowing it – and devoutly hoped I hadn't.

One was acutely uncomfortable, no more than that. A discomfort mainly due to the intense cold, but further – at least so far as I was concerned – to the fact that, being a very bad sailor, when presently a little swell got up, I was seasick. I remember, as I sat in the water, I thought out an improvement which I considered should be adopted for all lifebelts. There should be, I thought, a little bottle of chloroform strapped into each belt, so that one could inhale it and lose consciousness when one wished to. I must have been exceedingly uncomfortable before I thought of that.

The swell of the sea had the effect of causing the close-packed island of wreckage and people to drift apart. Presently I was a hundred yards or more away from anyone else. I looked up at the sun, which was high in the sky, and wished that I might lose consciousness. I don't know how long after that I did lose it, but that is the last thing I remember in the water.—

I heard afterwards that I had been picked up at dusk by a rowing-boat; that in the gathering darkness they had very nearly missed me, but that by some curious chance a wicker chair had floated up under me (it must have happened after I lost consciousness); that this had both helped to raise me further out of the water than I should otherwise have floated (and so likely enough saved my life by lessening the strain on me) and had made a slightly larger mark which had been noticed in the water, and they had rowed to it. The little boat had transferred me to *The Bluebell*. I was handed up to it along with a lot of dead bodies, but the midshipman who handed me on board said, 'I rather think there's some life in this woman; you'd better try and see.' So they did.

VISCOUNTESS RHONDDA

How We Lived Then

The sinking of the 'Lusitania' was a ghastly example of the hideousness of modern warfare and a piece of extraordinary stupidity on the part of the German Government, which apparently had not realized the effect such an action would have on

American public opinion and on her attitude towards the war—
Whether or no the 'Lusitania' was a defenceless passenger ship
flying the American flag and bearing only civilian passengers
and an ordinary cargo possibly now will never be known—
Whatever may be the truth, the fact remains that the great ship
sank in eighteen minutes, and that 1198 men, women and children perished. This tragedy was used all over the world for
propaganda purposes. A powerful cartoon appeared in the *New
York World*, depicting the piteous forms of little children rising
from the sea, holding out their hands and asking of the Kaiser,
'But why did you kill *us*?' This had a great effect upon American
opinion.

The result in this country of the sinking of the 'Lusitania' was
to inflame public opinion bitterly against Germany and those
Germans who until this time had remained unmolested and in
possession of businesses. In Liverpool it became necessary to
intern all Germans and Austrians for their own protection, for
shops were wrecked and the police had to be called out to protect
their owners. Rioting took place in other towns, and in London
feeling was extremely strong.

Mrs C. S. Peel

An English Wife in Berlin

Berlin, May 1915.

May 8, 1915, will live vividly in my memory for the shock that we
received by the sinking of the *Lusitania*. How can I find words to
write about it? And yet I cannot pass over the event that caused
more sensation throughout the world than the greatest victory or
the greatest defeat. 'Sinking of the *Lusitania* by a German submarine' was the headline in our German paper that morning,
without any details of importance. A great loss of life had been
the just punishment for that liner that was carrying munitions to
the enemy of Germany. Neutral America was providing these

munitions (a breach of neutrality, said Germany), and what sacrifice could be too great a punishment for that!

The Germans themselves were amazed – oh yes; but proud – proud of what one little submarine could do, of what power a few men in a little nutshell under the water could wield – what a wonderful method of warfare it was, and how soon England must give in if confronted with this power. At last the world would recognize the awfulness of the German navy, and see that Germany must become mistress of the seas, as she could prevent others from crossing the water in safety whenever she pleased. In one respect the Germans were right. The world does recognize the awfulness of that kind of warfare, but not with admiration!

The Americans here in the hotel, and those of the Embassy staff, had always professed to be neutral. They had been cordial and friendly towards the Germans they met, had gone out together, had played tennis, and so forth. But a sudden change now took place. The Americans openly avoided the Germans, almost cutting their friends of the day before. Friendly intercourse was absolutely out of the question. Their rage and horror at the idea that Americans had been killed knew no bounds, and they gave vent to their views in unguarded terms. One German turned to me and said, 'You and other English ladies here have self-control, but these American ladies, once they are roused, do not care how or where they express their feelings.'

EVELYN, PRINCESS BLÜCHER

Home Service Corps Review, 27 August, 1915

Current Events

Two H.S.C. Drummers on the 'Arabic'
It will be of interest to the drilling members of the Home Service Corps to learn that two of the Corps drummers, Miss Violet and Miss Olive Kelk, are among the survivors of the 'Arabic.'

Interviewed upon her return from Queenstown, Miss Violet Kelk gave the following description of the happenings of August 19th:–

'We went on board on Wednesday at 2 o'clock, and saw nothing out of the ordinary until after breakfast on Thursday morning. It was about 9.30 and we were all sitting on deck, when my brother came round with the news that the "Dunsley," a tramp steamer, had been shelled and was sinking. We could see her quite clearly with her bare deck and no sign of life anywhere, and were so intent on watching and talking of her fate, that we were startled to hear a sudden alarm that we ourselves were the object of an attack from a German torpedo. I saw the thin track of light green in the water, and then heard a heavy thud – it was nothing more; though they say there was a big explosion as it cut into the engine room. Everything happened so quickly that I do not think any-body had time to be really frightened. The bugle sounded an alarm on deck and then we ran for our lifebelts. I wish we had been told how to put them on; it is not easy when one knows that everything depends on speed. By this time we were listing heavily to starboard; this, however, righted itself and, after a slight list in the other direction, we straightened up and started to sink at the stern. My sister and I made for one of the boats; it was already full but I managed to push her in and see her into safety; and then I, with my elder sister, found a place in a second boat.

'We did not seem in luck's way, for our boat stuck and refused to get clear of the "Arabic." Somebody shouted that we were all too much on one side, which, of course, made everyone move at once in the opposite direction; and then, I do not know exactly how it happened – some said we capsized, others that the boat broke clean in two – anyhow, I found myself in the water and being sucked down by the vessel. I did not sink far; but, I suppose it was owing to my lifebelt, rose and struck my head on something floating on the surface. I looked up but it was very dark, so I sank again and tried to swim out into the open. The thing above me seemed hugely big, and I came to the conclusion that I was caught somehow under the wreck, and that the best thing to do was to try to end things quickly by swallowing water. At that moment, though, I saw a gleam of clear green, and making one more attempt, I reached it and rose close to an empty boat, into which I was helped by the ship's doctor and two other men, who had themselves been in the water with me. We were very wet, of course, and threw away everything that we did not absolutely need. There was no sign of the "Arabic" – she sank in twelve minutes – and only our little boats were left. We were four hours there, and none of us could use the oars until another boat lent us a man to keep us from drifting. I had time to count all the things I had lost! We were picked up at last by the "Primrose," and taken to Queenstown, where the whole place turned out to meet us, and we were told off to buy whatever was necessary for our return to England. Afterwards we heard that the crew of the sinking "Dunsley" had set out in a lifeboat to warn the "Arabic" of the German submarine, but they had been shelled and were unable to reach us.'

Serbia and the Great Retreat

Miracles and Adventures

Funerals of Nurse Ferriss and Mrs Dearmer: Serbia, Summer 1915

First walked a Serbian soldier carrying a Cross, on which was written the name of the dead, also a wreath, with flaring pink ribbons; then Dr. Dearmer, carrying his Prayer Book in one hand, and a brown, lighted candle – given him by a Serbian official – in the other. Candles play an important part in Serbian death ceremonies. Next I followed as chief mourner, and our British Military Attaché, who kindly offered to stay by me, Dr. Coxon, who had attended Nurse Ferriss, then the other doctors, and Captain Yovannovitch, the Unit, officers, representatives of the town, and general sympathizers.

This was the first walk that I had taken since my illness. The sun was scorching – at three in the afternoon – and the walk, at snail's pace, on the rough cobbled streets, seemed interminable. But the streets were lined with townsfolk, and I felt it was necessary to look stoical. I thought how it might easily have been myself instead of poor Ferris inside that ugly nailed-down box. But I would have changed places if I could. Then I thought of

Ferriss's mother, and of her fiancé; perhaps they were writing to her at this moment, planning all kinds of future happiness; and there she was lying, just in front of me, in a Serbian coffin, indifferent to it all.

Now that she was dead, she was saluted by passing officers and soldiers. I wondered if she wasn't a little pleased at the posthumous honour, and whether it would always be necessary to reserve honours for women till after they are dead.

MURIEL ST CLAIR STOBART

Journal

Serbia 1915

A whole nation, not merely an army, was retreating before the enemy along the only way open to them, that one leading over those ghastly Albanian mountains, roadless, deep in snow, with no sustenance for man or beast & continually swept by blizzards at this time of the year.

At Ipec we slept in the huge military hospital in a ward meant to accommodate 80 cases arranged in four rows, but already there were 95 people in the room, sleeping on hay on the floor. There were Serbian officers, railway officials, refugees, men, women & children, about 30 of the Scottish unit, nurses, doctors & orderlies, about 30 Stobarts, besides numbers of other units — Here also we had come to the place where Col. Mickolivitch said ponies & pack horses would be provided for us, but when we made enquiries nothing had been done & indeed there were very few to buy — The prices were enormous. For the ponies one had to pay £20 to £30 & for the pack donkeys from £12. However, they had to be had—

I was still feeling dreadfully ill & I knew that I as well as the other invalids would not be able to travel as quickly as the strong ones, so I begged all of them to go on — after a great deal of discussion they did consent to go & early one morning they started off & our little party numbering seven started two days afterwards with three ponies & three donkeys & a saddle pony to ride. The morning was warm & sunny for a change, & everything seemed brighter, in fact we quite enjoyed ourselves as we tramped along & very soon were on the steep mountain paths & the real climb began – that grim ascent that took the heart out of man & beast — We walked until 4.30 & then, having come to a very convenient place in a valley near to the river & also near a woodcutter's hut where we could get plenty of wood for our fire, we pitched our three wee tents, tethered our beasts, made our supper & went to bed. About 9.30 p.m. the wind got up, cold biting wind bringing sleet & snow, & by the time dawn came everything was thickly covered, & cold & shivering we lighted our fire, made some cocoa to drink with our breakfast of bread & a hard boiled egg, packed up our blankets, loaded up the beasts & started off. The paths became narrower & narrower as we went, & very slippery—

That night we once more pitched our tents, in the deep snow at the foot of Mount Velico 7800ft. above sea level. Over the snow we spread our groundsheets on which we lay rolled up in our blankets. You cannot imagine how miserable it is to try to light a fire & to boil water in a snowstorm, let alone unpacking the store box to get out necessary food. Everything got covered with snow as fast as we took them out—During the night all these things froze together into one huge lump! We were to start next morning at 7 – then began the ascent of Velico.

The rest houses became fewer & further apart, & we lost our first donkey – it slipped over the edge with all it carried – luckily not food & blankets.

The bound Journal is lavishly illustrated. At this point there is a vivid picture of the girls hanging on to the animals' tails to try to prevent their falling into the ravines.

An awful blizzard began to blow. All day we laboured on & on, slipping & slithering on the icy paths. When night came, we were only half way up the mountain, & the wet and misery was awful, too awful to find words to explain. This terrible suffering made children of us all again. We cowered together, holding each other's hands through the long dark bitter night.

—The next morning at 8.30 we started off again, thank goodness the blizzard had stopped for a while, & this day was the first of the awful experiences & sights that we became quite accustomed to for the rest of the trek. Dead horses, ponies & donkeys lay by the side of paths and at first I could not imagine as the poor beasts had merely died of starvation and cold, why they should be so cut about, but presently the problem was solved. Often the snow was stained red with the blood of these poor beasts and from as yet warm bodies, the prisoners, Bulgarians, Austrians and Germans who were in front of us, cut chunks of flesh and ate it raw and warm. These prisoners were a pitiable sight, they were no longer men at all, but dumb and driven animals and they too fell by the roadside dying from exhaustion & hunger, & their comrades would strip off clothes even before life had really left their poor shrunken frames. It was a common sight to see hands & feet protruding from the snow drifts – the feet never had shoes or boots on – they were far too valuable to be left there. Oh! it was awful, day after day & night after night the same—

One most pathetic sight I saw. It was a Serbian mother staggering along beneath the weight of a highly coloured wooden cradle which was strapped on to her back across her shoulders, its occupant, an infant of a few months was feebly wailing. On either side of her stumbled a wee child, not more than five & six keeping up a perpetual cry of 'Leibes-Leibes' (bread-bread). At her breast she clutched a yet smaller child two years or so. Not a particle of food had she with her – not a single bundle of any kind, & there she was, struggling along hoping to reach shelter before the night overtook her, hoping also to get food there too—

I never remember how I got to the top of Mount Velico, or however I got down. I was quite exhausted with walking & had been riding for some time & when Miss Dickinson looked at me, she saw I was unconscious, absolutely frozen onto the saddle & my legs were frozen onto the stirrups & leathers. They got me off, & it was Miss Dickinson who saved my life by carrying me in her arms down the mountains to shelter out of the blizzard. However she managed it, no one knows. She seemed to possess super-human strength.

—Before I had seen these mountains, I always thought that the sea was our only earthly picture of infinite space, but no sea could speak of distance so plainly as those ranges of mountains, one peak showing beyond another, & we knew perfectly well that when we reached the next summit we should see just such another beyond us – everlastingly another & yet another on the far horizon, & on & on we went our weary miserable way, following in that awful trail of dead things by the roadside—

GERTRUDE HOLLAND

Miracles and Adventures

Serbia 1915

There was no longer a defined way; the whole earth was now an untrodden track, from or to perdition. Whichever way you looked, oxen, horses, and human beings were struggling, and rolling, and stumbling, all day long in ice and snow. Soon after we started, I saw a long Column ascending the steep hill-side; near the top a horse slipped, and knocked down the man who was leading it; they both fell, and as they rolled down the slope, they knocked down all the other men and horses in the line, and these all fell like ninepins, one after the other, all the way down the mountain-side.

—No one knows or will ever know accurately how many people perished, but it is believed that not less than 100,000 human beings lie sepulchred in those mountains. The route of escape which led through Monastir to Durazzo was even more disastrous. From amongst the army reserve of 30,000, composed of boys below, and of men above, military age, 10,000 only reached Durazzo.

MURIEL ST CLAIR STOBART

Report from a Scottish Women's Hospital Nursing Sister

Albania 7th December 1915

The state of confusion here is beyond description —It has taken the HQ staff 12 days to do what we did in six and we had a fearful snow storm and after that the following days of frost to face, so they did not show any great zeal to face the situation. No doubt their women folk delayed them. It is a fearful journey I must own —From the moment the enemy crossed the Danube they (the Serbians) dropped all pretence and displayed openly their dislike of foreigners and it was with the utmost difficulty we managed to get transport, in fact we had to make all our own arrangements and in the final retreat through the mountains in spite of explicit promises we could not get either ponies forage or food. All was taken for the families of the general staff. Both Serbs and Montenegrins kept warning us about the Albanians but we came along unguarded and unarmed and were guided and fed by these unfortunate people on the ground. We were British in whose word they still believe — The British minister for Serbia is here very highly strung. He still appears to believe what the Serbians state *(? word unclear)*, which passes comprehension. They are incapable of speaking the truth as we know it, their vanity is beyond belief, they refuse to learn anything from anyone—The whole treatment of the hundreds of British ladies and nurses by the Serbian Government civil and military has been disgraceful.

MISS M. T. BARCLAY

Christmas with the Second Serbian Regiment: 1915

The Serbian Christmas is not till thirteen days later than ours, but we celebrated my English Christmas Eve over the camp fire that night. A plate of beans and dry bread had to take the place of roast beef and plum pudding, but we drank Christmas healths in a small flask of cognac, after which I played 'God Save the King' on the violin and we all stood up and sang it. This violin went into a long, narrow kit bag, which was carried in a pack-horse and had managed to survive its travels, though the damp had not improved its tone.

Flora Sandes

1916

1916 was a terrible year. In February the Germans launched their attack on Verdun 'to bleed France white', correctly assessing that the French would defend to the death fortresses steeped in historic and strategic significance. In July, to relieve the pressure on Verdun, the British launched the Somme offensive against magnificently entrenched German forces.

Nobody knows how many soldiers died in the Great War but British losses on 1 July 1916 remain a world record for a single day, in round figures some 60,000, of whom 20,000 were killed. By the end of the year, when virtually nothing had been achieved on the Western Front, some 1.5 million young men had been slaughtered. The only major sea battle of the war, the inconclusive Battle of Jutland, was costly in both men and ships. The German High Seas fleet did not, however, again venture into open waters.

What also died in 1916 was the lingering hope of a clear-cut victory for either side, while for many the concept of 'bright glorious war' was severely tarnished. Even before the carnage of the Somme, the flow of eager volunteers had begun to dry up and the Military Service Act (i.e. conscription) was passed. Conscientious objection was, however, recognised. Despite the harsh treatment meted out to many 'conchies', Britain was the only nation to have this conscientious right.

On the Eastern Front, having suffered casualties that dwarfed those on the Western Front, the Russian army was disintegrating, while the long-suffering Russian nation had almost had enough of an incompetent autocracy. The entry of Romania on the Allies' side did nothing to assist the situation.

Striking at your enemy when he is otherwise engaged is a time-honoured tactic, which Irish Nationalists employed in Dublin. The doomed Easter Rising then had little popular support but retrospectively it can be seen as the crucial step on the road to an Irish Republic.

This would have been the ideal year for peace with some sort of honour but it was not a course any of the warring nations felt inclined to pursue. It became a matter of slogging on to the bitter end, of hoping that the British blockade would produce shortages the German population could not endure, or that renewed German submarine warfare would cut the British Isles' lifelines, and that the Americans would finally enter the war to swing the balance for the Allies with a fresh supply of cannon fodder.

To say it was a great year for women would be crassly offensive to anyone with any sensitivity, to those millions whose loved ones were killed or returned home blinded, with amputated limbs or shell-shocked minds. It *was* the year in which women took over more and more allegedly masculine jobs and proved that they could perform them as well as, if not better than, their menfolk.

'The Greatest Page in the History of Womanhood'

From a *Home Service Corps Review*
editorial by Phyllis Lovell

Home Service Corps Review, 4 January 1916

To Workers

It was easy, in the strong emotion of a war just begun, to throw ourselves whole-heartedly into the schemes for work, believing that in so doing we could release a man for active service. It was easy to picture oneself standing in his place, holding up the flag of home duties, while he held up another flag abroad.

The idea, as an idea, was really heroic and picturesque, and very pleasing to the imagination. Realities, however, are the shatterers of dreams. The women who offered themselves in the service of their country are finding now the meaning of real work. They are finding that pluck is needed at home just as much as in the trenches. They are finding that they have a battle to fight with themselves in order to keep their flag floating and unstained.

It is to the workers, therefore, that we must offer assistance; because they are finding that the work is difficult. Woman, as woman, is on trial, and it is well to bear this fact in mind as one struggles along against odds which did not appear on the horizon of a few months ago. Woman has claimed a place in the world's work; claimed it persistently, and that place has been granted.

Women! Remember who you are. Remember that the eyes of a nation are upon you. Remember that the flag you hold is the flag coveted so long by the women of the past. Whoever you are – be you the carrier of letters, the driver of a cart, the turner of soil, the puncher of tickets – remember you are a woman, and that you are helping to write the greatest page in the history of Womanhood.

Daily Mirror, 7 January 1916

Boys Replaced by 'Flappers'

Reuter's Agency have for some time past employed a corps of smartly-uniformed messenger girls and the District Messenger Company has engaged more than 150 girls over school age.

'We are well-satisfied with these girls,' the manager of the District Messenger Company told the Daily Mirror yesterday. 'They are intelligent, very polite, and compare favourably with the boy messengers.'

Daily Mirror, 9 February 1916

Miss Elaine Jenkins, the late Lord Glantawe's daughter, holds a unique position, for she has now been elected chairman of the Swansea and Mumbles railway Company, that queer little railway that runs by the shores of Swansea Bay. Miss Jenkins is spoken of by hard-headed business men as one of the cleverest women in the country.

Evening News, 16 February 1916

Another Shock for the City

The London City and Midland Bank has put girls on the 'walk round'. That is to say, it is now employing girls in the highly responsible work of collecting money from other banks and City houses against cheques and bills. It is a position of great trust, as sometimes the walk-clerk has to carry thousands of pounds in a wallet, and must possess considerable ability. The L.C. and M. is the only bank that has yet adopted the innovation. More than 60 per cent of the staff have gone to the war, and the deficiency has been largely made up by girls. Other banks are expected to follow suit.

Daily Telegraph, 7 February 1916

Women Welders

Two years ago the boldest would never have predicted the adaptability to the most diverse kinds of work that women have shown. They have now taken up the work of oxy-acetylene welding – an industry which is itself in its early stages. Ever since the Active Service Branch of the National Union of Women's Suffrage Societies was formed it has kept to the fore a programme effort, and in September last opened the first school for the teaching of this craft to women.

Daily Express, 22 November 1916

The trained handy woman has arrived. She came yesterday to mend my electric bells, and gave an interesting account of her war-time work. She is an adept at repairs on every sort of contrivance, and gave advice on the management of my sewing machine with the same aptitude as she put up a new roller-blind.

Pall Mall Gazette, October 1916

A woman stage-manager, women scene-shifters, and women working the limelight will be one of the interesting interior features about the production of a new play *Iris Intervenes* in which Miss Lena Ashwell appears next Saturday night at the Kingsway Theatre. 'These women have all gone through trying times,' she said. 'Some of them have husbands serving with the colours, and have been left with great responsibilities.'

Manchester Guardian, 23 November 1916

Two scholarships of £75 are offered by 'The Common Cause' (the organ of the National Union of Women's Suffrage Societies) to women who wish to qualify for positions as industrial chemists. Preference will be given to students willing to study at the Imperial College of Science and Technology, or the School of Technology, Manchester.

Daily Sketch, 2 December 1916

On the banks of the Wye at Chepstow many women are finding employment in bridge building. They scrape and paint the girders, and also find employment in the iron-factory as core-makers.

The Star, 2 December 1916

The lady lamplighter has arrived. She has not yet had time to think about a uniform, she tells me. All the same it is under consideration and by what I can learn it is going to be a very feminine one, as the work does not necessitate masculine garb at all.

Daily Express, 11 December 1916

Two and a half years ago the general public thought women unsuited for most occupations other than those of a strictly domestic character. Now it is quite commonly supposed that a woman can do anything after six weeks' training. There is little enough truth in either of these propositions, but they serve the man in the street, who likes his conclusions in a nutshell.

Daily News and Leader, 30 January 1917

Mrs Preston, of Grasmere, Westmorland, who liberated her workmen in the early days of the war, has since brought her own coals daily from Windermere, an 18 miles journey. During the year 1916 she has covered in this way 6,316 miles.

The Globe, 17 February 1916

The College de France now boasts a woman professor. Mme. le docteur Ioteyko is not a Frenchwoman, as may be gathered from her name. She is a Pole, who studied in Paris and has lectured in Brussels. According to one who attended her first lecture at the College de France, she achieved a great success. The hall was crowded with students, who gave her an enthusiastic reception. The capitulation of so ancient a masculine fortress as the College de France to the claims of true worth, irrespective of sex, ought to give hope to English women that our two conservative strongholds, Oxford and Cambridge, may in time abandon their prejudices in respect to granting degrees to women.

Home Service Corps Review, 11 July 1916

The Guard of Honour

Last month a pressing invitation came to the officers of the H.S.C. to form a Guard of Honour at the wedding of Miss Joyce Louise Hindle and Lieut. L. E. Lovell 3/9 Hants. As the invitation came from the bride and bridegroom, and as the corps has, if nothing else, a strong reputation for versatility, a message of acceptance was sent.—It is superfluous to add that the Guard of Honour fulfilled its duties to perfection. Surely the occasion was, in every sense of the word, unique. Is there another church in Liverpool, or anywhere else for that matter, that has ever been 'taken in hand' by uniformed women? Have guests ever been shown to their seats by women police? Has a bride ever made her way from the motor to the church between two rows of blue and khaki beings who were not men? Once more the H.S.C. has proved itself to be original!

The Better Fight: The Story of Dame Lilian Barker

Woolwich Arsenal

In the early days most of the girls were Londoners, but later girls were recruited from all over the country. My father, who sometimes used to meet them as they swarmed to work in the early morning, or streamed in the evenings towards Beresford Square, where there was a scramble for the coveted seats on the open upper deck of the trams (some intrepid females climbing the balustrade), said they were the toughest bunch of girls he had ever come across. But Mother, who worked with them, saw another side of the picture. She admired their gaiety and fortitude and their bright conversation. Everything about the Arsenal tended towards drabness and monotony, the work, the clothes, the long hours, but the girls strove to introduce a touch of variety and even frivolity. They loved to dress and rearrange their hair, so soon to be hidden by the Arsenal cap. The caps, too, which were simply a circular piece of material with a string round the edge (rather like a pudding cloth) could be arranged so skilfully that it seemed as though a dozen different headgears had been issued by the authorities. The regulation gowns were of khaki or blue (the blue ones being in great demand, though when both had faded a bit there was not much to choose between them) their only decoration a number stencilled on the back. The first fashion touch was a posy pinned to the gown, each shop having its own flower emblem; but as these were confiscated during working hours, someone got the idea of substituting brightly coloured ribbon for the government shoe laces. First the 'cap shop' girls strutted proudly with emerald green ribbon in their shoes, the 'new fuse' girls followed with yellow, and soon the whole Arsenal was in the fashion.

ELIZABETH GORE

Women War Workers

Munition Work

Most of us are up at 5 or 5.30 breaking the ice in our water-jugs. The dark winter mornings are cold and comfortless, but thousands of men are out in the open trenches, and the constant remembrance of them stifles our groans. It is not so bad in the spring-time and summer, for the early morning freshness is sweeter than ever because of the heat and toil to follow. We live together in hostels as a rule, for we find that from union economy results. Moreover, hardships are not so hard when a hundred others are sharing the hardness with you. If Miss Fuse, in the end cubicle, is breaking her ice with her toothbrush handle, it seems easier to creep from the warmth of the blankets and attack one's own with a hatpin. Alone in rooms the very idea is gruesome.

Six o'clock breakfast is a fashionable institution nowadays, but even this alteration has not destroyed the germ of unpunctuality so inherent in our race. It has, however, broadened our minds. Dozens of us who used to button our gloves before leaving the house are now seen running gloveless along the streets devouring pieces of bread and butter as we go. Many of our comrades, on the other hand, pause at the winkle stalls to take a relish to their breakfasts.

We move in crowds, except when we get jammed, and then we cannot move at all. As we near the factories the roads become congested, and our numbers are still swelling. There is a mad scrum around the trams and omnibuses, and from what one sees daily taking place one gathers that the Government has sadly erred in not recruiting women for the trenches. If the very tram-conductors quail before the gentler sex, how poorly would the Germans fare! At other times, however, we are a cheery, friendly team, and mighty proud of our work. Except in districts where the population is composed solely of ourselves, we meet with sympathy and admiration everywhere. We are not allowed to speak of anything but munition life, and we never do, so that at last even our relations gaze upon us with awe. We come flocking from every corner of the British Isles. Canada and Australia have joined us, and sad-faced Belgium.

Our garments are as varied as our tongues. Some prefer tweeds remarkable for their absence below the knee, shooting-boots and leather gaiters, but many incline to satin and *crêpe de Chine* of vivid hues, white kid boots, ostrich plumes, and no gloves. The majority, however, are neatly and quietly attired. The few really shabby ones are popularly supposed to be peeresses in their own right. Whether that is so or not it is certain that persons with glittering handles to their names have occasionally entered our ranks. One girl was overheard remarking to another: 'Say, young Doll, see that there lydy on the end machine? They do say as 'ow she's a Dook.'

Inside the gates we are all on a level. Duchesses or coster-girls, we are crammed into earth-coloured overalls, and hustled and jostled, winked at and sworn at in the most indiscriminate and realistic manner—

The day is long, the atmosphere is breathed and rebreathed, and the oil smells. Our hands are black with warm, thick oozings from the machines, which coat the work and, incidentally, the workers. We regard our horrible, begrimed members with disgust and secret pride. It is so realistic. Some of us remember our mud-pie days and rejoice. The genteel among us wear gloves. We vie with each other in finding the most up-to-date grease-removers, just as we used to vie about hats. Our hands are not alone in suffering from dirt. The shop sweepers strike one as remarkably faithful and diligent workers, and they never forget a single corner if it happens to be occupied. Their worn brooms tangle themselves among our feet, and their dust-clouds, filled with unwelcome life, find a resting-place in our lungs and noses—

Engineering mankind is possessed of the unshakable opinion that no woman can have the mechanical sense. If one of us asks humbly why such and such an alteration is not made to prevent this or that drawback to a machine, she is told, with a superior smile, that a man has worked her machine before her for years, and that therefore if there were any improvement possible it would have been made. As long as we do exactly what we are told and do not attempt to use our brains, we give entire satisfaction, and are treated as nice, good children. Any swerving from the easy path prepared for us by our males arouses the most scathing contempt in their manly bosoms. The exceptions are as delightful to meet as they are rare—

167

The enormous wages held out by the papers to the clutching hands of mammon-worshippers, as carrots before the noses of recalcitrant donkeys, melt somewhat upon inspection, or rather have a tendency to be given to no one nearer than a friend's sister's niece. However, there is no doubt that we do earn more than women have ever done before. We 'pick up' our three pounds a week and fall into a rage because we were expecting three pounds and tuppence. At the same time living is so very expensive in these days that three or four pounds are not what they seem.

NAOMI LOUGHNAN

Daily News and Leader, 14 December 1915

'Middle-Class Women in Factories'

Sir,—

When the middle-class woman has finished her 12 hours' shift in a munition factory she goes home to a comfortable house, and if she has been on a night shift, to a comfortable, aired bed in a quiet bedroom.

When the working-girl comes back in the early morning she finds in most cases an unaired bed, which the day-worker has only just left – for in houses containing three very small bedrooms (sometimes only two), with families of seven, eight, or nine persons in them, there is no room for single beds – and in a close, stuffy room. If the window is kept open the street smells, all worse since so many street-sweepers have enlisted, and the smells from factories fill the room, and the continual noise outside, the ceaseless crying of someone's baby somewhere near, the jolting of heavy lorries and waggons, the monotonous cries of the street sellers with little rattling carts, the perpetual sound of machinery, all these noises hinder sleep. Besides, the girl must, more often than not, help in the house work as well as sleep.

Hundreds of streets in one Yorkshire city, now making munitions, consist entirely of back-to-back houses. If anyone really wishes to understand industrial life, and be one with the workers, and not merely an outsider, they must sleep in a back-to-back house. They will never forget the haunting smell of closeness, nor how every sound in the house is heard everywhere in it. There is no quiet and no privacy possible in such dwellings.

As for the food – when tea has to be bought in small quantities it has an entirely different taste from tea bought in large quantities in a middle-class house. The milk! – well, one wonders what it is made of! But the well-to-do woman will seldom, if ever, experience these things; for if she goes into these houses she will be given the best of everything (only the poor understand the highest courtesy, I sometimes think), and a wall of politeness will cut her off from obtaining this pricelessly valuable knowledge. Unless she goes feeling within her that there is not one shadow of difference between her and her hosts, except that they know infinitely more about life and its teachings than she has ever known, and perhaps ever will know; and that they often in ordinary daily life have to rise, and do rise, to heights of courage, devotion, and self-sacrifice that she in her prosperous sheltered home may never realise or understand in the least. Then they will treat her as a friend and comrade.

But these things must be seen from the inside.

ISABELLA O. FORD

Land and Water, 7 December 1916

There is a curious air of calm and, with the exception of one or two processes, such as the riveting of the base plates and the setting of the shrapnel ball, of quiet in the shell shops. As I recall it now with its armies of overalled women bending industriously over their lathes it might well have been a cocoa factory; and certainly the production of cocoa tins would be an immeasurably noisier process. There seemed to be something peculiarly sinister in this astonishing quiet, and in the apparently supreme detachment of workers and management amid all these instruments of death and torture. For the lathes were grinding out death and worse; and the preoccupied girls were no other than gunners in the deadly silent batteries a little behind the lines. Yet stores of 18-pdr. shells look not unlike well-filled bins of an epicure's cellar, and the 15-in A.Ps standing upright higher than the average man like a new kind of gate post, convey no impression of deadliness.

The Times of India, undated cutting

Rip and his Pass
A Dog Munition Worker

Of late a new policeman has appeared at — and the beast started a regular feud against Rip. Dogs aren't allowed in the works, but all the other police constables discreetly looked the other way. Well, for about a week he raised a fuss every morning. At last he said, 'Now Miss, don't you bring that dog again because I won't let him in.' So I went in by another gate and to my horror met my old enemy again. I began to get desperate, but next time I saw Lady L—, the Welfare Superintendent, who inspects our canteens, I asked her if she could get Rip a pass. She said she'd try and in due course arrived a proper pass, signed by one of the big pots, which solemnly sets forth:-

Name – 'Rip' Miss W's dog

Destination – E 34a

Business – To assist in the preparation of meals for munition workers

Note – This pass is not transferable. Bearer must produce the same when required, and answer all questions put by the police or other persons in authority.

The Star, 7 December 1916

A Wandsworth jury yesterday returned a verdict that a girl of 16, a worker in an explosives factory, died from T.N.T. poisoning. A Government contractor said he had 2,000 employees, practically all girls, and this was the only death. No one under 18 or over 45 was engaged. The girl had said she was 18. They now had a new type of machinery, so that T.N.T. would be very little handled by the workers. The work would be done under glass screens, excluding dust. Dr. Legge said only a small class were susceptible to T.N.T. poisoning. This class were those under 18 and the Ministry of Munitions was taking steps to prevent the employment of anyone under 18. The jury suggested that girls should be required to provide their birth certificates.

NUWSS Bulletin, 12 December 1916

During the 6 months ending October 31st, 41 munition workers died from T.N.T. poisoning. Only a few days ago we read the account of an inquest on a girl of 16 who died from this form of poisoning and we could only marvel at the statement of the doctor who gave evidence that 'only a small class were susceptible to T.N.T. poisoning, and this was the class of those under 18.'

Manchester Guardian, 8 December 1916

Sisters of Courage

England is very proud of the pluck, endurance, and determination of her munition girls—The twenty-six women who were killed and the thirty wounded in that explosion in a North of England factory on Tuesday night had, like thousands of other munition workers, faced the possibility of that fate hourly, and probably faced it with jest. Yet knowing that, and realising their kinship with the men who keep their souls unshaken in the trenches, we may marvel at the courage, and above all at the perfect discipline, which after the disaster kept the other girls in the factory imperturbably at their work.

It fits in with stories one hears from all the deadliest departments of the factories, where, as is well known, the girls, breathing in danger as they work, are most reluctant to abandon the task at the end of the term prescribed. Zeppelin nights in some places have put a very hard strain on the nerves of these girls, who in some factories have spent hours waiting in black darkness, knowing that at any moment a bomb may explode the munitions piled beside them. One hears thrilling stories of what happens during those hours – there was, for instance, the singer working in a canteen who for two hours sang away the horror of the night – but the stories always end triumphantly. The girls have come through the ordeal without panic or collapse. They should all have medals for their war service, with special bars for Zeppelin night service.

Women Worker, February 1916

Our women munition workers ought to be proud! Mr Lloyd George has brought out a picture book about them! It is a large, handsome book, costing 1s, entirely full of pictures of women workers and all the processes they can do. According to Mr Lloyd George, never was there such useful workers as women munition workers. He says they can do bronzing and soldering, they can make 8-pounder shells, and some of them are very successful in making high explosive shells.

Well, it is very nice to be praised by so important a man, and it is even nicer that he should take the trouble to have a book filled with pictures of girls at work. We women, however, have always had a lurking suspicion that we were, after all, as clever as the men, and it is pleasant to hear Mr Lloyd George say so. But there is a conclusion to be drawn from all this. If girls are as important and as clever as the men, then they are as valuable to the employer. If this is so it becomes the duty of girls to see, now and always, whether on government work or not, that they receive the same pay as men.

Daily Express, 27 November 1916

Frenchwomen's War Tour

The French women munition workers who have been making a tour of our provincial war factories will take back to France delightful memories – and a pair of trousers. They arrived at the Hotel Cecil yesterday from visits to munition factories in the provinces and will spend a week in and around London before they return to France—

'We were so delighted with your women's neat and common-sense trousers and plain, workmanlike coats that the Clyde women gave us as samples of each to take back to France,' said a bright-faced French woman worker yesterday—

A hale, hearty woman added, 'Your canteens are fine. I know of nothing in France at present so organised. What is there in France that we think you might copy? Well, I think our women munition workers' crêches, which I have not seen in England.

'In connection with the large factories there are these crêches, and a woman worker, whether she comes on for work in the morning or the evening, can bring her babies. They are looked after by women of experience, who not only provide the proper food for "les petits", but also toys, and there are gardens and places with trees for them to play in, and at this time of the year those beyond babyhood can help in preparing Christmas-trees. If we copy your large, well-organised munition canteens, and you copy our crêches, what a delightful exchange between Britain and France!'

Interview with Mary Macarthur

'There are today nearly 350,000 women trade unionists, but the number of women who might be trade unionists is 5,500,000,' said Miss Mary Macarthur, secretary of the Women's Trade Union League. 'That figure includes domestic servants. Leaving them out, there are about 2,500,000 women eligible for trade unions. The Women's Trade Union League exists to help them to become trade unionists, and to help them form branches—I think it is very important that women workers should realise the desirability of becoming trade unionists. I also want everyone to realise that trade unions do not cause strikes. They reduce the number of strikes by helping to remove the grievances which cause strikes. The value of trade unionism is unquestionable. For instance, we succeeded in obtaining wages boards, under the Trade Boards Act, for fixing minimum wages for women in the sweated trades. We secured the appointment of women assessors in the munitions courts, and special tribunals for hearing women's grievances. We have obtained many concessions for women workers. Men ask: What will happen after the war? Will women cut down the rate of men's wages? It is a curious fact that while individual women may be willing to do men's work at less than men's rates, women workers as a whole are just as much against it as men. They look on it as women look on the conduct of a girl who walks out with a married man – it is "not the thing".'

The Times, 4 April 1916

Fisher Lasses in War-Time

The entire deep-sea industry, except for a few trawlers which risk their way to the Dogger and neighbouring banks, has come to a stand-still. The drifters, &c., are now numbers in the Auxiliary Fleet, and their search is for the submarine and the floating mine. There is no age-limit for such seafarers, and some villages have put their entire male population, from grandfathers down to schoolboys, into the task. But what of the folks left behind?

—The second war winter has shown the 'dependents' of the men on the nation's perilous service as slenderly provided for as before, and quite unable to assist their friends (often near relatives) to whom a second cessation of the fishing season has brought disaster.

—Some girls have adventured forth into munition factories – a terrible change for these daughters of the open air. How they must ardently wish for peace and for the free breeze coming up the harbour, the cold swish of hose-pipes in the cleaning tubs, the wild screams of the foraging gulls – in these sheds where steel dust fills the air, where the heat is of roasting metal, and there is the shrill flesh-twisting grind of machine tools at every moment. Such girls are 'doing their bit' and providing for themselves under difficult conditions.

Traveller's Prelude: Autobiography 1893–1927 vol. 1

Censorship

In late autumn two householders guaranteed me and I went on trial as a Censor. This consisted of three weeks' training during which the letters were re-censored by a supervisor. She was an embittered woman who spent her time in a long room full of desks telling us all what fools we were, but at the end of three weeks I was sent on into a building off the Strand, where I worked for thirty-five shillings a week—

The letters I passed now went on my own responsibility: if I saw anything suspicious I sent it up with a form where the reasons for suspicion were given, and if the higher department thought the matter worth investigating the form was returned with a red star attached. I used to get from one to five stars a day, but a very stupid girl next to me hardly got three a week, so I can't help thinking that a good many undesirable things slipped past her. I could read about 150 letters a day (German, French and Italian mail from or to Switzerland). They were mostly dull; no one would believe how often people say the same thing: we had a cold snap at the time, and 120 out of the 150 letters described bursting pipes. The suspicious letters were, of course, interesting: some one could make sure of – the morse code cut round stamp edges, the lining of envelopes, and the flourishes and underlinings used as guides to key words: but generally it was a sort of *instinct* which told me to look carefully, and I had some difficulty in finding words for my suspicions that I would write on the form: more often than not this vague feeling was right and a red star showed that the clue was being followed.

—At five in the evening one came out into darkness – dim-lighted buses like glow-worms, and searchlights and moonlight tangled and lovely over Trafalgar Square. The Strand was crowded with Colonial troops most anxious for company, and when I had a cold I discovered that any slight cough would bring two or three huge Australians looming out of the night like the hulls of ships, so that I had to hurry along, desperately sucking lozenges.

FREYA STARK

Women War Workers

'Fares Please'

The woman bus-conductor is a war-time impression. She is a sign of the days which have brought about those social changes which have resulted in women engaging in every kind of employment, from conducting buses to conducting businesses, and which have enabled them generally to occupy with success many places formerly filled exclusively by men—

On every other bus you see her standing jauntily on the step with a cheery smile and an independent don't care-if-it-snows kind of look. She generally stands jauntily, she nearly always smiles and her air of independence is superb. She is renowned throughout the Metropolis for her kind and courteous manner and for the neatness of her smart navy blue serge uniform, with its tight-fitting jacket, short skirt, leather leggings, and a 'Paddy' hat strapped loosely beneath her chin. She understands exactly how to measure out her sympathy to nervous old women, crochety old men, and jolly Tommies home on leave. She knows, in fact, how to handle all the odds and ends of humanity who swarm up and down the steps of her bus all day long—

The aspiring bus-conductor now receives tuition in all branches and parts of her future work. She is taught the detailed history of tickets and the geography of routes. She learns the points of the route upon which she will presently work until she knows their whereabouts by heart. Her ability to stop her bus at the proper places on a dark or foggy night vies with that of the Early Victorian housewife whose great boast was that 'she could lay her hands on the blue bag in the dark.' She is shown how to punch a ticket in the correct way – and there is more skill in punching a ticket properly than the casual observer would ever be led to believe. She is taken into a map room, where it is conveyed to her that, quite contrary to any ideas she previously held on the subject, the Crystal Palace and Hampton Court do not by any means lie in the same direction. Common sense aids her in her lessons on the handling of coins on a dark night, and she soon becomes expert in detecting the difference between a farthing and a sixpenny bit, a two-shilling piece and a penny, a French franc and a British shilling, merely by rubbing the coins in the palm of her hand. Films are shown for her benefit depicting the way in which accidents do happen to the worst regulated of buses, and how they might often be avoided. Other pictures describe in detail the faults of the bad bus-conductor and the qualifications essential to the good one, from which the pupil is left to draw her own conclusions. Practical instruction is given by a series of 'joy rides,' as the girl herself terms them. She goes with some of her colleagues for a ride along some forsaken route, and then she has to submit to the ordeal of standing all the joltings, shakings, and swervings which the average motor-bus is capable of performing.

During these rides she is shown the correct way to jump on and off a motor-bus – an art which only the most careful student of it can claim to bring to perfection, as the occasional user of motor-buses often discovers to his cost.

Kathleen Courlander

Deutsche Frauen Deutsche Treue

Train Driver

I volunteered for train duty. First I was employed for two years as a tram driver and then, when I had passed my exam, assigned to work on the suburban train. The first time I stood next to the locomotive driver on the locomotive of a heavy train, comprised of four four-axled carriages, to learn how to work the controls, it seemed almost impossible that a woman's hands would ever be able to tame this monster of iron and steel, and the idea that I would now be responsible for a passenger-filled train like this one, each carriage of which could carry 80 to 100 people, took my breath away. But we were brave and very willing, and with careful training it was accomplished.

Our duties varied considerably, but they always demanded the greatest responsibility, particularly on my Cologne to B. Gladbach line, which at that time was mainly single-track. As train drivers we were responsible for the whole train, in particular for the blocks, for stopping punctually at crossings and for delays; time could be made up only at the cost of operational safety. If we had forgotten just one thing, or not paid attention to what seemed like a minor detail, it would have meant destruction and death, not only for ourselves, but also for the passengers entrusted to our care.

Our duties became particularly difficult when a recently qualified, but still nervous driver was assigned to our locomotive. We had to monitor her every movement on her first few trips. The weather was another matter altogether. In fog or rain the tracks became slippery and it was not easy to halt, quickly if necessary, a train full of passengers, when the weight of the train exercised a strong counterforce on the brakes.

Most of us female train workers had several children whom we had to look after when our working day was over without domestic help of any kind. So when we got home, exhausted, we had to start work again until late into the night – and our husbands at the front had to get their letters and parcels too. We often worked 16-hour shifts or longer, but I never heard any of the women complain. And even if air-raids forced us to go down to the cellar once or twice a night, the next morning we were always on the workers' train on our way to the station at 4.25 on the dot.

MRS JAKOB SCHMITZ

The Globe, 21 July 1916

Trousers and the Vote

We are not aware that women in Prussia have the vote, but it is clear that they are well on the way to acquire it. Why else should women conductors and guards on the State railways be enjoined in future to wear ordinary service uniform, including 'dark grey wide trousers'? Quite plainly it is a step in the direction of full emancipation. If a woman dresses like a man she begins to think like him, and her aspirations tend towards a common goal. Such is the subtle influence of dress. Only on such a theory can we profess to interpret the otherwise dark ruling of the director. We observe that when the conductors and guards are off duty they will be allowed to relapse into mere feminine skittishness, if they are so disposed, by wearing skirts and so forth. But we cannot rid ourselves of the obsession that there is a profound political development in the official wear of the too-obviously divided nether garment.

Deutsche Frauen Deutsche Treue

Postwoman: Germany

Before 1916 I lived modestly but happily with my husband and six children. To his sorrow, a serious heart condition prevented my husband from going to war. But he worked at home harder than he should have done: he died in January 1916, and I was left alone with six children between the ages of one and nine. There we were, without a penny to our name, though I'm proud to say that despite my husband's illness, we never got into debt. My pain was great, but my worries about the future with six small children were greater and more difficult to bear. The welfare officer came and tried to persuade me to put my three youngest children into an orphanage. But I told him that as long as I was healthy and had two hands to work, my children would never be deprived of a mother's love. There was enough work in Germany at the time – for women too. So the first thing I did was to send an application to the Reich Post Office: two days later I was on duty. I became a postwoman. Every day I got up at 4 a.m. I had to report for work at 5 o'clock. When we had sorted the post, we left the post office building with fat post bags. We had a lot to carry, for in addition to the letters there were countless forces parcels, each of which weighed at least a pound. Usually we each had to carry between 25 and 28 of these, which was quite a weight.

Three times a day I set off through the streets of my beloved Munich, carrying glad and sad tidings from the battlefield into the blocks of flats, upstairs and down. I was paid 2 marks and 70 pfennigs per day – you could just about manage to keep a family as large as mine on that.

When I got home I had to start on my housework: darning, patching, washing, and cooking the food for the following day. My two elder daughters had to help: we would never have managed otherwise.

Eleven months later frostbitten feet forced me to give up work as a postwoman. I was transferred to office duties: I worked in the money and valuables office. We did day or night shifts there, so I still had time for my housework. I was not as tired as I had been from all that stair climbing.

ELISE SCHMIDT

Women War Workers

A Postwoman's Perambulations: England

On entering the busy sorting office from the quiet of the streets one forgets what time of day it is, and quickly takes one's place among the crowd of workers. Sometimes the surroundings make the Postwoman recruit feel rather like one of a flock of sheep, with the overseer as sheep-dog, for our sorting duties are carried out with great exactitude of regulation as each mail-van arrives with its fresh sacks of correspondence, and the nature of the work obliges the overseer to have an alert eye for any stragglers or shirkers from the sorting-desk fold. Sometimes a ship's deck is brought to the mind, so tidied up and empty does the hall look when letters are just dispatched and there is no cart expected.

When the mails come in every one is at work loading and unloading consignments of missives, where delay for a moment cannot be tolerated. Occasionally the state of the weather or other mischance causes a mail-van to arrive much later than its tabulated time, and it is then that the Postwoman has leisure to observe or talk with her companions, and there is a migration to the room set apart for tea-making, or a clustering round the stove in winter.

As far as I have seen, these women are a happy crowd. Many of them have husbands at the Front, and they strike me *en masse* as having largely the characteristics of 'Tommy Atkins' himself. One foggy evening, during an unusually prolonged wait for an overdue mail-van, a desire for a waltz was expressed by some one; by way of orchestra a comb and piece of tissue paper were produced by a 'Peter Pan' of a girl, who perched herself up, using one of the sorting troughs as music gallery, and produced sounds of weird portent in squally gusts. Such dance music was never heard before, but couples gyrated round in the solid Post Office boots, with a wary eye on the power in office—

For myself the most unhappy moment of my official life was when I saw the boots we are expected to wear. They are of a weight and of a fearsome rigidity that the foot accustomed to lighter shoes cannot easily endure. Some few of the women wear them readily enough; others complain that they are crippled by them. The pair allotted to me, after a long treatment with oil, which was absorbed greedily, looked as adamantine and unyielding as ever, and I would as lief be clamped in the village stocks as put on this footgear. Were I the Postmaster-General the women should be treated like the men and have an allowance for shoe-leather, with freedom to purchase the kind of boot that suits the individual wearer. Probably the answer to this suggestion would be that the women would buy flimsy, high-heeled shoes, quite unsuitable for work in all weathers. But really the woman whose vocation calls for much walking may, I think, be trusted not to go about in the tottering, trussed feet of the Chinese image; she will be only too ready to wear serviceable and comfortable shoes befitting her work. But enough about the feet!—

The rest of the uniform is comfortable and sensible, and a

good protection from the elements is afforded by the tarpaulin capes and hat-coverings which are supplied. We sometimes long for the time when a little electric lamp can be provided in place of the unwieldy antediluvian oil lantern which we now dangle at our button-holes at night—

Had Bacon lived now an essay 'On Letter-boxes' would perhaps have been added to the treasury of his writings. Making acquaintance with the other side of the letter-box is an experience that 'gives one to think,' especially after the experiment of pushing letters into divers rat-trap-like receptacles.

The perambulation of some roads depositing letters is quite as exciting as exploration, and I have one letter-box lid especially in my mind which, in the ingenuity of its trickiness, fills me with awe, and which has committed serious ravages on my gloves, though I don't allow it to 'skin my fingers' in the manner graphically described by a fellow-Postwoman the other day. When there are no letters for the house which this horrible letter-box adorns I sing a pæan of praise. Walking up to some lordly portal expecting a generous mouth open to engulf what you have to offer, after much search you often find a slit fit only for the reception of an early Victorian *billet-doux*, and you feel that to thrust in some bulky trade advertisement will be shattering to its sense of reserve and propriety. Architects, apparently, have not, as a rule, given much thought to letter-boxes and the just proportion they should bear to the size of the door. Often the long-suffering Postwoman has a bad time of it when the newspaper boy or girl has been in advance of her and tried to ram the newspapers into the small cavern meant for letters.

Of all the official duties, to me the most *gênant* is collecting the surcharges on insufficiently stamped letters, and since the new postal rates this is a thing of frequent occurrence. At the early morning delivery men in pyjamas and women in dressing-jackets have, to all seeming, to raid every corner of the house or flat to find pennies—

In my own rounds (technically called 'walks' in the Post Office) there is many a house where some one is on the look-out for a letter from the Front, and, 'Anything from my boy to-day?' is an eager question that often greets one. After an inquiry like this one is always glad to see an envelope with the magic O.A.S. on it for that particular house. Sometimes a battered returned envelope has to be put in the letter-box, having as grim superscription, 'Killed in action,' with the additional, and one would think unnecessary sentence, 'Undelivered for this reason.'

MARY HUGHES

Women War Workers

Delivering the Goods

On my part it required a certain amount of pluck to present myself at that butcher's shop at 8.30 on that memorable Saturday morning, and to mount that high cart with a man beside me, feeling and knowing that dozens of pairs of eyes were looking at me from behind curtains and but partly shuttered windows; but when once mounted, seated, and started my courage returned, and after an hour or two on the round I felt as though I had been thus employed for years.

The man whose place I was going to fill accompanied me for about three weeks. During that time I had to note down names and addresses of customers in an order book, which I invariably lost at the start and which was always returned in due course to the shop, and awaited me on arrival back. During this period of 'instruction' the weather was the very worst of the whole year, and for many days I was driving in blinding snow and gales of wind which even the horse found it difficult to face. Proving strong enough to stand the exposure myself, I was soon 'promoted' to delivering as well as driving, and when my tutor was called up I took over his 'round' completely, and although I disliked handling meat of any kind I resolved to suppress that feeling, knowing that this was necessary if I was ever to become a successful 'butcheress.'

The people who had hitherto just seen me driving the cart were evidently not prepared for this further shock, and gazed at me with dumb amazement when I appeared at their doors with the *meat* and the question, 'Any orders for the butcher, please?'

One or two incidents of my first reception are still very fresh in my memory. Calling at one house with some soup-bones, the astonished damsel who opened the door to me fled in dismay to her mistress, saying, 'If you please'm there's a lady at the door with bones: what shall I do with them?' On being told to take them from me she returned and did so, gazing at me meanwhile as if I were a spirit from an unknown world!

For my work I wear a waterproof uniform, consisting of a short coat, breeches, and leggings. This costume I find most suitable for climbing up and down the cart, especially in wet weather. Appearing thus apparelled at one old lady's door I encountered a very shocked yet interested stare, so I said: 'I hope you are not shocked at this sensible uniform?' She replied, 'My dear, to the pure all things are pure,' and now I am sure she often wishes she wore the same costume herself.

One grumpy old man, who was always very difficult with my predecessor, declared at first that he 'wouldn't have no women messing about his doors for orders,' and it was with great difficulty that I could get him to give me an order at all. He preferred to write it most illegibly on a piece of paper and stick it on a remote bush in his garden, every time choosing a different bush, and when I failed once to find his paper and asked him for it, he indignantly replied: 'Can't 'ee see the order up tree?' which proved to be a big elm tree, and the order *was* a considerable distance 'up tree'! By bringing him an especially good joint weekly I have made him one of my most loyal friends and supporters, and now he gives me his orders verbally and I no longer have to hunt 'up tree' for his scraps of paper.

To begin with, some women were just as pessimistic in their

views as to the capability of a female to deliver their goods correctly, but that was soon overcome and they quickly began to put confidence in me. They even began to trust me to take payment for their meat.

With some of the poorer people it is customary for them to pay their bills weekly or daily, as the case may be. My experiences in collecting these small payments were often most amusing. On one occasion, when the customer was out and unable to take the meat and pay me in person, this note greeted me: 'Plase put meat en plate en mangle the money is their becos of the flies.' The reader may perhaps interpret the meaning of this missive better than I did, for I could find no plate, no mangle, and no money!

MARGARET E. CARDELL

Daily News and Leader, 15 February 1916

Great Appeal for Land Workers

Already the country has raised an Army, say, 4,000,000 men for the front. It has organised another army, still rapidly growing, of 250,000 women for munition factories. There now remains the problem of mobilising yet a third army of 400,000 women for the land. For several reasons this last is the most difficult problem of all. Work on the land is not popular among those best fitted to do it — No woman can be expected to enjoy milking cows at four on a winter morning, or spreading manure, or cleaning a pigsty. It is frankly admitted indeed, that much of the most necessary work is hard and unpleasant, and by no means extravagantly paid. That is why the appeal is made exclusively to the patriotism of women.

Recollections of the Land Army

I went to a building, I think was at St Paul's churchyard, London, a woman doctor gave a brief examination of the body & passed me. I then received notice to catch a certain train at Victoria station for Basingstoke Hants, and to go to Wicks Farm at Old Basing about three miles from the station. My father (who was on leave from the army) & my mother came to see me off & we found that there were some other girls going to the same place so I joined them. My father was quite happy at my joining the W.L.A. He was later sent to France. Our uniform was sent by parcel post which we had to collect from the post office. We did not all have the size meant for, as it was all together there was quite a tussle & some of the smaller sizes were snatched & we weaker ones had to accept what was left. However the quality was quite good, mackintosh, oilskin coat & twill breeches, pullover & smock, & gaiters & boots. We received another set of brown velvet breeches later—

Our only training for weeks were, weeding in the cornfields, with an W.L.A. to instruct us, a farmer's daughter I think very nice to get on with. Some girls were disappointed at this—

We lived in an old cottage (a row of them) very nice & clean & we went through a churchyard to get to it. A sort of dormitory upstairs with single iron beds (very clean, scrubbed boards on floor) a large table downstairs & a woman from the village came & cooked our meals, butter etc from the farm. Bullet holes in walls from Cromwells men. We had wages for about two weeks & then nearly enough to pay our fare home for a week-end.

- The boots gave me blisters & Farmer Wigg's sister, a nice elderly lady gave me some vaseline & bandage. There were no social activities as such. Had to send personal washing home by post to my mother.

When the weeding was finished we had rail tickets to go to Somerset near Bridgewater, & we were under canvass for several weeks. Six to a tent, all feet to the pole, sack filled with clean straw to lie on. We were driven out by army lorry each morning to fields to pull flax for aeroplane wings & linseed oil. Lined across the fields we pulled it up and laid it down as we went. It came out easy from the red soil. A farmer came along one day & gave us a flagon of cider. Our meals in big marquee was poor, cold ham, green in parts, uneatable. We sat in our tent all Sunday in pouring rain. We were then sent to different places.

—Some of us had tickets to West Malling in Kent. There we were put in a building & given a sack to fill with straw, & taken to a shop with a large room upstairs & on the table were bowls of rock buns. We had tea & helped ourselves to the buns & that was our breakfast & tea-time the same & we marched to orchards & were given paper cut to size & string, to do tree banding. There were gypsies there fruit picking — From there we [were] broken up again & some of us went to Meopham in Kent, to help the threshing machine time & we had nice digs & met nice friends & when the Armistice came I asked to leave & get back to a city job — My resignation was received with thanks & told I could retain my uniform.

Mrs M. Harrold née Britton

Diary

Women's Timber Corps

Tuesday week (*Undated, 1915 or '16*) We left Tonbridge after doing odd jobs about the house, for Chilgrove Camp — We made for Charing Cross and made friends in the carriage with some fine Canadian soldier boys. We arrived at noon and caught the 1.36 to Horsham for Midhurst and from there we went to Lavant. There was a snow storm raging and we arrived at 5 p.m. and the carrier's cart took us six miles along a very dark road under water. It was dark and cold and unusual for us to be really miserable. But to crown all joys we had to walk along a very dark road to the camp in the snow. With all our luggage and feeling cold and not knowing our road we felt very fed up. Finally we arrived at the huts at 7.30 p.m. We got something to eat and sat round the fire to get dry. We were glad to get to bed but we did not sleep. Our beds are just off the floor on a wooden frame, a straw mattress and pillow and five blankets. We woke to find a foot of snow on the ground. There are seven huts (like the ordinary YMCA hut). One is the Mess hut, one for the staff and one for the Stores and one for the Church and Hospital. The camp is miles from anywhere, absolutely isolated. One would never imagine such a place existed. The snow was too thick to work so we carried wood from the piling stations and sawed it for indoor use in case we should get snowed up. We have breakfast at 6.30 and another at 9.30—After lunch we went to the woods and started our new work. It is great, axeing at great trees. We were given a bill hook, an axe, a saw and a cord measure.

Thursday

Today has been grand. Very cold but the work is fine. It is great to watch a grand old tree crash to the earth and feel that you did it alone —Life is just what I have always longed for. After dinner tonight we had some music. It was strange to see the girls dancing, breeches and jerseys, in a log hut with a stove in the middle. It will be glorious here in the spring. Even now with snow clad hills all around it is a gorgeous sight.

Friday

Enamel plates and mugs and tin knives and forks. It is a strange life but absolutely great. We made for the woods this morning and made a big log fire. It snowed all day. We have not seen a soul since we arrived, outside camp people. A fire in the woods and such figures as we cut would frighten anybody. We dress in sou'westers and short oilskin coats and no smock. We look like Skipper Sardines.

MISS B. BENNETT

189

Women as Army Surgeons

The Opening of Endell Street Hospital, London

A glass-covered passage ran down the centre of the square and across to either block. It was fenced in with high iron railings, and the free space on either side was divided by more railings into little pens. The little pens had padlocked gates and were labelled: 'Old Males,' 'Young Males,' 'Old Females,' 'Young Females;' and it was in these cages that the inmates of the workhouse had sought fresh air and recreation. There was a little gate office next to the mortuary, where a set of pigeon holes, constructed out of slate slabs, was designed to receive coffins, and where the gas meter took up most of the room. Behind the main buildings were the children's home – modern and well built – and the Guardians' offices, opening on to Broad Street. Part of the administrative block bore the date 1727, and St. Giles was said to have been the workhouse described by Dickens in *Oliver Twist*. A long room, with a fireplace at either end, still exists in the oldest part, where Oliver is supposed to have been interviewed by the Guardians; and the cellars or basements under this section of the building are of the most ancient and grimy description. The hospital blocks were five stories high, with good air space and large wards. There were windows on both sides of these wards, and more sunshine and fresh air were available than was expected in that locality. The warehouses next door were in the hands of the A.S.C.M.T., and all round lay the teeming, crowded streets of Soho and Drury Lane.

Extensive structural alterations were necessary. Lifts capable of carrying stretchers were put in; the sanitation was renewed, and electric light and modern cooking apparatus were installed. The building was cleaned and painted throughout, but there was an extraordinary amount of old furniture and disused apparatus which the Guardians had left behind, and the presence of piles of lumber was embarrassing. The fittings of padded rooms and curious pieces of furniture, designed to restrain the insane, came out of the lunacy block; antique baths and obsolete drain-pipes were cast out by the builders, and in their place ward kitchens and bath-rooms were arranged on every floor; and operating theatres, X-ray room, laboratories, dispensaries and store-rooms were completed.

FLORA MURRAY

Daily Sketch, 6 July 1916

Somme Offensive

*WOUNDED MEN IN HOSPITAL STAFFED BY WOMEN
MORE ANXIOUS TO PRAISE DOCTORS THAN TO TALK OF
THE BIG PUSH*

During the last three days one London hospital has accepted and is now treating 300 British Tommies wounded in the Great Advance.

The number is by no means excessive, but is interesting because the hospital – Endell-street Military Hospital – is run by a medical staff of women.

At the outset the hospital was viewed with suspicion and suffered a great deal from prejudice, but difficulties were quickly removed when the results of the magnificent work done by the women were seen.

To-day Endell-street hospital is perhaps the most popular in London.

Daily Chronicle, 6 November 1916

Another matter on which no sane person has had to change his or her opinion is feminism. It is enough to make any feminist dance with rage to hear the continual exclamations of surprise at the fact that women can do practically everything. We told you so again and again, and you would not believe it. When England's Worst Woman Novelist and a bevy of peeresses signed manifestos to say they were not conscious of having any capacity, you wagged your heads and said that of course woman's place was the home.

But are you conscious of what you owe to the suffragettes?

I admit that the silly campaign of arson and violence which was in full swing at the beginning of the war, must have contributed to the effect of lawlessness which made Germany think it a propitious moment for the outbreak of hostilities. I admit that one bows one's head with shame when one hears of former officials of the Women's Social and Political Union mobbing Lord Haldane with idiot cries of treachery. But if the suffragettes and suffragists had not conducted their campaign there would not have been the vast and willing army of women which is taking men's places all over the country.

The very rough-and-tumble of the movement had its merits; in Palace Yard or at the street corners they acquired a courage which now they use in the service of their country.

The story of the work of the Scottish Suffrage Societies' hospital in Serbia and Rumania is immortal. The biggest factory in France which supplies an article most necessary to our armies is under the sole charge of a woman under thirty, who was formerly a suffrage organiser. One could cite many such cases. And one doubts that women would have gone into the dangerous high explosive factories, the engineering shops and the fields, and worked with quite such fidelity and enthusiasm if it had not been so vigorously affirmed by the suffragists in the last few years that women ought to be independent and courageous and capable.

REBECCA WEST

Senlis

Modern warfare is so monstrous, all-engrossing and complex, that there is a sense, and a very real sense, in which hardly a civilian stands outside it; where the strife is to the death with an equal opponent the non-combatant ceases to exist. No modern nation could fight for its life with its men in uniform only; it must mobilize, nominally or not, every class of its population for a struggle too great and too deadly for the combatant to carry on alone. The 'unfit' who step into the shoes of the fit, the old men who fill the gaps left by their sons, the women who press into fields and workshops – all these keep the fighting line going, and without them the fighting line must fail; and hence, under modern conditions of war, an increasing difficulty in drawing the line that protects the civilian from open attack by the soldier. A munition factory staffed by women, a laboratory where some weakling discovers a chemical compound, may be deadlier instruments of death and destruction than thousands of horses and men. Further, where each party to the strife enlists the services of his entire population – puts forth, in a word, his utmost – the question of national exhaustion looms far larger than it did in the day of the professional soldier and the army running to thousands. Consciously or unconsciously, while the armies are at grips, the civilians of one nation are outstripping, exhausting the other – or are being outstripped and exhausted in the struggle for resources and replenishment. The work and resources of a civilian population have always been an indirect factor in every military situation; but to-day they are a factor direct and declared, to-day the exempt and the woman are openly mobilized and enlisted. One sees that this direct intervention of the civilian in warfare must entail a certain loss of his immunity from direct attack and punishment, and that a leader hard pressed or unscrupulous may deem himself entitled to interpret the fundamental maxim enjoining him to cut his enemy's communications in a fashion undreamed of by those who framed rules for a conflict confined to the soldier.

CICELY HAMILTON

Japanese Women and the War

English women's work in the war is another great stimulus for Japanese women. Well educated English mothers, wisely bringing up their children, and working in unison with their husbands, have hitherto been the admiration and ideal of Japanese young women. And the living example of her Majesty Queen Mary, followed by the ladies of rank and the women professors and students of the colleges and universities, is an inspiration to them, and they recognize in them the good results of education. So nowadays a stronger desire for higher education is generally felt among the women of our country, and public opinion is in sympathy with it—

Our women have also begun to realize that heaven has ordained the women of the 20th century for a great mission, and though they are weak and insignificant, still they have mighty powers, deeply hidden in their hearts which will unfold if they only can believe. Israel was a small country, but there the religion of the world was born. Greece was a tiny peninsula, but the greatest art of the world was cultivated there. So God may choose to use His frail vessels to accomplish His good will.

With a conviction that there is a domain which only women can and must reclaim in this century, Japanese women, though very young in the history of modern education and the experiences of women's movements, are no longer narrow-minded, ignorant, self-interested beings. Their eyes are open to the living facts of the day, and now they are busily qualifying themselves, by culture and education, for this mighty mission. And their ardent spirit is ready to join hands with that of their elder sisters of the West, and to follow them, if they would lead, in the accomplishment of the work of restoring international peace and promoting the true happiness and welfare of man.

JINZO NARUSE, PRESIDENT OF THE JAPAN WOMEN'S UNIVERSITY

'We Regret to Inform You'

Chronicle of Youth:
Vera Brittain's War Diary 1913–17

[January 13th] Keymer

I arrived at a very opportune though very awful moment. All R.'s things had just been sent back from the front and they were all lying on the floor. I had no idea before of the aftermath of an officer's death, or what the returned kit, about which so many letters have been written in the papers, really meant. It was terrible. Mrs Leighton and Clare were both crying as bitterly as on the day we heard of His death. There were his clothes – the clothes in which he came home from the front last time – another set rather less worn, and underclothing & accessories of various descriptions. Everything was damp & worn & simply caked with mud. All the sepulchres and catacombs of Rome could not make me realise mortality & decay & corruption as vividly as did the smell of those clothes. I know now what he meant when he used to write 'this refuse-heap of a country' or 'a trench that is nothing but a charnel-house'. And the wonder is, not that he temporarily lost the extremest refinements of his personality, as Mrs Leighton says he did, but that he ever kept any of it at all – let alone nearly the whole. He was more marvellous than even I ever dreamed.

All that was left of his toilet luxuries came back – a regular chemist's shop – scented soap, solidified Eau-de-Cologne etc. We no longer wondered why he wanted them. One wants the most expensive things money can buy to combat that corruption. Even all the little things had the same faint smell, and were damp and mouldy. The only things untouched by damp or mud or mould were my photographs, kept carefully in an envelope, & his leather cigarette case, with a few cigarettes, a tiny photo of his Mother & George Meredith, & the three little snapshots Miss Bervon took of us, inside. He must have had those things always on him, & the warmth of his body overruled the general damp & decay. There was his haversack crammed full of letters – he seemed to keep all he received. I found the rest of mine, & also several of Edward's. There were letters from officers of the Norfolks, from Mrs Bennett at Uppingham, & one or two very pathetic & grateful epistles from the mothers of Tommies, thanking him for his sympathy & careful record of details, & hoping he would come safely through.

Letters to Lieutenant Oscar Eckhard, Manchester Regiment

Battle of the Somme 1916

Harrow-on-the-Hill
July 30th 1916

Dear Mr Eckhard,

I am very, very grateful to you for your letter of the 25th received this morning, and for the sympathy from you & 'those who are left'. I can quite understand the reason of the delay in getting any information & under the circumstances we cannot expect more, or, but little. I wrote to the Chaplain attached to the 12th Manchesters and I am hoping I may hear through him, that my dear Boys body was buried, and where. He meant *so much* to my sisters and me, for whether at home or outside his home, he was, from a little boy, *always* the same cheery, unselfish nature. Again thanking you for taking so much trouble.

Your's very truly

M<small>ARY</small> E. A<small>LDERTON</small>

Altrincham
Aug 6th 1916

Sir,

I received your kind letter telling me about Henry. I have had cards from him he is suffering from shell shock at Con Camp Bouglone *(sic)* Had he been here Sir I feel like saying All the Kings Horses and All the Kings Men shall not get him to France again. I am very thankful God has spared him to me once again. Oh may it be ended soon to me it is so wicked to kill our Good lads 12 months tomorrow my oldest son fell. I hope God will spare you Lieut. Eckhard to return to your mother.

I am Sir
Yours obedient

S. R<small>HODES</small>

Autobiography

Death of the Prime Minister's Son

On Sunday, September the 17th, we were entertaining a week-end party—While we were playing tennis in the afternoon my husband went for a drive with my cousin, Nan Tennant. He looked well, and had been delighted with his visit to the front and all he saw of the improvement in our organisation there: the tanks and the troops as well as the guns. Our Offensive for the time being was going amazingly well. The French were fighting magnificently, the House of Commons was shut, the Cabinet more united, and from what we heard on good authority the Germans more discouraged. Henry told us about Raymond, whom he had seen as recently as the 6th at Tricourt.

As it was my little son's last Sunday before going back to Winchester I told him he might run across from the Barn in his pyjamas after dinner and sit with us while the men were in the dining-room.

While we were playing games Clouder, our servant—came in to say that I was wanted.

I left the room, and the moment I took up the telephone I said to myself, 'Raymond is killed.'

With the receiver in my hand, I asked what it was, and if the news was bad.

Our secretary, Davies, answered, 'Terrible, terrible news. Raymond was shot dead on the 15th. Haig writes full of sympathy, but no details. The Guards were in and he was shot leading his men the moment he had gone over the parapet.'

I put back the receiver and sat down. I heard Elizabeth's delicious laugh, and a hum of talk and smell of cigars came down the passage from the dining-room.

I went back into the sitting-room.

'Raymond is dead,' I said, 'he was shot leading his men over the top on Friday.'

Puffin got up from his game and hanging his head took my hand; Elizabeth burst into tears, for though she had not seen Raymond since her return from Munich she was devoted to him.—I walked away with the two children and rang the bell:

'Tell the Prime Minister to come and speak to me,' I said to the servant.

Leaving the children, I paused at the end of the dining-room passage; Henry opened the door and we stood facing each other. He saw my thin wet face, and while he put his arm around me I said:

'Terrible, terrible news.'

At this he stopped me and said:

'I know . . . I've known it . . . Raymond is dead.'

He put his hands over his face and we walked into an empty room and sat down in silence.

MARGOT ASQUITH

Marriage and Widowhood

1917

Then the blow fell. On the afternoon of September 4th – too late to get married that day – a further telegram arrived ordering Jack to leave Victoria for service overseas early on the 7th. There was nothing to be done, but to cancel the honeymoon plans, while one of Jack's friends discovered a farm which would be willing to take us after the wedding next day. This was near Haslingfield, a village about six miles from Cambridge, where in my school days I had often sat reading by a stream on solitary bicycle rides.

So, after our marriage on the 5th, to Haslingfield we went in the autumn sunshine, with the last of the corn stooks standing in the fields. Jack was twenty-six and I was twenty, and both of us were, I think, very young for our ages. In the tense emotional climate of the time, we had little conception of what we were doing and little idea of what we might be committing ourselves to. We were indeed strangers and afraid in a world we never made.

The next afternoon we took the train to London, staying overnight at the Rubens Hotel so as to be near the station for Jack's departure next day. Early the following morning, a day and a half after our marriage, I saw him off from Victoria along with a train-load of other cannon fodder.

Five weeks later the War Office 'regretted to inform me' that Capt. J. W. Wootton of the 11th Battalion Suffolk Regiment had died of wounds. He had been shot through the eye and died forty-eight hours later on an ambulance train; and in due course his blood-stained kit was punctiliously returned to me.

Thus before I had reached my twenty-first birthday, I had experienced the deaths of my father, my brother, my favourite school friend and the husband to whom I had been married in theory for five weeks and in practice for something less than forty-eight hours. In ten years I had learned little about life, much about death. In spite of the contemporary doctrine that personality is formed in early infancy, and that nothing that happens afterwards can greatly change it, I do not think that anyone can live through such experiences without some significant and permanent marks remaining. Had these years been different, I am sure that I should have been different too, even to-day. But at least I entered upon my adult life with a realistic sense of the impermanence of earthly relationships.

My troubles were, of course, in no way unusual. What happened to me happened also, in one form or another, to thousands of my contemporaries; and that fact served at least to hold in check any temptation I might otherwise have had to dramatise my tragic situation. Indeed what infuriated many of us, when Vera Brittain published her *Testament of Youth*, was the impression she conveyed that she alone of the nurses with whom she worked had to endure the anxiety of knowing that her beloved was at the front. My upbringing, too, had left no room for self-pity: none of the adults in our family circle would ever have dreamed of using misfortune or unhappiness as an excuse for shortcomings. Whatever happened, one was expected to go ahead and make the best of whatever the next job might be.

In this the attitude of our elders, though somewhat exacting, was, I think, much to be preferred to the contemporary practice of encouraging the young to dwell upon any early misfortunes that may have befallen them and to use these as explanations, if not as excuses for, their own subsequent deficiencies. To the young, particularly, it should be the future, not the past, that counts.

BARBARA WOOTTON

A Reaction to Grief

In the time of dogs and novels, tennis rackets and golf, and some-times even a spare hour spent with our babies, we talked of munitions as we had talked before of the North Pole. The papers spoke of shells and tool-setters, of enormous wages and cheery canteens, happy hostels and gay girl-workers, but how one found the key to this useful wonderland we knew not. We were sick of frivolling, we wanted to do something big and hard, because of our boys and of England. When the dreaded telegram came at last and everything was grey and bitter, we gave up talking and made our way to the lowest level – the gates of the nearest ammunition factory. A sentry looked at us, and we went in. A scrubby little man with a grimy collar smote a grimier fist upon the grimiest of palms. 'Take it or leave it,' said he, ''tain't nothin' to me. Fifteen shillin's a week and war bonus; hours 6 to 2, or 2 to 10, or 10 to 6. Them's the facts. It's for you to choose.'

Naomi Loughnan

How We Lived Then

'A 'Appy Time for Us'

One woman with a very bad husband owned frankly that she would not be sorry if he were killed. 'But I 'spose he'll be spared, and other as'd be missed 'll be taken, for that's the way of things,' said she. 'It's the only time as I and the children 'ad peace. The war's been a 'appy time for us.'

Mrs C. S. Peel

Numbers of new Bridge Clubs, at some of which poker also was played, came into being, and were greatly patronized, partly because there were no parties to go to, partly because, owing to the difficulty of obtaining coal, people were glad to keep warm at the club's expense and economize their fuel, and partly because the game took their minds off their anxieties, though the tension of life made tempers irritable and disagreements not uncommon.

'I was playing bridge at the — one afternoon, putting in time before going on to my canteen, when a servant came up to my partner and said "Mrs. — would like to speak to you outside, please." The poor woman's face went white. Her cards fell out of her shaking hands. I thought she was going to faint, but she got up and went out of the room. It was the telegram . . . her son had been killed. One of the proprietors of the club came in to take her place, and we went on playing,' writes a woman whose only son was killed a few weeks later.

Mrs. C. S. Peel

Sex and Cinema Violence

Arbeiter Zeitung, 15 October 1916

Sexual Mores: Germany

We women have certainly made marvellous progress during the last twenty years; so at least says the world of the bourgeoisie. We are not only allowed to earn our bread by the sweat of our brow but the State is graciously pleased to allow us to enter into the state of matrimony, and to bear children. Further, we are assured on all sides that our enfranchisement is only a question of time and those of us who are blessed with strong constitutions may perhaps live to see women admitted to political organisations and given precedence over criminals and lunatics. Even now women of good family whose fathers can afford it are allowed to study medicine and philosophy and perhaps eventually jurisprudence.

One right is, however, denied to us women, a simple and natural one, but still the most sacred right. Why is no protection given to us in our sexual existence? Why are we outside the law as regards our special function as women? If a man burns down a rotten barn, or breaks a few lathes, or a broken fence, the law punishes him; but he can marry a young healthy innocent girl, destroy her morally and physically, and no law can call him to account—

Perhaps I should not have realised the full crime which is so light-heartedly committed against my sex if chance had not taken me to a Polish town in the military area. Soldiers naturally attract large numbers of prostitutes, but in Poland the line between the professional prostitute and the so-called respectable woman is not so clearly drawn as with us — Over there we learn many things of which a respectable protected woman is generally ignorant. We hear of hospitals for venereal diseases—We see girls brought up on the stated days for examinations by the doctors and removed to the hospital weeping and wailing. All this strengthens our conviction that medical examinations should be compulsory for men as well as women, for it is a fact that men acknowledge no responsibility as regards prostitutes. A decent minded man may take all care that he does not propagate disease either within or without marriage, but is the world exclusively composed of decent minded men?

There can be no doubt that the question is now an urgent one. All the men who return to their families at the end of the war will have been away for months or years from their homes. The spiritual shocks, the bodily strains, will have naturally blunted their delicacy of feeling, confused the issues of right and wrong and weakened their powers of resistance to evil. They must be helped—

I am not a lawyer, nor a doctor, and I do not know how this can be done, but this I know, it is the least that a woman could ask of the community.

Home Service Corps Review, 22 October 1915

The Very Latest!

Prompted by fear for the future preservation of the nation, comes a timid suggestion from a body of Bristol clergymen. Once again English women are to be called upon to sacrifice. Of course, sacrifice is becoming such a daily occurrence to women that another small item on the programme is neither here nor there. This time women are asked to send in their names, under conditions of the strictest secrecy, to this clerical party in Bristol, intimating that they are willing to meet, and subsequently marry and support, a wounded soldier. Then, all things proving satisfactory, the founders of the scheme will provide opportunities for the bringing together of both parties. 'Love,' we are told, 'is consecrated by pity,' and we are bidden to bear in mind the example of Othello who accounted for the affection of Desdemona by explaining that 'She loved me for the dangers I had passed, and I loved her that she did pity them.' Excellent reasoning, certainly, from the standpoint of the man; but how about the women?

Woman has sacrificed all along the line, but that is insufficient. Now a group of men ask that she shall sacrifice still further; that she shall deliver over the rest of her existence because the future of the nation is in danger. Impossible! Woman is not a machine. Woman has her rights, and in this day is learning to realise what is meant by individuality. We wonder how many names the Bristol clergymen will secure!

Co-operative News, 2 February 1916

Women's Corner

We are told that something will have to be done to make up the horrible 'wastage' caused by the war. We are informed that the State requires babies – and still more babies! If that is so, why doesn't the State look after the babies which are born, and which die off every year for lack of nourishment and warmth?

—Now, no man or woman of independent spirit desires to appeal for State aid for the rearing of their children. Also, no intelligent married couple will wilfully bring into the world more children than they can properly feed and clothe. That is one of the chief reasons for the falling birth-rate. The wages of the bulk of the workers are not large enough to admit of their rearing *properly* a large family.

It is only the most ignorant among the working class who burden themselves with large families; and they suffer for it, too, though, they and their innocent little ones. Let me give you a couple of instances; these are *facts*, not fancy.

A man and his wife have supplied the State with eight babies in nine years. The husband's wages are 28s per week. They have only two beds for the whole family! When the last baby was born (about two months ago) the midwife had not received her fee for the previous confinement, which occurred only ten and a half months before the last. The whole family were half-fed and ill-clad. *And the State wants babies!*

The other case is that of a couple who have brought six children into the world. The husband is a farm labourer; wages about 24s per week. The children are all delicate, they are insufficiently nourished, and are always needing the doctor. The poor, harassed mother owes a doctor's bill for almost £30 which she can see no prospect of ever being able to pay. One of the children, aged four and a half years, is suffering from consumption of the throat, and the doctor has ordered it plenty of good nourishment – new milk, fresh-laid eggs, etc.! The husband was off work for almost three months during the summer with a broken leg, and the only money they had coming in was 10s from his State insurance!

Is there any encouragement for working folks to increase and multiply? If the State wants babies, would it not pay it to look after such families as these, and to see that these little ones were supplied with plenty of the necessaries of life?—

As for the women who are shirking their duty – the Government and the press hirelings who rave about the falling birth-rate will storm and threaten in vain! For these 'shirkers' are not fools – they are the intelligent portion of the working class. I know several of them, young, healthy, in every way capable of rearing a brood of bonnie boys and girls – if they had the wherewithal to feed and clothe them. But they have not, and so their families consist of one or two, in cases none at all—

No matter how loud and insistent the cry for more babies, the most intelligent of the workers will continue to shirk their duty – and small blame to them.

A WORKING WOMAN

Memorial to IWSA
President Mrs Chapman Catt, 1916

Enquiry into the Cinema

In the name of the International Alliance we are asking you to take an initiative which could have important moral repercussions across the world: namely the question of an international agreement (initially worked out by women) to reform film production.

In France we are greatly concerned about crime films which have a disastrous effect on children and even adults—especially since the release of such films as *The Vampires*, *The Secrets of New York*, *The Phantoms*, etc. juvenile crime has risen.

As a result of our conference we have therefore taken the initiative in forming an active working party composed of feminist societies, of leagues concerned with public morality and the raising of teaching standards, etc. After several meetings, a delegation led by senators and deputies went to the Minister of the Interior to present our conclusions.

The Minister received us with the utmost courtesy. He already knew of our efforts from newspaper reports and promised to take measures to improve the situation in our country (by the creation of a national censorship committee to issue certificates authorising films, press publication of its composition and the instructions sent to Prefects and Mayors throughout France).

But the Minister pointed out that without international agreement we should never obtain our objectives. How can we ban the production of French 'films policier' to sell abroad, without harming the commercial prospects of our major film studios, if Italy, America or England etc. are allowed to produce them? This argument has validity and that is why we think it would be interesting if simultaneously in all countries women prepare the way for an international agreement for the reform of film production.

It seems to us, Madame President, that you could usefully take the lead in this movement. An article from you in *Jus Suffragii* could explain the objective of such an enterprise. Questionnaires would be sent to all the national societies affiliated to the Alliance and *Jus Suffragii* would publish the responses from all the Presidents.

We should thus know exactly how each country stood on the question.

We believe, Madame President, that nothing is more helpful to the suffrage cause itself than *an international union of women taking moral action*. Desiring to prevent minds being depraved by salacious and unhealthy spectacles is to prepare the world for a better tomorrow. It is in a certain sense to work for world peace, as scenes of crime, of murder, of robbery can only serve to excite the lowest, the most cruel sentiments, contrary to all that we wish for the future. We also believe, Madame President, that the International Alliance through the medium of *Jus Suffragii* should become the means of such enquiries which will serve to further the community of ideas and interests of the women of all countries. To achieve women's suffrage, each country will have its own methods, its own ways of going about things, but except on principle there will be little chance of communal action.

On the contrary, an agreement on moral and economic questions is not only possible, it is essential. Perhaps you will think the International Council of Women should undertake this action, but we believe that the Alliance is more enterprising, more flexible, and could only gain by taking the lead in such an action.

p.p. L'Union Française pour le Suffrage des Femmes
Mme. de Witt Schlumberger

The Cinematograph

This conference *(of Women's Enfranchisement Association of South Africa)* views with alarm the harmful influence of the cinematograph upon young children, and is of the opinion that the time has arrived when the Government should restrict performances for children for afternoons only, and that the pictures screened should be approved by local or otherwise elected censorship.

The Times, 23 October 1916

Venereal Disease

WOMEN SOCIAL WORKERS' APPEAL

Having knowledge of the terrible ravages venereal disease is making, we feel it our duty, as women, and on behalf of the present and future generations of the Empire, to urge that speedy steps be taken to assure more effective action now, although fully realizing the excellent work the Commission is doing as regards educating the public, and pressing forward provision for free treatment for the sufferers.

We wish specially to plead the extreme urgency of the question owing to the number of men passing through England. The Commissioners report that these diseases produce blindness, deafness, insanity, feeble mind, sterility in women, many forms of nervous diseases, and skin and bone diseases. Sir William Osler holds that of killing diseases they come third or fourth—

The disease is certainly spreading, and that is why we suggest that something should be done immediately. Soldiers' mothers write that they have given their sons willingly to die for the Empire, but not like this. It seems almost incredible that men and women, known to be infectious, should be at liberty to spread the contagion when and where they will. Yet so it is. In many cases, even warnings are libellous before the law. It *cannot* be generally known that the disease is now very largely spread by girls of between 15 and 18 years of age. Can we wait while these mere children, caught perhaps innocently, or in a moment of madness, become the mothers of the future generation, and give birth to children more miserable than themselves?

The proposed remedy for this state of things is the education of the public by lectures and by private admonition, but will you by these means get hold of one per thousand of the public you desire to educate? Will they come to the lectures? Who will be able to admonish the larger part of them? How can we wait to educate the young men and girls who are already infected? Who will educate the prostitutes, especially the foreign ones, who do not understand our language? Only through legislation can the whole community be really educated and imbued with a full sense of responsibility towards the race.

The obvious remedies for every contagious disease are notification and compulsory treatment, and other dangerous and contagious diseases are thus treated.

The evidence is so strong under our personal observation that we believe when the general public become alive to the grave dangers arising, notification of all infected persons will be *demanded*, as the Commission states. Time is short, and that demand should be made now, or it will be too late.

The Spectator, 18 November 1916

Secrecy and Disease

Sir, I regret exceedingly that last week there were no letters on the subject of your article 'Secrecy and Disease.' I hoped to have seen writing from abler pens than mine. Surely this matter is viewed from a wrong standpoint. Of those who write: 'It *cannot* be generally known that the disease is now very largely spread by girls of between fifteen and eighteen years of age,' you say: 'The appeal cannot be praised too highly for its splendid courage.' Does no one see the injustice of the accusation against young girls in their teens that on this question of immorality and the spread of venereal disease they are the most blameworthy? Does any one of their accusers really think that a girl or woman can spread this particular disease by prostitution without being first of all contaminated by some man? The young women complained of are the product of our educational system, for many are only just over school age. Their education has, with few exceptions, been 'completed' without any instruction in the all-important things of their natural life – without any warning of the dangers to which as women they are subject. To-day hundreds of them are said to be little better than common prostitutes; but how can we justly attribute the entire blame to them? They are all supposed to be protected by the law of the land until sixteen years of age, yet before that age they have been ruined by men (many of them in the King's uniform) and no action has been taken against their destroyers. In some cases where they have willingly rushed into danger, it is because their minds have been soiled by the shady pictures of the cinemas and the scarcely veiled filthiness of the cheap comic papers. But the soldiers, for whom so many are crying out for protection against these young women, are all men of military age. How can they be thought of as needing protection from girls younger than themselves? And further, it seems absurd to me to call for the education of the older prostitutes. They are already educated by reproach and despair, and they know that the wages of sin is death. The vital question to my mind is, Who will educate our young men? Who can protect them from their own evil minds and lewd conversation? Who will protect them from their own authorities who now distribute [and] broadcast among them shields and prophylactics that they may hope to be thereby protected in, instead of restrained from, vice? Who will stir these same authorities to take action by imparting information and giving strong warning to those under their care and at least endeavouring to restrain the polluters of our race? Many restrictions are placed upon soldiers that it is not possible to place upon civilians. Would it not therefore be wise to refuse leave to any man known to be in a condition likely to impart disease either to his own wife or to another woman? As to the arguments in favour of compulsory notification, these do not seem to me to be logical. Notification for other infectious diseases was called for in order that the medical authorities might be able effectually to isolate for the time being the individual cases; but the chief difficulty with regard to venereal disease is that the patients shrink from calling in a medical man. Indeed, they are often in ignorance of the necessity for doing so. It is not anticipated that these patients can notify themselves. This is not, in my judgment, the moment to call for fresh legislation, but much improvement might surely and quickly be effected by a more equal and energetic administration of statutes already coded, and especially by effective treatment and comfortable accommodation being provided for all sufferers from this disease whether innocent or guilty.—

I am, Sir, &c.,

FLORENCE E. BOOTH

The Backwash of War

Women and Wives

You know, they won't let wives come to the Front. Women can come into the War Zone, on various pretexts, but wives cannot. Wives, it appears, are bad for the morale of the Army. They come with their troubles, to talk of how business is failing, of how things are going to the bad at home, because of the war; of how great the struggle, how bitter the trials and the poverty and hardship. They establish the connecting link between the soldier and his life at home, his life that he is compelled to resign. Letters can be censored and all disturbing items cut out, but if a wife is permitted to come to the War Zone, to see her husband, there is no censoring the things she may tell him. The disquieting, disturbing things. So she herself must be censored, not permitted to come. So for long weary months men must remain at the Front, on active inactivity, and their wives cannot come to see them. Only other people's wives may come. It is not the woman but the wife that is objected to. There is a difference. In war, it is very great.

There are many women at the Front. How do they get there, to the Zone of the Armies? On various pretexts – to see sick relatives, in such and such hospitals, or to see other relatives, brothers, uncles, cousins, other people's husbands – oh, there are many reasons which make it possible for them to come. And always there are the Belgian women, who live in the War Zone, for at present there is a little strip of Belgium left, and all the civilians have not been evacuated from the Army Zone. So there are plenty of women, first and last. Better ones for the officers, naturally, just as the officers' mess is of better quality than that of the common soldiers. But always there are plenty of women. Never wives, who mean responsibility, but just women, who only mean distraction and amusement, just as food and wine. So wives are forbidden, because lowering to the morale, but women are winked at, because they cheer and refresh the troops. After the war, it is hoped that all unmarried soldiers will marry, but doubtless they will not marry these women who have served and cheered them in the War Zone. That, again, would be depressing to the country's morale. It is rather paradoxical, but there are those who can explain it perfectly.

Ellen N. LaMotte

The Latest Excitements in Britain and Ireland

Diary 1905–1924

8 April, 1916 [41 Grosvenor Road]
The Friends Meeting House in Devonshire House Hotel, a large ugly circular hall with a big gallery running round it, was packed with some 2,000 young men – the National Convention of the No-Conscription Fellowship—Among the 2,000 were many diverse types. The intellectual pietist, slender in figure, delicate in feature and complexion, benevolent in expression, was the dominant type. These youths were saliently conscious of their own righteousness. That they are superior alike in heart and intelligence to the 'average sensual man' is an undoubted fact: ought one to quarrel with them for being aware of it? And yet the constant expression, in word and manner, of the sentiment avowed by one of them: 'We are the people whose eyes are open,' was unpleasing. There were not a few professional rebels, out to smash the Military Service Act, because it was the latest and biggest embodiment of authority hostile to the conduct of their own lives according to their own desires. Here and there were misguided youths who had been swept into the movement because 'conscientious objection' had served to excuse their refusal to enlist and possibly might save them from the terrors

and discomforts of fighting – pasty-faced furtive boys, who looked dazed at the amount of heroism that was being expected from them. They were obviously scared by the unanimity with which it was decided 'to refuse alternative service', and they will certainly take advantage of the resolution declaring that every member of the Fellowship must follow his own conscience in this matter. On the platform were the sympathizers with the movement – exactly the persons you would expect to find at such a meeting, older pacifists and older rebels – Bertrand Russell, Robert Trevelyan, George Lansbury, Olive Schreiner, Lupton, Stephen and Rosa Hobhouse, Dr Clifford, C. H. Norman, Miss Llewelyn Davies and the Snowdens: the pacifist predominating over the rebel element—

The muddled mixture of motives – the claim to be exempt from a given legal obligation, and the use of this privilege as a weapon against the carrying out of the will of the majority – marred the persuasive effect of this demonstration of the No-Conscription Fellowship. The first argument advanced by all the speakers was: 'I believe war to be an evil thing: killing our fellow men is expressly forbidden by my religion, and by the religion, by law established, of my country. Under the Military Service Act *bona fide* conscientious objectors are granted unconditional exemption: I claim this exemption.'

But this plea did not satisfy the militant majority. They declared their intention to defy the Act, so that the Act should become inoperative, even if all the conscientious objectors, on religious grounds, should be relieved from service. They *want* to be martyrs, so as to bring about a revulsion of feeling against any prosecution of the war. They are as hostile to voluntary recruiting as they are to conscription. If the government decided to rely on the recruiting sergeant, they would send a missionary down to oppose him. These men are not so much conscientious objectors as a militant minority of elects, intent on thwarting the will of the majority of ordinary citizens expressed in a national policy.

Now it seems clear that organized society could not continue to be organized, if every citizen had the right to be a conscientious objector to some part of our social order and insisted that he should be permitted not only to break the law himself but to persuade other citizens to break it. Moreover, when the conscientious objection is to carrying out an unpleasant social obligation like defending your country or paying taxes, conscience may become the cover for cowardice, greed or any other form of selfishness. Hence the state, in defence, must make the alternative to fulfilling the common obligation sufficiently irksome to test the conscience of the objectors — The social salvation of the twentieth century is not coming by the dissidence of dissent. Democracy means either discipline or anarchy.

BEATRICE WEBB

Diary

Daylight Saving Arrives

21 May 1916

The latest excitement has been the *Daylight Saving Bill*. Some years ago the originator of the scheme, one Willett by name who lived in Chislehurst, tried hard to get the government to adopt it, but with their usual dislike of anything new (even should it be of the utmost benefit to mankind!) they would have none of it. But now that poor Willett has been in his grave for some years, and as the war has brought home to our stupid government the utmost need of saving coal and gas, the Bill has not only been thought advisable, but brought in and passed. So on Saturday night, or rather on Sunday morning the 21st May, at 2 o'clock, all clocks and watches had to be set at 3 o'clock! We altered all our timepieces however at 9.30 on Sat evening, and then went to bed as we had made it 10.30!! so we got all right without any difficulty, and without any loss of sleep! though there were several dolts in England who 'raised objections'. I believe there are people who will want to argue and make objections when the Last Day comes! We benefit in many ways by the new arrangement — But the greatest benefit of all is after dinner, when it is broad daylight till close on ten! — Taking it all round, everyone has reason to bless the name of Willett.

Thrilling Times: A New Prime Minister

14 December 1916

Another Christmas dawning! and yet no signs of peace. The butchery and the carnage, and suffering and death, continue with relentless fury. Men seem to have lost all sense of manhood and decency in their lust for blood. Not only has the conflict been more deadly than ever of late, but England has been torn with political troubles at home. But a totally inefficient government couldn't be allowed to go on, and within the last few days great events have been happening. Mr Asquith has discreetly (!) resigned and Lloyd George is now Prime Minister. He is a man of actions (though I'd never trust a Welshman) and heaven knows the time has come when we need action – sharp, swift, and decisive. I fancy we are in for a thrilling time at home!

ETHEL M. BILBOROUGH

Letters to her son Fred

Fulham, May 13 1916

The Belgians here are causing a lot of trouble. On Sunday they nearly murdered a policeman & a soldier & yesterday the English people & kids collected in hundreds in Lillee Road where a lot of the Belgians have opened shops & last night the scene was beyond description. They have served them like they served Landau's & the other Germans. Windows & shops smashed up everywhere. What with the Germans & the Irish & now the Belgians, we have our share of the troubles.

Last week Fulham began their *allotments* but of course there were hundreds more applications than were in hand, & one lot near Kingwood Road have had to shift tons of hard core and rubbish, throw that up one side, then get out the mould and reverse the mixture. The poor beggars will deserve all they get off *that* ground. The Bishop talks out big about people tilling the right soil, but when they approached him, for the use of his meadow he said the military were in possession of it. Of course they could not tell him '*point blank*' that he was a perverter of the truth; but they let him know they did not believe him.

Fulham, March 27 1917

Rumour had it that the Germans had landed at Scotland & Lowestoft. On Saturday all the special constables were called up, also volunteers. Buses were stopped & sent in *one* direction 'somewhere in England" & of course that gave wings to the rumours. But – like the Russians – there is a reason for letting it float – over the East End the food riots began on Sat evening, & they set fire to some of the shops. There is almost sure to be some trouble if the food gets scarce. We have been laying in some stores, for every one else seems to be looking after themselves. No – I have not been in any potato fights yet. Several people got slightly damaged last Sat in Dawes Rd, while trying to get some.

   Your ever loving mother

E. FERNSIDE

Letters to a Beloved Husband

Walthamstow E17, Sept 17 1916

My Dearest one and only,

   Oh for the sight of your dear face, I feel it more everyday, it seems years since you were here and took dear Baby and I in your arms and when I look out and see the pouring rain my heart feels fit to break to think of you in the cold dismal tent, while I am at home with a nice fire. Oh dear it does seem terrible to me and you've done nothing to deserve it. Sunday seems the same as every day but worse today its the 17th dear. Well dear matey I have sent this parcel and hope you will like them, they are plain this time and also kerchieves and another undervest, which in unfolding be careful, as I've put a little something in to celebrate the anniversery instead of sending cigs — Well darling I can't think of any more new just now but let me know if anything you are needing, by the way would you like a couple of pig's bladders to fill your breeches out, they'd make fine cushions as well, that's the worst of these cheap bums. Heaps of love and kisses from your dear little Baby and everloving devoted wifie

June 25, 1917

My Own dear Hubby,

You dear letter of Sat. just received — Well darling mine I have just a little news to tell you which I'm sure you will regret to hear. Poor Harry Saville has gone under, news have just come through that he was shot on the 10th & died of his wounds on the 15th & they never had notice he was wounded even, so it was a terrible shock to them, poor Mrs S. is properly knocked over & Mrs Styles son lays at Bournemouth badly wounded from France. Oh darling it seems so terrible if only it would end and send you back to me. I should know you were safe, it seems age & ages since your dear face was before me & when one hears bad news it makes you feel so downhearted Excuse this scrawl as I've got Baby in my arms asleep and it's rather difficult — Cheer up sweetheart all my dearest love to you darling & heaps of kisses from your dear little treasure who says daddy's gone to fight the naughty shermans & she wont love em. Your everloving everlonging & devoted to you wife and Babs

My own dearest one,

At last thank God I have heard from you, from Durban dated Sept 19 & 20 & one posted at sea all 3 arrived together on 30 october & silk hanky as well, after long weary months of waiting my patients were rewarded & thanks awfully darling it was so sweet of you, to see your dear writing once more was like a hidden treasure. What an experience for you dearest & what a lot you will have to tell dear babby & I when you return to us again, & how many an evening we shall sit in the dear firelight listening to all your travells. What a time that will be dear, one can hardly realise it, if only it was for some other purpose, one could be so very much happier, but there dear that's the way of this wicked war, so I must buck up for your dear sake, & we will make up for all this when you come back to us which I pray please God will not be much longer now as we are all fed up with it—And your sweet little daughter joins me with all our dearest, best & devoted love to you dear & lots of loving kisses, & hope you will come safely home to us soon.

ANONYMOUS

How We Lived Then

'. . . For Tomorrow We Die'

The style of dancing altered during these years, and Jazz bands multiplied and flourished. In all classes war brought about a loosening of social convention, and as time went on, and girls who had never before earned money or been free of chaperonage found themselves independent, their elders sometimes were horrified by their behaviour.

As the casualty lists lengthened, 'Life is short, let us enjoy it whilst we may' became the motto of the young, and it was inevitable that this should be so—

The following letter of a young married woman, at that time a girl of eighteen who in normal circumstances would have led a carefully chaperoned social existence, but who, owing to the war, was almost as free as her brothers, presents an interesting picture of those days.

'Looking back on the war years,' she writes, 'we – that is, the young people of my set and day – seem to have been very callous. We were so very young then. I expect the men we knew were often terribly frightened, but of course they never said so, and we didn't think about it very much. It used to be hateful if one went to see them off by that horrid leave train. But generally they didn't want one to, thank goodness.

'Although most of us did some kind of war work – indeed, one despised girls who didn't – we used to dance almost every night. I remember going to a dance at Lady S—'s, and the refreshments were lemonade and squashed fly biscuits – you know those crunchy little biscuits with currants in them. At most of the dances the refreshments were more lavish – sandwiches, jellies and cup – but somehow although the food *looked* like food it soon left one hungry again. I can't think where people got the things to make sandwiches of. I suppose they used potted meat – that wasn't rationed, was it?

'Sometimes at these dances there was a small band, often only a piano. The men looked so nice in uniform, and I loved the Guards' overcoats, grey with a red lining. If it was warm we used to walk in the street between the dances and sit on doorsteps. It was awfully difficult to get taxis; they would only take you where *they* wanted to go unless they were bribed heavily. I often came home in a taxi with six inside and three or four on the roof! And still oftener we had to walk home, and then perhaps stopped for a cup of coffee at the Junior Turf Club, as we called the all-night refreshment stall at Hyde Park Corner.

'I do not remember many dinner-parties – I suppose people couldn't get enough food – though some things weren't rationed, were they? Giblets and entrails of kinds. But we used to dine at restaurants. An officer at one time might not spend more than a fixed sum for meals, so would hand over his money to you and let you order and pay. You might treat them – 3s. 6d. for lunch, 5s. 6d. for dinner.

'There were no chaperones: they were hard at work canteening and so on, and people who gave parties didn't want to feed and water them! And if they were elderly they didn't feel like having to walk home after late nights. I think one could do much as one pleased, but we had our standard, and the men were very careful of you if they thought you deserved to be looked after. I personally never dined alone with any of my men friends: we used to go about in fours or still larger groups.'

MRS C. S. PEEL

Constance Markievicz: An Independent Life

Easter Rising: Dublin 1916

Dr Lynn's open two-seater drove up to City Hall with Constance in high spirits, standing up and waving her plumed hat, and shouting 'Go at it boys' to her old Fianna graduates. The women of the Citizen Army lacked Con's grand daring in wearing breeches and had ripped their long skirts when they climbed over the iron gates of City Hall. Inside, Helena Moloney was in charge of the commissariat in the caretaker's kitchen and the Red Cross station, while men had scaled the roof and were exchanging fire with the military in the Castle Yard. From this vantage, they controlled the entrance to the Castle, so the place was effectively under siege, if not incommunicado—

Constance went on alone to Jacob's, yelling exuberantly when she got there, 'The Citizen Army are taking the Green, Dublin Castle is falling.' She then went on to Stephen's Green, driving the car boldly inside—

The revolution there—was proceeding in a relatively playful

and decorous manner. Mary Hyland and Kathleen Cleary had taken over the summer-house for their commissariat and had laid out a tasteful array of sandwiches, hams, cheeses and cakes. Madeleine Ffrench-Mullen had taken the glass conservatory as her first-aid shelter. Inside the railings that bounded the Green, men were busy digging trenches in the fashion of Flanders. On her arrival, Constance was told by Commandant Mallin, silk-weaver and musician in his everyday life, that she could not be spared as a liaison officer but must take her turn as a sniper. To this, she was proud to assent. Soon, Mallin appointed her his second-in-command.

For some time, to the bemused audience squinting through the railings, the scene had the appearance of a charade. The women laying out the picnic-teas, the men digging with the warm sun on their backs; the air laden with the scent of spring flowers and the hum of insects; and Mallin and Markievicz, guns at the ready, authoritatively pacing around—

Constance had a sister sniper in Margaret Skinnider, who had brought the detonators from Glasgow at Christmas and had been lately summoned by Con as promised. It was Margaret who later crossed the road again with a tricolour which was hoisted on the roof of the college—

However, most Dubliners did not know what to think of the day's events and the audacity of the Sinn Feiners, or Shinners as the revolutionaries were known colloquially. Many of them would, by tradition, support in theory, a rebellion – but when it was for real, and inconvenient and dangerous . . . Others, the South Dublin middle class, for example, were, with exceptions, outraged, and trusted it would be quelled with all haste and firmness. Very few, apart from the participants, were actually keen on it. As dusk drew on, people re-entering the city from their day out with tired, whimpering children in tow, were irate to find the trams not running – the stations had been seized and the lines ripped up at some points to hinder the movements of troops – certain streets impassable, and the city preparing for siege. In

223

the following days, as the shops remained closed and food and milk deliveries were interrupted and rumours spread and tales were told of uninvolved citizens getting shot and killed, they grew more irate still—

Food was a problem for insurgent and citizen alike. Many of the rebels, hidden away on roofs and in isolated outposts, did not eat for days on end. Mothers and sisters turned up at back entrances to present food parcels. In Boland's, they had any amount of bread and flour and fruit cake. In Jacob's, they had the cream crackers and the ham all battalions seem to have stocked up with, and some 'chocolate slab stuff' they used for cocoa. In City Hall, Helena Moloney found some oatmeal and made porridge. The rebels occupying the Pillar Cafe in Sackville Street had bacon and eggs for breakfast every day. In Jacob's, they had a 'great stew' when a side of beef was commandeered – Maire ni Shiubhlaigh sent out 'a great little fellow Bob Donohue' to find some onions.

Often food supplies travelling about the city were requisitioned by the rebels who ventured into the streets, usually on bicycles, to waylay the carts. In Stephen's Green, two young Citizen Army women, Lily Kempson and Mary Hyland, held up a milk float at gunpoint. Three women arriving at the College from the GPO with some ammunition also had bread, cheese and oxo cubes, bought with money James Connolly gave them for provisions. Hanna Sheehy-Skeffington brought bread, potatoes and oxo cubes, with which they made bouillon. But hunger was endemic, especially in the GPO. As the week went on, rebels began to hallucinate, to imagine things, to see faces in the sky, and to fall asleep at their posts—

There was one group of women who were vituperative in their hostility to the rebellion – perhaps the women Stephens heard speak out against it in the streets. These were the so-called 'separation women', the wives of Irishmen who had joined up for the duration of the war and who were fearful that the rebellion would jeopardise their 'separation allowances'. One such woman who attacked a Volunteer reporting to Jacob's on the first day of the rebellion was shot dead in front of Stephens. The starkly differing reactions of the Dublin populace astonished the military who were new to Ireland and did not know what to expect.

A young rebel called Brighid Lyons spent the last night hours of the rising in the Four Courts, wrapped in the ermine and sable robes of the judges. On Sunday morning, she and some other women were loaded into an army truck going to Richmond Barracks, and that evening when they were lined up for the march to Kilmainham Prison, she found herself beside Countess Markievicz in her elegant uniform. The rebels were glad, for once, of their military escort because, as they left the Barracks, they were met with a clamour of insults from the 'Separation Women' who had not been paid that week due to the cessation of normal life and its bureaucracies and feared they would not be paid again. A lot of the hatred, said Brighid Lyons, seemed to be directed at the Countess's breeches.

ANNE HAVERTY

Foreign Fields and High Seas

Pall Mall Gazette, March 1916

The Three Graces: French Women Who Followed Their Men to War

A muster of Zouaves near Paris was the undoing of three desolated females who had followed their men to war.

The Zouaves' baggy breeks and full, ample tunics serve the purposes of women and girls anxious to masquerade as soldiers; and the women had been for some days in the fort before they were detected. The place serves more as a drafting depot than a barracks, and this enabled 'the three graces' as the men had dubbed them, to elude detection longer than would have been thought possible.

When, yesterday, all ranks were ordered to muster for selection of reliefs for the front, they were unmasked, and, as military law is inexorable, they were locked up on charges of illegally wearing uniform and on suspicion of espionnage *(sic)*. Moreover, the men they sacrificed everything for, including their wavy locks, were placed under arrest for aiding and abetting them.

French Heroine

Yesterday in the Sorbonne, at a meeting to celebrate the heroic deeds of Frenchwomen in the present war, M. Klotz paid warm tribute to a young Frenchwoman named Marcelle Semmer, who has been decorated with the War Cross and the Cross of the Legion of Honour.

The exploit which made Marcelle Semmer famous was after the Battle of Charleroi, when the French troops tried to hold back the Germans on the Somme, but, being few in numbers, had to retire across the canal at Eclusier. When they were safely across this young girl of 19, under fire from the enemy, opened the lock and then threw the key into the canal, thus preventing the Germans from crossing for nearly 24 hours and making the retreat of the French possible.

M. Klotz referred to the action of the British General who later in the year occupied Eclusier, to show respect to the youthful heroine he ordered his men to salute her when she passed, and never address her unless they were first spoken to.

The Battle of Jutland

Diary of a Nursing Sister:
Grand Fleet Hospital Ship *Plassy*

31 May 1916

Today the whole fleet of battle cruisers & cruisers have gone out, we watched them steaming up, & wondered if there is really anything doing this time, there having been so many false alarms. This evening after dinner two or three officers arrived in board with note books etc to find out what accommodation we had got for the wounded, how many cots, how many stretchers etc &

later on we got a signal to get full steam going, so as to sail off at a moment's notice. It really looked as if there was going to be some work at last, we were very busy in the wards getting dressings ready. We waited up until 11–12 then the P.M.O. said we had better turn in as there was no more news and we could easily be called.

June 1st 1916

Still no news of patients — It has been a weird sort of day, waiting about the whole time & afraid to settle to anything for fear of any sudden news. This afternoon it has been raining in torrents, almost tropical, which did not tend to cheer us up. It seems almost certain there has been a fight of some sort, but where, or how severe, no one knows. We all felt fearfully mouldy, as all sorts of rumours kept on coming — We were all up on deck after dinner watching & waiting, when we saw through the mist & rain, two destroyers come under the Forth Bridge and following them very slowly but still in stately manner the first battle-scarred heroine.

2nd

We received orders early to proceed at once down to the Forth Bridge to prepare to take on patients as the ships came in. There has been the most tremendous battle—As we got to anchor the ships began to come in — crowded on the decks in most varied rig, were survivors from the poor lost ships — I much regret that I did not take photographs, but we were expecting patients any moment, so I did not dare go away. Soon they began to arrive, drifters by the dozen, six and seven deep on the port and starboard sides waiting to unload their sad burdens — by 12.30 had taken in over 100 and they said the worst ones were still to come. We got them all into bed as quickly as possible, no easy job sometimes, & fed them with beef tea & the bad ones with brandy — then the bad cases began to come in, poor things it was pitiful to see some of them, with legs & arms off, & some fearfully burnt, face, arms, legs & body. We even had destroyers up alongside discharging patients directly on board. A tremendous thunderstorm came up in the afternoon, which didn't assist matters as everything got wringing wet; by about 3.30 they were all in board — I had the most in my ward with 46 acute cases — we started about 5 to do the dressings — some of the poor things hadn't been touched since Wed night when the first fight took place & had only the first pictic dressings on their burns. It must have been agonies taking the dressings off, but very few of them made a moan. I never saw such bravery in my life.

3rd

I did not get to bed till 3 o'clock this morning — We started work at 8.30 and finished at 10.30 tonight, with short intervals for meals & 5 minutes blow on deck after lunch. The smell of burns is awful, one gets almost nauseated sometimes — the poor things have nearly all to be fed as nearly all have both hands tied up and masks on their faces — It is unfortunately true about the Queen Mary (lost) & besides that the Indefatigable, the Invincible, the Defence, the Warrior, the Black Prince — all gone in one fell swoop, & the loss of life must be ghastly.

Mary Clarke

Personal Correspondence

23 August 1916

Dear Mother,

You will probably think me quite mad when I tell you I have decided to go to Russia with the Scottish Women's Hospital people. We went to see the War pictures at the Scala Theatre on Monday night and as a result of that I felt it to be my duty to offer my services to Dr. Inglis. I never thought they would be accepted.

As a matter of fact, she, or rather her deputy, Dr. Chesney, jumped at the offer, as it appears they are very short-handed and find it exceedingly difficult to get people. The Russian government have asked for four units from this country.

They say they are going to sail on Monday next but I don't suppose they really will. I hope you won't think it very foolish of me to go. It seems to me there is no reason for me not to go and I haven't moved a little finger so far to help in any way.

Yours
Ellie

From HMS *(name censored but it was in fact the* Huntspill*)* 7.9.1916

Dearest Mother,

I can't remember what I told you in my last letter. In case I didn't describe the party to you then I will do so again as it is essential you should understand what we consist of. The unit is under the command of Dr. Elsie Inglis. It is divided into two sections.

1. The Motor Section under Mrs Haverfield. This consists of:

A. First class drivers B. Second class drivers C. Cooks D. Secretary E. Interpreter Uniform – khaki

They almost all have short hair. They are popularly called 'The Buffs'. They are very smart and very conceited. Mrs Haverfield is a great stickler for discipline, obedience, etc., etc.

2. The Hospital Section under Dr. Inglis. Uniform – Gray.

It consists of: Doctors, Administrator, Matron and Assistant matron, Sisters, Orderlies, Sanitary Inspector, X-ray assistant (myself), Cooks, Laundresses, Interpreter.

On Sunday morning at 7.30 there was some excitement because a German submarine passed about 10 miles away. Luckily she ignored us —later one of the marines saw a whale which he mistook for a torpedo and he was with difficulty prevented from firing at it. We have three guns on board. We have come a tremendous round in order to escape from torpedoes and mines —We do a zig-zag course the whole time. For two days it was bitterly cold but otherwise we have had lovely weather. The other night there was a very fine display of the Northern lights.

Love

Ellie

7.9.1916

Dear Betty,

This is a wild adventure I am on— Dr. Inglis likes a great deal of deference paid to her as head of the unit and she goes in for roll-calls, cabin inspection etc. We have to stand to attention etc. and at roll-call she has given the order that we are to say 'Here ma'am' — The sisters – as in military hospitals all the nurses are sisters here – are the oddest collection of old dug-outs. Most of them apparently were private nurses & haven't been near a hospital for years. They look anything but smart — There is actually an old and toothless harridan who rouges shamelessly. The Assistant matron who is rather a bright spot told me that they had found it very difficult to get nurses. All the best ones have been snapped up long ago. These creatures will never have much authority over the orderlies. The orderlies are active, intelligent, educated specimens. The sisters are essentially uneducated.

FRANCES ELEANOR (ELLIE) RENDEL

War Diary: Scottish Women's Hospital: Romania, 1916

We were about forty miles from the front and soldiers were constantly coming and going. One of the most wonderful things was to see and hear a Russian regiment go by. Their march was a much slower one than ours, they covered the ground well, but in long slow strides. Somehow it always reminded me of the slink of a panther. As they marched they sang, and *how* beautifully — Once in Romania I came round a corner in the car on to a Cossack cavalry regiment singing too divinely. The leader of the regiment

231

had a sort of little canopy of silver bells over his horse's head. They carried lances with little pennants. It was a blue, sunny day and the brilliance of the sunlight on the lance points, the shimmering sound of the silver bells and the haunting lilt of the men's voices make up one of those golden memories of which one has, alas, far too few.

Another Nation in Retreat

We all started off at ten o'clock in pitch darkness along dreadful roads, went about ten miles, then the road was so hopeless, enormous cavities and river to ford, etc., that we all struck and said 'Blast the enemy, we'll camp the night on the road in the cars', which we did, and at 4 a.m. we set off again across country, making for a place where we were to meet the First Serbian division and get further orders. All the time we were going we heard guns nearer and nearer, as we were going to another part of the front near Constansa. Well, we eventually found the General in a field in a valley with crowds of soldiers and guns etc. We waited there an hour and all the time just over the hill the shells were bursting and flames from the burning town and oil wells could be seen. Two or three shells burst over us while we waited. Then the order was given to get on, *retreat*, and all the soldiers had to go first. We were the very last of all and when we'd got about a quarter of a mile our blasted car stopped and wouldn't budge, so with great calmness (!!) with shells coming nearer and nearer, we cleaned the plugs, oiled various bits and pieces and eventually after half an hour's playing about, she started, and we raced after the others. We went about ten miles on, all this mind you, across *fields*, no road at all. Then we halted again while the military authorities burbled to each other. It was getting towards sunset, there was a scarlet sky, a vast undulating plain ahead —Again orders to move, and again we were kept to the last and it began to pour. Off we went, and I shall always see that sinister plain and the rain and grey ghostlike figures of the soldiers and guns retreating.

Well, we had gone for about two hours when we discovered that one of our big lorries had stuck. We waited and waited while they tried to get it going and the shells got closer and closer. At last we had to abandon it after smashing the engine with a hammer, removing the magneto etc. Then we went on until about 10 p.m., when we came to a village and we slept in the cars there, as were all done in and couldn't see an inch, and besides no one knew where to go — That village was pandemonium all night, guns, guns, guns crashing and Roumanian, Russian and Serbian troops all mixed up in hopeless confusion in the retreat, not knowing where to go or what to do.

At 4 a.m. we started off again, and from then until we got here it was *Hell*. Imagine to yourself an enormous stretch of country like the back of the Downs, only gigantic, and through the centre of it one not very wide or good main road, running to the River Danube and the Frontier, and from *every* direction on this plain as far as you could see, behind and before and all around, streams and streams of carts and horses and women, men, children, herds of cattle and sheep, soldiers, guns, bullock wagons, every conceivable thing, and *all* converging on this one road!

A Nation in Retreat and only *one* road. The wretched peasants in rough carts made of a few planks roped together, and on them all their worldly goods; furniture, pigs, geese and children all huddled together. Old women and young with babies in their arms trudging along beside them. There were five or six carts deep across the road, we had awful difficulty in moving at all and every yard we were beseeched to take people. We couldn't, we had wounded with us in most cars and the others were full up with stores, petrol etc. Every hundred yards or so you would see a tragic group of wailing women over one of those wretched carts which had broken, and there were all the things they possessed fallen in the mud and ditch, being trampled on by the passing crowds. It was dreadful.

And then about 10 a.m. a rumour spread that Bulgarian cavalry were coming over the hills at our back, and then panic seized the poor wretches. The soldiers and their wagons whipped up their horses and drove furiously on over everything and everyone. All the people began to *scream* and *scream* and run for their lives — Never can I forget the terror on the faces of those people — to add to its horrors we saw a poor woman lying in the agonies of childbirth in the ditch—

We heard afterwards that the road was shelled to pieces later in the day, just after we, on the advice of George, had left it and struck across country, which proved our salvation. Two Roumanian business men plagued us for lifts and we let them hang on to the steps of the car. During one of the halts they went to Mrs. Haverfield and said that of course we must all be demi-mondaines and some of us were quite pretty, and how much did she want for the pretty ones!!!

We were incredibly hungry, we had had practically nothing but a little black bread and some Brand's beef lozenges for some considerable time, and tired doesn't describe it, to say nothing of the dirt. At last we got to the Danube, where the congestion was again frightful. Literally thousands camped on the banks, not knowing where to go or what to do. Eventually we got over the river and into Braille. The first little restaurant on the outskirts of the town which we saw, we fell upon and ate a huge meal. Then still exhausted beyond description and simply filthy from head to foot, we hadn't washed for a week, we proceeded into the heart of the town. It was perfectly crazy, that's the only way I can describe how I felt. Out of all that terror and anguish and chaos, we suddenly emerged into an open flower bedded garden place in the centre of the city with gay restaurants and brilliantly lit shops all around. We parked our cars beside the gardens. Suddenly crowds of people arrived and began to cheer us, throw flowers at us and before we knew where we were someone, I don't know who, had taken all of us into an enormous brightly lit restaurant filled with smartly dressed people. We were installed at a long table in the centre of the room, people stood on chairs in order to see us. A magnificent meal was brought to us which, needless to say, after the one we had just eaten, we could scarcely swallow. We were so tired we could hardly hold up our heads. We felt perfect fools and looked ghastly in our filthy muddy uniforms amongst this extremely chic crowd. People gave us more flowers, cigarettes, chocolates, crowds surrounded us and we were literally mobbed as we struggled through pushing, cheering masses on our way to the place in which we were to sleep. We experienced no pleasure, as far as I can remember, from the enthusiastic reception given to us, merely a feeling of sick fatigue and a complete incomprehension of the apparent insensibility of these people to the shattering horrors from which we had just emerged.

KATHERINE HODGES

My War Experiences in Two Continents

The Armenian Massacres

Erivan. 20 January *(1916)*
Last night's experiences were certainly very 'Russian.' We had wired for rooms, but although the message had been received nothing was prepared. The miserable rooms were an inch thick in dust, there were no fires, and no sheets on the beds! We went to a restaurant – fortunately no Russian goes to bed early – and found the queerest place, empty save for a band and a lady. The lady and the band were having supper. She, poor soul, was painted and dyed, but she offered her services to translate my French for me when the waiters could understand nothing but Russian. I was thankful to eat something and go to bed under my fur coat.

To-day we have been busy seeing the Armenian refugees. There are 17,000 of them in this city of 30,000 inhabitants. We went from one place to another, and always one saw the same things and heard the same tales.

Since the war broke out I think I have seen the actual breaking of the wave of anguish which has swept over the world (I often wonder if I can 'feel' much more!). There was Dunkirk and its shambles, there was ruined Belgium, and there was, above all, the field hospital at Furnes, with its horrible courtyard, the burning heap of bandages, and the mattresses set on edge to drip the blood off them and then laid on some bed again. I can never forget it. I was helping a nurse once, and all the time I was sitting on a dead man and never knew it!

And now I am hearing of one million Armenians slaughtered in cold blood. The pitiful women in the shelters were saying, 'We are safe because we are old and ugly; all the young ones went to the harems.' Nearly all the men were massacred. The surplus children and unwanted women were put into houses and burned alive. Everywhere one heard, 'We were 4,000 in one village, and only 143 escaped;' 'There were 30 of us, and now only a few children remain;' 'All the men are killed.' These were things one saw for oneself, heard for oneself. There was nothing sensational in the way the women told their stories.

The Armenians are hated. I wonder Christ doesn't do more for them considering they were the first nation in the world to embrace Christianity; but then, one wonders about so many things during this war. Oh, if we could stamp out the madness that seems to accompany religion, and just live, sober, kind, sensible lives, how good it would be; but the Turks must burn women and children, alive, because, poor souls, they think one thing and the Turks think another! And men and women are hating and killing each other because Christ, says one, had a nature both human and divine, and, says another, the two were merged in one. And a third says that Christ was equal to the Father, while a whole Church separated itself on the question of Sabellianism, or 'The Procession of the Son.'

Poor Christ, once crucified, and now dismembered by your own disciples, are you glad you came to earth, or do you still think God forsook you, and did you, too, die an unbeliever? The crucifixion will never be understood until men know that its

236

worst agony consisted in the disbelief which first of all doubts God and then must, by all reason, doubt itself. The resurrection comes when we discover that we are God and He is us.

SARAH MACNAUGHTAN

A *History of the Scottish Women's Hospital*

Salonika Front: 1916

'Passed right along the very edge of the water for several kilometres and stopped at the station of Ostrovo. White sand on the shore of the lake bright in the moonlight – a row of tall poplars shadowed against the water beyond. Not a soul to be seen on the platform at first; later on a girl with a lantern in a straw hat appeared – R— of the Harley Unit. Mrs. Harley, General French's sister, had a motor ambulance Unit here at Ostrovo, sent out by the S.W.H. She also ran a kind of canteen for feeding the soldiers to and from the front, as they came through in the trains — A short wait of two hours – from 2 till 4 a.m. at R—'s camp fire, at one end of the station – cocoa and gingerbread. Drive to Dr. Bennett's Hospital, about four and half kilos back along the side of the lake, in a Ford van driven by a girl with short hair and very short skirts, at a furious pace along the roughest of tracks, with awful bumps and bounces.

'Arrived at Hospital camp very much shaken up. White tents amongst a clump of great green trees – moonlight – white-capped night Sisters with lanterns. Lay down in their tent till the morning. Morning light in the elm trees – magpies – white tents – high mountains beyond. Cocks crowing hoarsely. Guns from behind a big mountain range in the north, Kaimatchalan. Interviews with Miss Jack, administrator, and afterwards with Dr. Bennett. On duty in the wards . . .

'The Hospital ambulances – at that time four were running – and the cars of the Harley Unit at Ostrovo village brought the wounded in from the dressing-stations. One of these was high up on the slopes of the mountain of Kaimatchalan, which had been captured by the Serbs a week or two earlier – the other one at the foot of the mountain—

1st November

'Went up to the upper dressing-station as attendant orderly in a car driven by one of the chauffeurs. An awful climb and tremendously rough and narrow tracks up the mountain – boiling engines. A great and wonderful view over the Macedonian Plain towards Mount Olympus, and of the whole lake of Ostrovo. Track up the hill crowded with many-coloured throngs of transport of various nations – Serb, French, British, native Turks, and Macedonian. Donkeys, mules, oxen, horses, carts, Ford vans, and our ambulances. The little village of Batechin half-way up, the inhabitants of which are Roumanian. Curiosity of native children about our clothes, especially our stockings. They kept lifting the hems of our skirts to see exactly what we wore on our legs. A great desire to know whether we had any hair on our heads under our caps.'

AN ORDERLY'S DIARY

1917

Long-standing political and social tensions, exacerbated by the military disasters of 1916, started to simmer ominously, or came to the boil. In February and March the first Russian revolution occurred, when the liberal intelligentsia formed a provisional government, forced the Tsar to abdicate, and Kerensky became prime minister. It was at this period, with thousands of Russian soldiers laying down their arms, that the women's 'Battalion of Death' was founded. In October the Bolsheviks seized power and in December they negotiated a cease-fire which ended Russia's involvement in the war.

Early in the year units of the French Army baaed like sheep as they refused to obey orders and be led to the abattoir. On the Western Front the mutinous contagion did not spread, but the soldiers of Britain and her Empire thereafter bore the brunt of battle. The murderous mudbath of the Third Battle of Ypres, otherwise known as Passchendaele, joined Verdun and the Somme as paradigms of senseless slaughter. Terrible casualties marked the Battle of Caporetta, when a German-Austrian force smashed the Italian army.

Also in the autumn there was a brief mutiny at Étaples, the massive British base camp on the French coast near Le Touquet. French women 'mutinied' too, or at least, led by the Parisian *midinettes*, thousands of war workers went on strike for '*la semaine anglaise*'. Ostensibly this was the Saturday half-holiday enjoyed by their English counterparts but it was a demand for better conditions and wages. There was growing industrial unrest in both Britain and Germany.

Women continued more than to plug the gaps left by men but with the male casualty rates mounting, the British government took the revolutionary step of forming first the Women's Auxiliary Army Corps, then the Women's Royal Naval Service and the Women's Royal Air Force. Service with the armed forces added a new dimension to the parliamentary debate about women's suffrage.

In tandem with the Bolshevik takeover of Russia (which was by no means a longer-term certainty in 1917) the major event of the year – in April – was the United States' entry into the war on the Allies' side. The reactions of American women followed the same pattern as their European sisters, a small hard core of pacifists but the majority, with varying degrees of conviction and enthusiasm, supporting their country's war effort.

'A Microcosmology in Which Woman Replaces Man'

Subheading of Gilbert Stone's *Women War Workers*

Daily Mirror, 3 January 1917

The dustwoman has now arrived. Willesden Borough Council has lost so many men as the result of enlistments that they are now employing women as 'dustmen'. People have ceased to be surprised now when they see women in new posts.

Unidentified press cutting

Women Dustmen: Low Carts and Small Baskets

When Wandsworth Tribunal were asked today for an extension of the exemption granted to two dustmen, both passed for general service, Mr Boller, the representative of the contractor to the Borough Council, declared that they could not be replaced.

The Mayor: You will have to do what they are doing in other boroughs, and get some of these Amazonian women who wear trousers.

Mr Boller: Women are wearing trousers all right, but I don't think they will do as dustmen.

The Mayor: Women are acting as dustmen in other boroughs —

I suggest that women can do this work if you use low carts and small baskets.

Both claims were disallowed, but the men not to be called up for two months.

Evening Standard and St James's Gazette, 26 January 1917

The Royal Flying Corps always leads the way in matters of invention and experiment, and I hear it is taking up the only solution of the man-power problem with energy, that is to say, the employment of women.

Daily Sketch, 18 January 1917

The woman chauffeur has reached the height of her ambitions – she is to be allowed at last to drive the royal mail vans. A start will be made in London next Monday, beginning with the eleven o'clock night shift, when six women drivers, wearing the uniform of the Women's Volunteer Reserve, will drive the one-ton lorries which convey the outgoing mails from the G.P.O. to the railway stations, where they will wait for the incoming mails. The six are only the pioneers of a large number of women drivers wanted to drive the royal mail vans, in order to release as many as possible of the 300 men now employed. The first women drivers of H.M. Stationery Office wear uniforms of a military character.

NUWSS Bulletin, 6 March 1917

Women Taxicab Drivers

The Home Secretary's recent announcement that qualified

women will be licensed to drive public vehicles in London has resulted in large numbers applying for posts as taxi-drivers. At 2 schools of motoring altogether about 100 women are now studying the 'knowledge of London' test which has to be passed before Scotland Yard grants a licence. Meanwhile men members of the London and Provincial Union of Licensed Vehicle Workers are taking a ballot on the proposal to cease work directly the first woman appears in London as a driver of a licensed vehicle. The result of this step remains to be seen.

Daily Telegraph, 14 February 1917

Are women capable of driving at night?

The Times, 22 January 1917

The woman window-dresser, strange as it may seem, is a war novelty — There has also been a great influx into the drapery trade of women buyers, shopwalkers, and commercial travellers – branches in which some women had already displayed considerable ability.

The Times, April 1917

Women at Lloyd's: Question of Fitness for 'Rush and Turmoil'

Daily Express, 4 July 1917

Miss Gertrude Lowthian Bell, the famous Eastern traveller, is acting as assistant Political Officer for the British Government in Bagdad. This is the first time that any woman has filled such a post, and no one could have been chosen better qualified to fill it.

The Times, 14 August 1917

The Architectural Association, of which the King is patron, will open its school for the first time to women students this autumn.

Manchester Guardian, 23 October 1917

More pit-brow lasses were started yesterday at colleries in the Bolton, Atherton, Tyldesley and Leigh districts. In some cases they take the place of men who have been called up for military service. Girls and young women who have been thrown idle through the operations of the Cotton Control Board are going to the pits, and there are now over 3,000 in the South Lancashire coalfield.

Unidentified press cutting 1917

Army Spectacles

THE GIRL WORKERS OF CLIFFORD'S INN
The Army Spectacle Depôt is within a girl's stone-throw of Fleet-street, yet Fleet-street hardly realizes its existence. It is tucked away in Clifford's Inn, which during some centuries of existence has been put to various uses, but none so remarkable as this. The old Hall is occupied by drawers and dockets, by showcases of lenses, frames, and artificial eyes, and by busy girls in brown overalls. In chambers adjoining accountancy and other secretarial work is being done. The garden, to which Dickens alluded in 'Our Mutual Friend' as a 'mouldy little plantation or cat pre-serve,' is covered by a factory as clean, tidy, and well-equipped as any in the country. The visitor is reminded of one of those estab-lishments where people are happy and industrious in quietude

described in the pages of the Utopian novelist. But there are few visitors, and the passer-by in Clifford's Inn murmurs only 'More Government huts!' without a suspicion of what they cover.

The staff numbers about 100, and, with the exception of Mr. J. H. Sutcliffe, the superintendent, and three or four R.A.M.C. optician mechanics and foremen, is female. Setting aside some of the senior accountants and typists, all these girls have been trained entirely in the depôt. As a rule, they begin at 14, coming straight from school or 'blind alley' occupations; and the present average age is 18—

In the factory a beginner is taken through the stages of screwing up lenses, altering, repairing, and making frames, lens edging and engraving, lens surfacing. The optical trade has hitherto regarded this last as exclusively a male occupation. To the warehouse staff falls the charge of the ophthalmological apparatus, and of the big stock of about 1,000,000 lenses; together with the duty of examining lenses for blemishes and flaws. The artificial eye department, employing six to eight girls, has a stock of 30,000 eyes, from which the military hospitals are supplied on demand—

The foundation of the depôt was the consequence of the formation of a citizen Army. The old Army, generally speaking, did not require glasses. With universal service, the alternative was presented of admitting spectacled soldiers or rejecting large numbers who suffered from astigmatism and kindred visual defects—

Recollections of a Wartime Bank Clerk

I was born in London in 1894 and at the age of fourteen I started work as a lowly shop assistant at Selfridges in Oxford Street. When the war broke out I was in the corset department (I remember demonstrating an American model called *Nemo*). By 1917 corset sales had dropped dramatically and I was sacked. Somebody told me they were looking for girl clerks at a branch of the Bank of England in Lombard Street so I went along and in February I was taken on, without any references, but I had beautiful handwriting.

There were two shifts 8 a.m.–3 p.m. and 3 p.m.–10 p.m. and we were paid £3.7.6d. per week, with 2/6 per hour overtime. There were some older men there but most of the clerical staff were by then women. We worked in a huge room at trestle tables and never mixed with the men! Each section had a woman team leader who had to ensure nobody made any mistakes but the big bosses were all men. I remember Lord Cunliffe coming round. He was apparently so incensed at seeing flowers on the tables and us girls in summer dresses that he banned the flowers and issued instructions that we all had to wear overalls. The bank provided the overalls free and after a week or two the flowers reappeared and nobody said anything.

In June 1918 I was chosen to boost war loans – I was very pretty then and I'd had my hair cut into the latest fashion 'bob'. My picture appeared in the *Daily Graphic* as 'The £50-million Dividend Girl'. I was ever so chuffed!

All in all I enjoyed my period at the bank. The pay was certainly much better than at Selfridges. When the war ended some girls were kept on but I left for fresh woods and pastures new.

ADELA HALL

Daily Mail, 12 July 1917

Woman Diplomatist

Great interest was aroused by the statement that a woman was one of the six British official representatives at the Anglo-German Conference at the Hague on prisoners of war. Yesterday afternoon Mrs Darley Livingstone, the first woman to sit at a table of diplomatic negotiations, successfully devoted all her not inconsiderable diplomatic talent to diverting conversation from her unique experience. Young, charming, vivacious, an American married to a British officer, she said yesterday, 'Yes, people did seem surprised to find a woman among the British representatives. I am sure I don't know why, because there is really nothing that women are not doing in England today, is there? I had no means of telling what the German representative thought, because, of course, we didn't talk to each other, not socially, I mean.'

Diary 1916–17

Munitions: Police Work

Nov 2 1916

Then we heard that women police were badly needed, so we went off to their offices to see what that was like. All the W.ps we saw looked very smart in a very dapper uniform of navy blue. We were interviewed by an inspector who gave us the job details. They are anxious to get W. police recognised as an official part of the police service. They would deal especially with women and children. So far, they have not got the recognition, only a sort of toleration but certain county and borough councils have employed w. police on their own responsibility. These are paid out of local funds, & work independently of the men police & are not sworn in — but the Government (i.e. Ministry of Munitions) are employing w.ps inside munition factories to control the women workers, & it is for that work they want recruits. Pay is £2 a week, but recruits have to buy their own uniforms. They have taken up our references, & if we are accepted I think we shall take it on.

Dec 4th

There about 20 other recruits — Most are ladies or middle class women, all are in a better class than the average policeman. We had a lecture & drill, tomorrow we go to a police court.

Jan 5 1917

Marching orders again! This time promotion, Buckie to sub insp & me to sergeant. We both go to Pembrey in S. Wales.

Jan 14th

Pembrey is the back of beyond, a little coal mining village with a minute harbour, & the remains of a large silver works. The factory is 3½ miles from the town. The town mostly consists of rather dismal looking cement houses, some larger, some smaller, but most fairly pretentious. They have gas laid on everywhere, & smart little tiled paths leading to the doors, but no water & no drains. Very Welsh! The factory is built on the Burrows (i.e. sand-hills), the most desolate spot in the world.

—The factory sheds are built with a large mound of sand all round them, & are entered by a small tunnel through this mound. In this way the sheds are quite invisible from outside, & the place looks more like a gigantic rabbit warren than anything else. In the sifting rooms only 5 or 6 workers are allowed at a time, & if an extra person wants to go in, one of those inside must come out. The factory makes TNT, G. cotton, cordite & ballistite.

March 10th

The girls here are very rough, so are the conditions. Their language is sometimes too terrible. But they are also very impressionable, shrieking with rage one minute, & on quite friendly terms the next. The previous Sub Insp had only one sergeant & three constables under her, & they managed to get themselves heartily detested by the workers, with the result that for a policewoman to so much as show herself was a signal for all the girls to shriek & boo. They several times threatened to duck the Sub Insp, & did once throw a basin of dirty water over her.

—The ether in the cordite affects the girls. It gives some headaches, hysteria, & sometimes fits. If the worker has the least tendency to epilepsy, even if she has never shown it before, the ether will bring it out. There are 15 or 20 girls who get these epileptic fits. On a heavy windless day we sometimes have 30 girls overcome by the fumes in one way or another. Girls who show signs of epilepsy ought really to be discharged, or found other work — Some of the girls have 12 fits or more one after the other. It generally falls to our lot to take the sick girls to the surgery — In this way we have begun to win their confidence, & some who are most aggressive at first are beginning to be friendly.

The girls here are much more interesting than those at Chester. They are more full of life, & there are so many different types down here. There are about 3,800 women workers in all sections on both shifts. Some of them come down from the sheep farms in the mountains, & speak only Welsh, or a very little broken English. Then there are the relatives of miners from the Rhondda & other coal pits near. They are full of socialistic theories & very great on getting up strikes. But they are very easily influenced by a little oratory, & go back to work like lambs if you shout at them long enough. A number of the girls are from the Swansea docks, a different type from the other, with a good deal of German blood with a large admixture of other races, including blacks. There is one girl here, half negress who is a most extraordinary mimic. She keeps the other girls in fits while she imitates the matrons, foremen, chemist, women police etc. She also gets up concerts during meal times, beating time with her spoon. She has a very fine voice, as have many of the others, so that the concerts are worth listening to.

Miss G. M. West

Daily Express, 14 February 1917

Revolt of Seven Shell Girls

EXPLOSIVE THEY WOULD NOT HANDLE
Seven girl munition workers were charged before the London Munitions Tribunal yesterday with refusing to obey a lawful order – to go on 'C.E. work.'

The girls, who had previously been employed on T.N.T. shell filling, objected to 'C.E. work' because one of the consequences might be discoloration. Some also said they were unfit, but it was explained that they were Class A girls, passed as fit for T.N.T. and C.E. work. Four of the girls left the factory, and have not returned.

'You were aware that it is very urgent?' said Mr J. G. Talbot, the chairman, to the girls.

'Yes,' replied one of them.

Mr Talbot: We know it is badly wanted for our men at the front. Still, you are not willing to help? – No, sir.

She added that she was willing to go on T.N.T. filling.

Another girl said they thought they ought to have masks, but the works manager said the doctors argued against respirators, gloves, or veils for C.E. work because they increased the liability to dermatitis.

The chairman fined the girls 15s. each.

'The work is very important although the circumstances are disagreeable,' he said. 'I should have thought all would be anxious to do what they can, even at some discomfort and inconvenience to themselves, to supply this explosive which is so much wanted for our soldiers.'

The clerk: Do you want time to pay?

'We won't pay,' shouted the girls in chorus. 'We refuse to pay. We are not labour conscripts, we are volunteers.'

Arbeiter Jugend, 2nd June 1917

One cannot count the number of young girls making poisonous gases and acids, manufacturing inflammable and explosive materials. And there is no ten-hour day any more, no early finishing on a Saturday, no Sunday off and no ban on night shifts. In day and night shifts, Sundays and holidays our young comrades are hard at work. Night shifts of twelve hours with only two half-hour breaks are common. Young girls are even asked to do 24-hour shifts—

In hot rooms, filled with noise and poisonous fumes, these young girls in their prime spend their lives, their youth. The good ladies and gentlemen, sitting at the marble tables in cafés, hardly think of this when they tell stories of how these 'young things' earn eight and ten marks per shift. That the young females are sacrificing the happiness and strength of youth, their girlish laughter for the pieces of paper they receive on pay day, does not occur to the ladies and gentlemen, who would be terrified if they had to send their own daughter into a munitions factory just for one night. And how shocked they would be if the young miss returned from the poison factories with her skin turned Mongol yellow and her hair green!

Recollections of Munitions 1917 – A Factory Explosion

—Still hating the restrictions and abuse from my employers I volunteered for 'munitions' as it was called, and at the end of 1916 I was sent to a factory near Morecambe Bay — We were billeted in sea-side boarding houses, but the landladies who took us in wanted us out before holiday makers came in. We slept five in a room and never got enough to eat. On all night shift (seven to seven) we had a few slices of bread & margarine for our main meal which we ate between eleven & twelve. We had to pay the landladies twenty-five shillings out of the twenty-seven we received, and there were no facilities for laundry. We had to walk three miles each way to the factory, which was a filling factory packed with explosives.

Many railway lines traversed the area which was three miles across and nine miles in circumference. Shells of all sizes came in to be filled, many of them nine inches across 9.2s. The filling was a boring and laborious task. A large amount of powder stood by each shell, and this had to be rammed into the shell using a piece of wood & wooden hammer. Often it seemed impossible to ram in any more powder but with the mallet and stem another small hole had to be made into the powder & more inserted. This was called stemming. Many girls fainted in the T.N.T. room but I was not affected, so was often exposed to that deadly poison.

It was in this factory that to my disgust I was told how babies were made. I refused to believe it and told those women in no uncertain terms what I thought of them, remarking, 'My mum & dad would never do that!' How those women laughed!

—On the evening of October 1st 1917 a rocket was seen to leave the middle of the works & go over the sea — At eleven p.m. just as we went to the canteen for our dinner a fire alarm sounded & we saw flames. We never expected the fire to spread, as each building was separated from the next by a long corridor with water sprinklers. Actually we girls hoped it would last for a while as we would not have to resume work until it was safe. However, the fire did spread rapidly soon huge explosions shook everything. There was quite a lot of panic as the twelve foot high gates remained closed. The police on the gates were never permitted to open them until soldiers surrounded the factory & the line to the camp had been cut. The rush for the gates had the weaker people on the ground, yet others still climbed over them to try & climb the gates while the police tried to hold them back. A few girls were working to dislodge the girls on the ground and carry them to the canteen. I had no hopes of escaping that holocaust, but somehow I was not scared. We were shut in the wing with those explosions for several hours. The buildings had strong walls & weak roofs so the roofs would go up rather than the walls. Truck loads of benzine & dangerous chemicals were exploding, too, and several people threw themselves into a river which ran at the back of the works. We never knew how many died. At the end of the week with that huge place still smouldering we were paid off and given a railway ticket for home from the Labour Exchange.

OLIVE MAY TAYLOR

'Miss Adventure'

Last week a series of articles by Harold Begbie, entitled 'Miss Adventure' appeared in the 'Daily Chronicle'. The 'Miss' in question is the girl of 1917, and her adventures are her experiences in the new sphere of work that is now open to her. Mr. Begbie describes the girl on the bus, on the van, in the tube; the office girl who, after hours, devotes her free time to taking blind soldiers for walks, which not infrequently end at the registry-office; the bank-clerk girl who has come to stay on the lower slopes of finance though, in the guise of fortune-teller he cannot predict for her a triumphant stand on its summit.

Mr. Begbie dilates upon all the attractions of the 1917 girl, her pluck, her courtesy, her adaptability, her clothes, her appearance. His flattery stands in need of the proverbial grain of salt, but underlying his innumerable flippancies there is a fairly comprehensive sketch of the kind of work girls are doing that used to be considered only possible for men, and much shrewd – if delicately conveyed – criticism.

Mr. Begbie lays great stress on the fact that the majority of bus conductor girls and girl van-drivers are drawn from the ranks of domestic service. Now that they have become inured to the roughness of their out-of-door life, they will be most unwilling to relinquish its variety and independence for the monotony of the kitchen. This is a point which will demand consideration after the war. Besides these bus girls are earning about 48/- a week – 'good money' as they call it – and will not find it easy or pleasant to adapt themselves to the old régime. Mr. Begbie draws a contrast between the girl on the bus, and the 'young lady' in the bank who is starving herself on 22/- a week. These clerks are of two kinds, he says; the girl who is trying to better herself – the genuine worker – and the girl who has gone into business as a piece of patriotism. Here he is touching upon one of the most serious problems connected with women's war-work, and one which promises to complicate that process of industrial reconstruction which must follow the war.

The so-called patriotic girl, who is not dependent on what she earns for her livelihood and who cheerfully accepts 22/- or 25/- a week, is doing the real worker an irreparable injury. Far from saving the State expense, she is running up a heavy bill which sooner or later must be paid. She is forcing down the wage-rate so that it is insufficient for the self-dependent worker, who cannot however hold out for higher pay as there is always another patriot ready to undersell her labour. The result is loss of efficiency to the worker and so to the State, and further the prospect of still greater hardship after the war when labour is no longer at a premium.

What is wanted is to bring the 'patriotic worker' to some reali-sation of what she is doing, so that she may be induced to refuse a wage on which she cannot live. She need not fear she is costing the State more than she need. If she has surplus wealth at her dis-posal she can invest it in the war loan. Meanwhile she is converting her pseudo-patriotism into the genuine article. Incidentally she will probably increase the market-value of her own labour. The work of a girl who is neither taking herself nor her occupation seriously cannot be the best of which she is capable.

Manchester Guardian, 21 November 1917

Chaos of Women's War Work

FEMININE AUTOCRATS
—I find that there has long been among the most experienced and far-seeing women a conviction that the time had come to secure some sort of co-operation, with the establishment of a cen-tral directorate, which should leave the various main services free to carry on their work, but which should devise some scheme to

avoid the endless overlapping and rivalry, establish a standard of efficiency, and see that the work women are urgently required for is carried on on democratic and sensible lines.

The great hindrance is felt to be the aristocratic or autocratic woman's determination to hang on to the prestige and power accruing from her position in the amateur society, and her fixed conviction that the purple-blooded war-worker is designed by nature for higher things than comradeship and equality with the less delicately nurtured; that she may earnestly desire to devote herself to the nation's need, but that she cannot be expected to enter any service through the portals of the labour exchanges. This has been the real trouble with the V.A.D.'s – the stubborn determination of the governing committee not to surrender a particle of its power or privilege.

In London alone there are at least eighty-six women's societies, each with its own more or less expensive offices, propaganda, and administration, doing war work of more or less value, and work that is more or less distinct, but that could quite well come in under a scheme of wide co-operation. This might be sufficiently amusing and harmless in ordinary circumstances, but at present it means, as leading women have assured me, that the best and most important work of the country is being held up, and plans of supreme importance are being thwarted at every turn, with a certain prospect that in the immediate future things will become infinitely worse.

By a Woman Correspondent

Deutsche Frauen Deutsche Treue

Four Months as a Munitions Worker

As the war went on, the 'WUMBA' (Berlin Weapons and Munitions Production Office for Field Artillery) ordered two large munitions factories to be built right next to our town too. But very soon there was a shortage of male workers there. And so, at the end of April 1917, all the town's women and girls were asked to come and work in these factories. At the time this seemed to be the most important assistance one could offer, and when we heard from the captain running the factories that no one from the educated classes had yet volunteered, and that hundreds of workers were urgently required, our decision was made. Together with two friends, my sister and I volunteered for duty immediately.

All we had to do was make the necessary purchases: large long-sleeved aprons; an enamel dish and spoon for our evening meal; a coffee pot and mug and a light straw bag in which all these items could be properly stowed away, together with our bread and margarine. Then, somewhat apprehensively, given the completely unknown situation that lay before us, we set off for the factory for the first time.

We began with an eight-hour shift from 3 in the afternoon until 11 in the evening. We were supposed to have changed shifts the following week, but we agreed with our work-mates that we would always work the 'night shift'.

Every day we left our parental home at just after 2pm. A twenty-minute walk took us to a small temporary station, where we boarded a worker's train for a fifteen-minute ride which took us close to the factory; then we had another five-minute walk to the work-sheds of the Bürgerfelde Munitions Factory.

Initially we were all put in the sewing room, where day after day we had to sew thousands of little bags which were then filled with barrel powder for the cartridges in another department. We felt as if we had been transported back to our school days – except that our school benches had been far more comfortable than the rough wooden benches without back rests on which we had to sit here. We sewed without interruption – apart from a short coffee break and a half-hour supper break, when we could straighten ourselves up again and stretch our legs. Supervisors walked up and down, inspecting our sewing and making sure that the conversation amongst the more than 100 female workers gathered in the room didn't grow too loud. Our backs often hurt from this unaccustomed sitting. Our heads often ached terribly in the bad air, which you could almost have cut with a knife. But we carried out this uninteresting work very conscientiously. We scored a psychological success too. Following our example, around 70 young girls volunteered for duty.

After a few days my sister was posted to the office, which was in urgent need of assistance. She had passed her Abitur and teaching exams, so she was best suited to fill this post. She was responsible for working out the quantities of powder, cartridge cases and fuses needed for the ammunition trains commissioned, and for ensuring that any materials the factory was short of were ordered in good time—

After a few weeks, at our own request, we were moved on to 'heavy work', where we had to put the howitzer shells together with the brass cases containing the powder, and equip them with fuses.—It was hard work and required a good deal of energy; all the more so because the air in the relatively low barrack was often unbearable. For despite the heat – it was July by now – we were not allowed to air the rooms, even during our meal breaks. Doors and windows had to be kept permanently shut because of the danger of explosions. But we prided ourselves on never slacking, on always keeping up with the professional workers. Here too the harmonious relationships we enjoyed with them was clear. For if ever this completely unaccustomed work proved too much for one of us, one of the workers would help out as a matter of course, smiling, 'Leave that to me, miss – it's far too hard for you!' We never really thought about the immediate danger we were in. But during this time three young girls, who had recently started work in the other munitions factory, were fatally injured by a grenade which fell and exploded.

Even today we still like to think back to the time when we were able to serve the Fatherland, working with our hands at one with the people.

EDITHA VON KRELL

The Victorious Midinette

The successful strike of the 'midinettes' of Paris is an outcome of the war, and more especially of the Franco-British alliance, with which every Englishman who knows his Paris will sympathise. The midinette is the assistant in the dressmaking business for which Paris is world-famous. Without her the 'creations' that rule fashion in time of peace could not be. She has formed the 'beauty chorus' of half a dozen British musical comedies with scenes in Paris, and has been the central figure of a score of sentimental novels about Paris by writers who did not trouble to give more than one side of the picture of her life. With her neat costume, rakish hat, and bandbox over her arm she has typified Paris for the Englishman in many a drawing that was more gay than truthful. Paris, as the 'Temps' said the other day, is as proud of her as Venice of its pigeons, 'but while the pigeons serve only to orna-ment the Place of St. Mark, the midinettes work for the wealth of Paris.' Hitherto they have worked six full days a week for a wage that would not content their English sisters. They have struck for the English week-end and a rise in wages to meet the cost of living. They have had processions through the streets and demonstrations in their favourite restaurants, and they have main-tained their demand with a spirit, a gaiety, and a determination that have won them general support and secured for them a rise of a franc a day and the promise of a 'loi sur la semaine anglaise' which will set them free, on a full day's pay, from mid-day on Saturdays. The strike culminated appropriately enough in a riotously merry reception given by the girls to a British Guards' band which has gone to play in Paris and which has been smoth-ered in flowers and flags. This extension of the British working week to the most famous body of French work-women is a pleas-ant fruit of the Entente. Next time it may well be our turn to borrow from France.

From Field Marshal Sir Douglas Haig, General Headquarters, British Army in France

Concerts at the Front

June 1917

The Concerts at the Front, organised by Miss Lena Ashwell, have been a source of endless pleasure and relaxation for many thousands of soldiers. I am personally very grateful for the untiring efforts of those who have contributed to make them such a success, and I know that I am only voicing the opinion of all ranks of the army in France in wishing that your scheme may not collapse through lack of funds.

Deutsche Frauen Deutsche Treue

During the War in German East Africa

War was declared. The whole country was in a state of turmoil and excitement. No one had much time to think. Most importantly, we had to equip the colony for defence, for no country ever went to war less prepared than German East Africa.

Trusting that international treaties would be adhered to even in times of war, Germany had envisaged its African defence forces only for the suppression of native uprisings, since the Congo Acts had excluded the possibility of a European war extending to African territory. But our eyes were opened early in August 1914. English ships appeared on the coast of Dar-es-Salaam, demanding the unconditional surrender of the colony, which, of course, was refused.

The demands now made on German women were great. Had they not joined in the defence of the nation as a matter of course, such a long and lasting war would never have been possible—

Everywhere, women had to help with the work: in the hospitals, where the 16 nurses of the Red Cross had long since been insufficient; in the difficult supply of foodstuffs, which, once the remaining European supplies had run out, had to be produced entirely from the land—The women on the larger plantations in the tropical areas planted maize, sweet potatoes (mohogao) and beans to supply the Askaris and porter convoys. This was no easy task, because outdoor work in the heat of the sun was exhausting and the overseeing of large gangs of workers required a considerable degree of authority. Our men were in the battle field, too far away to reach, each individual plantation lay hours away from the next. It would have been so easy for the Negroes to refuse to obey the women and cause all sorts of problems. Yet nothing of the kind happened. The blacks worked willingly and faithfully under the command of the white 'Bibi'. Then, in the summer of 1916 all that came to an end, when the English brought in reinforcements from all over the world to fight against our little army—

Late in the evening of 6 June I had to leave quickly on the orders of the commander of the Northern Troops, since the enemy was advancing. That very night the bridges and the level crossings on the Usambara railway, which I myself had just crossed, were blown up, the trains were crashed or driven into the Pangani River, and anything which could help the enemy's advance was destroyed. The following day he was already marching through our plantation and had taken the railway line. After 17 days of uninterrupted marching on foot, right across the country, accompanied by my faithful boy Omari and a group of my best black people and porters, I reached the town of Morogoro on the midland railway—

Those were terrible days! Our German troops had moved south. The night before they left they blew up the station and the bridges, munitions stores and all store rooms. We were left behind in this hellish noise, which we could only interpret as enemy fire— It was not until 48 hours later that the first English patrol came through the town, their revolvers outstretched, believing Lettow-Vorbeck himself to be behind every house. We stared in wonder at the beautiful horses. In the whole campaign we had only had two mounted companies, and the faithful horses had long ago fallen victim to the insidious tsetse illness. We became even more amazed when car after car arrived and countless motor bikes raced through the hitherto peaceful little town, making a deafening noise day and night. Troops from all arms of the services and in all colours and shades, on foot and on horseback, moved through the town, on a scale larger than all our forces in the colony put together. We had always been proud of Lettow-Vorbeck and the achievements of our soldiers, but at the sight of this massive troop contingent, and the modern war machinery with which they were equipped, which seemed almost fantastical in our eyes, but which nevertheless had not been able to force our little army to surrender, we were doubly proud and grateful to our admirable defenders.

In their disappointment at finding nothing but women and children and not a single healthy man in the whole town, the English and their allied Boors *(sic)* tried to take revenge on us day after day by bullying and harassing us—

The enemy commander-in-chief, General Smuts, remained in Morogoro for weeks. I must say in his honour that in spite of everything, we owe him a great deal. It was due to his strict order that any soldier who came too close to a woman would be severely punished, that only minor incidents occurred, at least in this respect.

I lived in my tent in Morogoro until October of that year – every room in every house was filled with refugees. Then I received permission to return to our plantation. After a four-day journey in a car with no suspension, sitting at the front next to the driver, my boy Omari sitting at the back on top of my luggage, we travelled for twelve hours a day on a reckless journey up mountains and down valleys, through swamps and rivers, over stones and tree stumps, through sand and over rocks, in the unbearable heat of the sun. As far as possible, the friendly driver tried to make the journey easy for me. But worse than the strains of the journey were the terrible things we saw on the way. Death had reaped a dreadful harvest among the English thoroughbred horses, who were far too refined for this country, and among cows, goats and sheep who had been no match for the forced marches demanded of them. Hundreds of corpses in all stages of decay filled the roads and made the air almost unbearable. Swarms of flies and vultures fought with hyenas over the disgusting plundering of bodies, or hung around mortally ill animals who waited for their end, shivering, their eyes begging for help.

And above all this horror was the stifling, merciless sun! More dead than alive myself, I arrived near our plantation and learned that our house had been completely robbed and destroyed.

After much to-ing and fro-ing, accommodation was found for me in Wugiri, in a convalescent home established by the German woman's association of the Red Cross in the western Usambara region, where a number of women and children were already massed.

Thus began the third and darkest period of my stay in German East Africa: my period of imprisonment! Cut off from the whole world, with no news of our men (all we knew was that the wounded and sick had been transported to India), with no links with the small remnants of our heroic army still fighting, we spent the years between hope and fear—

Two and a half years! Then came our hour of liberation. But what a liberation! Expelled from the country like criminals, we were loaded on lighters with our luggage, in front of our boys and the many other natives who had remained loyal to us to the end, taken on board an Australian troop transporter and, squashed together, we were sent off home. German women have probably never been treated in a more humiliating way than we were then by the allegedly most chivalrous nation in the world. Nevertheless, I often think back on the war years in East Africa with great pride, and am grateful that I was one of the German women who were able to take part in the great struggle. And I will never stop hoping and working for the day when our wonderful country becomes German again.

HILDEGARDE VON LECKOW

Air Raids and Rations

A *Zeppelin Shot Down*

4 September 1916

Dearest Mums,

I will now tell you about the Raid last night – the sight of my life!

It was the second night of London lighting or rather no-lighting orders. At 2.30 I was wakened by a terrific explosion & was at the window in one bound when another deafening one shook the house. Nearly above us sailed a cigar of bright silver in the full glare of about 20 magnificent search lights. A few lights roamed round trying to pick up her companion. Our guns made a deafening row & shells burst all around her. For some extraordinary reason she was dropping no bombs. The night was absolutely still with a few splendid stars. It was a magnificent sight & the whole of London was looking on holding its breath. She was only a little way to the east of me & I had a topping view as there's a stone balcony outside the window. I yelled for field glasses to Captain Hermani *(?)* but he was escorting the whole household to the cellars cook was howling *(word indecipherable)* so sat on the window ledge in my dressing gown. The Zepp headed slowly north amid a rain of shells & crashing artillery fire from all

quarters. She was pretty high up but was enormous 600ft long I
shd say. Capt. H came up & joined me & we watched for another
5 minutes when suddenly her nose dropped & I yelled
'Getroffen'. But she righted again & went into a cloud (or possibly she made herself!) Then the searchlights scientifically
examined that cloud to help the airmen but she didn't appear &
we thought the fun was over as the guns stopped. Then – from
the direction of Barnet & very high a brilliant red light appeared
(we thought it was an English fire balloon for a minute!) Then
we saw it was the Zepp-diving head first. *That* was quite a sight.
She dived slowly at first as only the foremost ballonet was on fire.
Then the second burst & the flames tore up into the sky & then
the third & cheers thundered all round us from every direction.
The glare lit up all London & was rose red. Those deaths must
be the most dramatic in the worlds history. They fell – a cone of
blazing wreckage thousands of feet – watched by millions of
their enemies.

It was magnificent the most thrilling scene imaginable.

This afternoon I went out to Barnet (so did 3/4 of London!)
The wreck covers only 30ft of ground & the dead are under a tarpaulin. The engineer was gripping the steering wheel and one
man was headless. I hope they will be buried with full military
honours. They were brave men. R.I.P! — The engine is at the
W/O. The Zepp fell close to Cuffley Church & telescoped when
she hit the ground.

MURIEL DAYRELL-BROWNING

Letter Home

Buckingham Palace
25th September 1917

We had a tremendous raid last night, at least it seemed tremendous because they came so much nearer to me, personally, than
they have ever done before. There is a huge hole in the Green

Park just by the Ritz Entrance and all the back windows of Arlington Street are shivered to atoms, and I am told there is a hole in the Courtyard of Devonshire House. I don't know much about the extent of the damage, but they appear to have got Highbury and Highgate very badly again. It was most exciting as a lot of our own aeroplanes were up last night and there were tremendous fights going on in the darkness though I have not heard that any were brought down. The forecourt of B.P. was scattered with bits of shrapnel, and they picked up the nose of a shell in the garden this morning. Rather a narrow shave for poor Kingie, who was watching the whole performance with great interest from his window.

CELIA CROFT

Diary

Waltham Abbey, Essex, 1917
Oct 20

I haven't had an instant to write up my diary owing to the constant raids. We had five in quick succession. It is not necessary to describe them all, but perhaps my first experience of a raid when on duty may be interesting. The hooters sounded about 6.30 before the girls' supper hour — There are no real shelters for the girls who have to leave the danger sheds & crouch under the clean-ways. There are raised gangways which lead from one shed to another. The ground underneath is often very wet, & covered with nettles, also there are some rats, & always plenty of slugs. These small matters make it extremely difficult to get the girls to go under cover, & still more difficult to keep them there.

MISS G. M. WEST

Lilian Baylis: The Lady of the Old Vic

About this time Lilian began to be known by the audience, largely as a result of the speeches she made to them. These began during the German air raids—And although it was some years before she learned to do it well, she seems to have enjoyed the exercise. Henry Kendall recalled her speech as going something like this: 'Now boys and girls, we're not going to let Kaiser Bill interfere with the Vic, and so we shall carry on with this beautiful play, and if you up there on the top shelf would feel any safer you can come down and sit in the stalls – and I won't charge you any extra.' Or, more brusquely, she would bark: 'Will all those who wish to leave please do so at once? *We* are carrying on.' She gave the company no option. Once, when bombs began to drop during an opera rehearsal, everyone on stage stopped and took shelter in the wings, until Miss Baylis appeared in a blazing temper. First, she had been made to stay in the Tube against her will. Now, she discovered that her company had deserted their posts. 'I'm ashamed of you all,' she shouted at them. 'If you have to be killed, at least die at your job.' A guilty witness reported that 'we all went back to work feeling that somehow we had failed'. One evening a raid began when Sybil Thorndike was on her way to play in *Richard II*. As she came out of the Tube at Waterloo she was stopped by a policeman.

'"I can't help the raid," I cried, clinging to his brass buttons. "The curtain's up at the Old Vic, and I shan't be on for my entrance."

'"Old Vic, is it," he said. "Oh, I know Miss Baylis; yes, you're right," and a lull coming in the bomb sounds, he gave me a push into Waterloo Road with a: "Now run for your life, and if you're killed, don't blame me – blame Her."

'I got to the pit door – first door I reached – and found Lilian in a fume and fret.

'"Why on earth weren't you in before this?"

'"A raid," I said. "Everything underground at Waterloo – everything impossible."

'"Raid," she snorted. "What's a raid when my curtain's up?"

The fact that the Vic played through the raids helped to give it an aura of special patriotism. On the first night of *King John*, in September 1917, the nine-year-old Agnes Carter, playing Prince Arthur, and Ben Greet, as Hubert, 'went through their scenes without turning a hair'; and the lines at the end

> This England never did, nor never shall
> Lie at the proud foot of a conqueror

brought the house down. These lines were put up above the proscenium arch for the rest of the war. A sign of the status so rapidly acquired by the Vic was that it was here – in February, 1918 – that a roll of honour was erected (somewhat prematurely) with the names of those musicians, actors and writers who had died in wartime service. The roll was placed above the stage door and unveiled by the Bishop of Southwark. Lewis Casson read out the 142 names. And every year thereafter a ceremony of remembrance was held on the eve of Armistice Day, after the performance, at which the Last Post was sounded, a hymn was sung, a wreath was laid and, later, a maroon was fired (or rather misfired) by the master-carpenter.

RICHARD FINDLATER

Memoir

During the air-raids, if we were on the night-shift at the factory we often kept working but if it got very noisy and the explosions sounded close, we trooped into a sort of garage place. It was my job as an 'examiner' to grab the first-aid box and check that all my girls were safe. If there was a night raid while I was working days, my mother insisted we all went to the crypt of our local All

Hallows Church. With so many people packed in and some of them cooking their suppers on primus stoves, the condensation poured down the walls like Niagara Falls. Later on, when the Zeppelin raids got worse, we went down into the tube at Mornington Crescent. People either slept on the platforms or, if they couldn't stand the smell and the snoring, travelled round and round on the tubes which kept running. So did the trams. They rattled up and down outside our factory in the Grays Inn Road throughout the raids.

By 1917 we had ration books for quite a lot of foods but we didn't register with shops, not like in the Second World War. You'd 'get the wire' that the Maypole or the Home and Colonial had extra stuff and you'd go and stand in line. While you were there you'd hear that Ridgeways had extra tea and you'd proceed to line up there. I don't remember using the world 'queue' then. If you had a soldier member of the family home on leave you'd send him to stand in line because the shop-keepers always served people in uniform first.

ALICE CONNOR NÉE KEDGE

How We Lived Then

The First National Kitchen: 21 May 1917

The Queen opened the first Ministry of Food national kitchen, and, helped by Princess Mary, served a number of customers. Her Majesty seemed quite agitated by one minute child, who, reaching up to receive its purchase from the counter, seemed in imminent danger of spilling a plateful of scalding rice pudding on to the top of its head. In those days people had not learned the art of buying their dinners at public kitchens, and many of them omitted to bring any kind of receptacle, and, in order that they should not be too late to be served by the Queen, rushed madly home again to fetch a jug or basin. Cornflour and rhubarb jelly was one of the sweets of the day, and a supply of this dish had been put ready on a lower shelf of a serving-table. The enterprising and social yellow dog, which attends all functions from race to missionary meetings, naturally decided to attend the opening of the Westminster Bridge kitchen, and was discovered, having dodged through a mass of legs and squeezed himself behind the counter, sitting licking a pink mould with the greatest appreciation. Presently one of the servers came and shoo'd him away, but did not remove the pudding. One wondered who ate that pudding, because the yellow dog had licked it very neatly, and it still looked shapely and shining.

While the Queen was ladling out food a very old man shambled up and bought meat, vegetables and pudding, which he proceeded to place all together on a very dirty plate and cover them with a still dirtier piece of newspaper. He then shambled out, never having realized who it was who had served him. The fact that it was the Queen must have been pointed out to him by the crowd outside, for shortly afterwards he returned, edged his way back to the serving counter and solemnly waved his hat three times.

Mrs C. S. Peel

Life's Enchanted Cup

At the Ministry of Food – and Pensions

There was no monotony about our work in Grosvenor House, and it had its humours. Changes were frequent both of staff and of rooms, and often one would hear snatches of conversations, such as: 'Where is so-and-so's secretary now?' 'Oh, he is in the Duchess's bathroom.' Or, 'Fats have moved, haven't they?' 'Yes, they are up in the nurseries.' 'Where have Public Meals got to?' 'They used to be in Number Nine, but exchange says Fish is there now,' and so forth.

Some of the hundreds of orders which were issued afforded mirth. One concerned poultry food, and ran as follows:—Scheme (B). 'Other birds, being hen birds, hatched since January 1st, 1916, and not receiving rations under Scheme (A) will be able to obtain certificates entitling their owners to purchase up to an amount per head per day (which will be less than two ounces per day) to be fixed from time to time, according to the quality of food stuffs available.'

Sometimes, too, one smiled at the strange manner in which duties were allotted to members of the staff. It appeared that if you were an expert in one subject, that seemed the best possible reason for not allowing you to deal with it. On going to a certain section one of our secretaries found a gentleman of her acquaintance. 'But what are you doing here?' she asked, 'I thought you were the greatest living authority on fish.' 'Precisely,' was the bland reply, 'and that is why I am controlling mangel-wurzels.' Life was even brighter in other Ministries – notably so, it is said, in the Air Ministry – while according to the accounts of a friend who worked in the Separation Allowance Department of the Ministry of Pensions, some of the letters received cheered the staff considerably. Our friend declared that the following examples were genuine:

'You have changed my little boy into a little girl. Will it make any difference?'

'My Bill has been put in charge of a spittoon. Will I get any more pay?'

'I am glad to tell you that my husband has now been repotted dead.'

'I have not received any pay since my husband was confined in a constipation camp in Germany.'

'If I don't get my husband's money soon, I shall be compelled to go on the streets and lead an imortal life.'

'In accordance with instructions on ring paper I have given birth to twins enclosed in envelope.'

'I have been in bed with the doctor for three days. He doesn't

seem to do me any good. If you don't send my money soon I
shall have to go to another one.'

Mrs C. S. Peel

Berliner Leben 1914–18

Memoir of a Woman Worker

Until the year 1915 things were just about OK. But then the starvation began. If you had children you received cabbage and some
food which you had to collect from Caseler Strasse. At work
horse-meat and sausages and margarine were handed out.
Because I wasn't doing any *war* work our allowance was very
small. And then there was the cold. Transport on the suburban
railway was catastrophic. Only when the compartments were full
to the brim could you get a little warmer. But the train often
stopped for an hour on the track and we froze again. At work ici-
cles formed on the windows. There was no coal. We had to work
with numb fingers and so we earned less. Now and then there
was coal at the Wissensee Goods Depot. I was lucky to own a
handcart. I found the largest sack I could and hurried there. Then
the battle to get close to the wagon began. You needed the utmost
strength to hold up the sack until it was full. If you started to drop
it you were ruthlessly pushed aside.

'Kups'

Revolution in Russia and Women Soldiers

War Diary: Russia, 1917

The Abdication of the Czar

One day we heard a rumour that the Czar had abdicated. No one paid much attention to it and no one seemed particularly interested, but a few days later I was off duty reading in my room, which looked on to the road and suddenly thought 'What an enormous number of soldiers there are on the move to-day.' I looked out of the window and regiment after regiment marched by. I went out and enquired into things, and was told that just outside the village in a large field there was a ceremonial parade and that the abdication of the Czar was to be read to the troops. It was very, very cold and my room was very warm and cosy. I nearly sat down to my book again, then thought 'Goodness, this is history, I mustn't miss it.' I tore on my gumboots etc., and rushed off in pursuit of the soldiers. I found thousands of them formed into a gigantic hollow square with various Generals and bigwigs and a bishop and priests in the centre. I edged my way in amongst the men as I was very curious to see what their reactions would be. Interminable prayers were read and long speeches were made. All the soldiers standing rigidly to attention were frozen to the bone, poor things, and when the great moment came and the abdication of the Czar was announced it was a complete anti-climax. Nothing happened at all. No one appeared to care in the least. The only thing they did care about was to get off the bitingly cold wind-swept field and back to some sort of warmth. Still it was very interesting to hear it. I was glad I had gone.

KATHERINE HODGES

Co-operative News, 3 June 1917

Women's Co-operative Guild Congress at Torquay: Resolution on the Russian Revolution

We women co-operators, assembled in Congress, rejoice with our Russian comrades at the dawn of a new day for freedom and brotherhood in their country. The revolution has brought new hope to us in England, and we trust that the social reforms foreshadowed will build up a co-operative state in Russia which will lay the foundation of the international co-operation essential to world-wide peace. We also welcome with admiration and enthusiasm the Russian appeal to the people of all nations to meet together to find a base for an international peace without conquest, which shall be founded on the free development of nations and shall lead to permanent international concord.

CARRIED BY 207 TO 73 VOTES

Daily Graphic, 8 June 1917

What I Shall Say to the Russians

I am going to Russia because I think our organisation can do some useful work in the cause of the Allies. We can make a special appeal to the Russian people—We are the real revolutionaries; we don't merely talk about it; we have had it; and we suspended our revolution because we realised that our first duty was to preserve our country and to be loyal to our Allies in the war. Someone said of me, 'I think it is a good thing she should go because she has been to her Siberia.' Because we have not been platform revolutionaries. We have suffered prison, forcible feeding, all these things; therefore they will be ready to hear what we have got to say. I should think I have addressed more public meetings on the war than almost anybody else; from the early days when we had our own recruiting compaign. A large number of them have been meetings in connection with industrial unrest; others have been special meetings for women, open-air meetings; meetings in halls, in drawing-rooms, in churches. I believe we can put the case for the war as it is felt by the ordinary men and women of this country.

There are people going over to Russia or trying to go, who will claim to speak in the name of the working-classes, but who do not represent the mass of the people. They represent only a very small minority, and they have no right whatever to speak either in the name of organised labour or the general mass of the people. What a pretty friend of humanity a man is who won't fight for his own country! And these British pacifists will make big claims in Petrograd to represent the people of this country, when the fact is there is not a constituency in this country where they could get elected. They dare not hold an open meeting.

Last Sunday I took the opinion of a big meeting in Hyde Park. I said I was going to Russia. One man asked that it should be put to the vote. I said that although I might not be in agreement with the audience on ordinary political questions, yet on the war I did represent them; that we were all united against an inconclusive peace, that we were in the war to avenge Belgium and Serbia and to win such a victory that the world would be free from the German menace. Only two hands were held up against me.

What I want to do is to make the Russian masses realise that the masses of the British people are of one mind for this war; that we are not in it for aggrandisement or anything of that sort, but that we are fighting against the enemies of freedom; that the whole future of civilisation depends upon whether the world is to be free or enslaved.

MRS PANKHURST

Yashka: My Life as Peasant, Exile and Soldier

The Women's 'Battalion of Death'

It was the evening of May 21, 1917. I was driven to the Mariynski Theatre and escorted by Captain Dementiev and his wife into the former Imperial box. The house was packed, the receipts of the ticket office amounting to thirty thousand roubles. Everybody seemed to be pointing at me, and it was with great difficulty that I controlled my nerves.

Kerensky appeared and was given a tremendous reception. He spoke only about ten minutes. Next on the programme was Madame Kerensky, and I was to follow her. Madame Kerensky, however, broke down as soon as she found herself confronted by the audience. That did not add to my courage. I was led forward as if in a trance.

'Men and women citizens!' I heard my voice say. 'Our mother is perishing. Our mother is Russia. I want to help to save her. I want women whose hearts are loyal, whose souls are pure, whose aims are high. With such women setting an example of self-sacrifice, you men will realize your duty in this grave hour!'—

Before I had time to realize it I was already in a photographer's studio, and there had my portrait taken. The following day this picture appeared at the head of big posters pasted all over the city, announcing my appearance at the Mariynski Theatre for the purpose of organizing a Women's Battalion of Death—

On the morning of May 26 all the recruits gathered in the grounds of the Institute. I had them placed in rows, so as to arrange them according to their height, and divided the whole body into two battalions of approximately one thousand each. Each battalion was divided into four companies, and each company subdivided into four platoons. There was a man instructor in command of every platoon, and in addition there was an officer in command of every company, so that altogether I had to increase the number of men instructors to forty.

I addressed the women again, informing them that from the moment that they entered upon their duties they were no longer women, but soldiers. I told them that they would not be allowed to leave the grounds, and that only between six and eight in the evening would they be permitted to receive relatives and friends. From among the more intelligent recruits – and there were many university graduates in the ranks – I selected a number for promotion to platoon and company officers, their duties being limited to the domestic supervision of the troop, since the men commanders were purely instructors, returning to their barracks at the end of the day's work.

Next I marched the recruits to four barbers' shops, where from five in the morning to twelve at noon a number of barbers cut short the hair of one woman after another. Crowds outside the shops watched this unaccustomed proceeding, greeting with jeers each woman as she emerged, with hair close cropped and perhaps with an aching heart, from the barber's saloon.

The same afternoon my soldiers received their first lessons in the large garden. A recruit was detailed to stand guard at the gate and not to admit anybody without the permission of the officer in charge. The watch was changed every two hours. A high fence surrounded the grounds, and the drilling went on without interference. Giggling was strictly forbidden, and I kept a sharp watch over the women. I had about thirty of them dismissed without ceremony the first day. Some were expelled for too much laughing, others for frivolities. Several of them threw themselves at my feet, begging for mercy. However, I made up my mind that without severity I might just as well give up my project at the beginning. If my word was to carry weight, it must be final and unalterable, I decided. How could one otherwise expect to manage two thousand women? As soon as one of them disobeyed an order I quickly removed her uniform and sent her away—

One day the sentry reported to the officer in charge that two women, one a famous Englishwoman, wanted to see me. I ordered the Battalion to remain at attention while I received the two callers, who were Emmeline Pankhurst and Princess Kikuatova, the latter of whom I knew.

Mrs Pankhurst was introduced to me, and I ordered the Battalion to salute the eminent visitor who had done so much for women and her country. Mrs Pankhurst became a frequent visitor to the Battalion, watching it with deep interest as it grew into a well-disciplined military unit. We became very much attached to each other. Mrs Pankhurst invited me to a dinner at the Astoria, the leading hotel in Petrograd, at which Kerensky and the various Allied representatives in the capital were to be present.

MARIA BOTCHKAREVA
(AS SET DOWN BY ISSAC DON LEVINE)

War Diary: Russia, 1917

I remember nothing about the journey from Kieff to Petrograd. When we reached the latter we went straight to the Anglo-Russian Hospital and Lady Muriel Paget very kindly invited us to stay there. I should like to say how very, very good Lady Muriel and her staff were to every British Unit wandering through the city —I then started a strenuous campaign through all sorts of Russian bureaus, the British Red Cross, the Consul, the British Permit Office, to try and get our papers in order for leaving the country — Every office seemed to be full of Samovars and tumblers of pale tea and lemon. When in doubt, drink tea, seems to be the Russian motto.

At one of the many interviews, the Russian bigwig to whom I

was talking asked me if H.G. and I would inspect the now Famous Women's Battalion of Death, as he thought that we, in our war uniforms, would be interesting to them. We were tremendously flattered at this and accepted with pleasure.

At the appointed time, H. G. and I furnished up to the best of our ability, proceeded to the meeting place, a huge building in the middle of the city. We progressed through several large rooms with all the women soldiers lined up for our inspection. We felt ourselves Generals at least, as we (*smartly* I trust), took the salute through each room. Every sort and class of woman seemed to be represented. They had not sufficient military uniforms, but they were all in breeches or trousers of sorts, some of them clad in the most amazing hotch-potch of garments. They were young and old, peasant and aristocrat, a most extraordinary mixture.

After the inspection we had an interview with the woman commanding. She asked us if we would stay and join the Battalion to organise a motor-unit for it. We told her we would let her know the next day. After thinking it over very carefully we decided that as she had no cars as yet, merely a vague promise for the future, and as we should have to teach the women how to drive and such mechanical knowledge as we possessed, all in Russian, we thought it was no use attempting it.

The Woman Commandant told us she did not expect women to be any real use as active combatants, but that her whole idea was to restore the morale of the ordinary troops by the force of example. This, I fear, did not work out according to plan for I was told, possibly untruly, I don't know, that when the Battalion left Petrograd for the Front there was a dreadful scene at the station, several of the women being badly man-handled, some deaths occurring as a result. I also heard that every woman carried cyanide potassium, to take if she was made prisoner & feared rape or torture.

KATHERINE HODGES

The Times, 26 July 1917

The Women's Soldiers of Russia

Mrs Rheta Childe Dorr, an American writer who has just returned from the Women's 'Battalion of Death', with which she went to the front, says:

—I lived with them for two weeks. There are women of all types, peasants, intellectuals, doctors, stenographers, telephone girls, and others. Whilst we were travelling from Petrograd crowds on the station made fun of us, asking 'Why do you girls want to fight?' 'Because you men are cowards,' retorted the women. The first night after we reached the front near Vilna there was a pounding on the door, and a Jewish girl sentinel gave the challenge. 'Aren't the girls in here?' asked some soldiers outside. 'We are not girls, we are soldiers,' said the sentinel, stepping out. 'If you don't go away we will shoot.' They went — It rained every day, but the women carried out their drill and practices in sharp-shooting unfailingly. They lived just as the men do, with this difference, that their commander, Mme. Botchkareva, who is now wounded, was about four times stricter — The only sign of mutiny I ever saw grew out of the demand made by the women to go into battle. When word came that they were to move nearer the front, their 'Hurrahs' lasted many minutes. These women have overthrown every convention and forgotten everything women have ever been taught. You have no idea how nice women can be when they are absolutely natural and unselfish — It had never occurred to me before that women ought to go to war, but I am convinced now that in any country under such conditions women ought to step into the breach, guns in hand. It is their country as much as the men's.

RHETA CHILDE DORR

Bolsheviks and the Battalion of Death

The committee and my friends, numbering about one hundred, insisted that I should be given a trial and not lynched. My girls were ready to die for me to the last one. I was taken out from the dugout by my defenders, who made an effort to lead me to safety for an open trial.

The mob, which had now increased, pressed closer and closer. The two sides were fighting for me. It was agreed that no weapons were to be used in the scramble. The mass of humanity swayed back and forth, my girls fighting with the strength of infuriated wild beasts to stave off the mob. Now and then a man would get close enough to strike a blow at me. As the struggle developed these blows increased in number till I was knocked senseless. In that state my friends dragged me away from the scene of the struggle.

My life was saved, although I was badly knocked about. It cost the lives of a loyal girl and an innocent friend—

Life for the Battalion was becoming absolutely unbearable, at least at this part of the front. It was difficult to understand the change which had come over the men in a few months. How long ago was it that they almost worshipped me, and I loved them? Now they seemed to have lost their senses.

The General advised me to disband the Battalion. But that would be to admit failure and despair as to my country's condition. I was not ready to make such admissions. No, I would not disband my unit. I would fight to the end.

MARIA BOTCHKAREVA
(AS SET DOWN BY ISSAC DON LEVINE)

Odessa: July 1917

It was at this juncture that Dr. Inglis conceived the plan of conveying to the home authorities some account of the real state of affairs, and at her suggestion Dr. Jambrishak (Member of the Jugo-Slav Committee) then in Odessa, drew up a report of the political situation as it affected the Serbs. This report was given to Miss Robinson and Miss Holme, members of the Transport, who were returning to England.

To carry away any written document, especially of such a confidential nature, was, however, impossible, so Miss Robinson committed it all, some 2500 words, to memory. On a small piece of paper about an inch square the headings of the report were written out and secreted by Miss Holme in a needle-case. In this manner a detailed account of the position of the Serbs was conveyed from Russia.

EVA SHAW MCLAREN

Daily Mail, 5 April 1917

The Woman Sergeant Major

Few women have had such exciting exploits in the great war as Miss Flora Sandes. She has been in all the Serbian campaigns, first as a nurse and then as a soldier. At Prilep she stayed to work in the hospital, the only English woman there, and she sat up in bed in the night with an electric torch in one hand and a service revolver in the other, as the Bulgarians were expected to come in and sack the town. During the retreat into the Albanian mountains she was taken on as an ordinary soldier and had her share of the desperate fighting.

She has now received the gold and silver cross of Karageorge –

a rare Serbian badge only given for conspicuous gallantry in the field. Here is her letter:

I daresay you've heard that I got knocked out by a Bulgar hand-bomb, so I never got into Monastir after all; but I've had a very good run for my money all the same, as I had three months' incessant fighting without a scratch.

The newspaper account of the fighting was all off the line. The fighting was a sight that day, but, unfortunately, I only saw the start of it. There was deep snow on the ground, the bugle was blowing the charge, and we were going up the steep hillside while the Bulgars, hidden by the early morning mist at the top, were firing down on us. The Bulgars had counter-attacked at dawn and driven our men back, and everybody was mixed up. There were no trenches or anything like that.

My company were peacefully sleeping in the snow behind a rock, as we were Battalion Reserve that night, when we were called up at dawn as reinforcements. Battalion Reserve is a rotten job. You get all the shell-fire that's going, and you never know what's going on in front until you are suddenly roused out and plunged into the thick of it, as you're only a few hundred yards back and you sleep with your rifle in your hand.

There's first a shout of '—Company forward,' and everyone's off like a streak. When we arrived on the scene the men were rallying for a counter-attack. The bugler had got 'cold feet,' and an officer had taken the bugle and was standing up against the skyline, where everyone could see him, a mark for every bullet, blowing for all he was worth. He wasn't blowing a bit the right notes, but everyone knew what it meant. We knew the position had to be retaken at any cost, as it meant the fall of Monastir if we could.

We went anyhow we liked, taking cover as we could. An officer and about a dozen men and myself got to the top, when some bombers dodged behind the rocks and hurled bombs at us at close range and scattered us.

I was left alone, as I couldn't move, but the officer crawled back right up to the enemy's lines and dragged me back over the snow by my hands to where two of my 'non-coms.' were waiting for him, and then they rolled me up in a piece of tent and half-dragged, half-carried me down the steep hillside to a safe place.

The Serbs are fine comrades. We thought once we should all get taken, but they wouldn't leave me! I've had ever so many cards from them asking when I'm coming back, but as I have twenty-four wounds and a broken arm the doctors seem to think I'll have to wait a bit yet.

'Over the Top in America'

Daily Express, 19 May 1917

The Vanguard of the U.S. Army

The first contingent of the American army for the war, in the shape of a medical unit, arrived in a British port today. This is regarded as a record in American hustling —Sixty-five nurses are with the unit, which numbers between 200 and 300. All are trained nurses from the Lakeside Hospital, the largest institution of the kind in the Middle West. They looked very smart in their blue uniforms, with a brilliant red cross over the left breast of the cloak. They include members of many distinguished American families.

Mobilizing Woman Power

The American woman is going over the top. Four hundred and more are busy on aeroplanes at the Curtiss works. The manager of a munition shop where to-day but fifty women are employed, is putting up a dormitory to accommodate five hundred. An index of expectation! Five thousand are employed by the Remington

Arms Company at Bridgeport. At the International Arms and Fuse Company at Bloomfield, New Jersey, two thousand, eight hundred are employed. The day I visited the place in one of the largest shops women had only just been put on the work, but it was expected that in less than a month they would be found handling all of the twelve hundred machines under that one roof alone.

The skill of the women staggers one. After a week or two they master the operations on the 'turret' gauging and routing machines. The best worker on the 'facing' machine is a woman. She is a piece worker, as many of the women are, and is paid at the same rate as men. This woman earned, the day I saw her, five dollars and forty cents. She tossed about the fuse parts, and played with that machine, as I would with a baby. Perhaps it was in somewhat the same spirit – she seemed to love her toy—

Nor are the railways neglecting to fill up gaps in their working force with women. The Pennsylvania road, it is said, has recruited some seven hundred of them. In the Erie Railroad women are not only engaged as 'work classifiers' in the locomotive clerical department, but hardy Polish women are employed in the car repair shops. They move great wheels as if possessed of the strength of Hercules—

The professional woman is going over the top, and with a good opinion of herself. 'I can do this work better than any man,' was the announcement made by a young woman from the Pacific Coast as she descended upon the city hall in an eastern town, credentials in her hand, and asked for the position of city chemist. There was not a microbe she did not know to its undoing, or a deadly poison she could not bring from its hiding place. The town had suffered from graft, and the mayor, thinking a woman might scare the thieves as well as the bacteria, appointed the chemist who believed in herself. And she is just one of many who have been taking up such work.

Formerly two-thirds of the positions filled by the New York Intercollegiate Bureau of Occupations were secretarial or teaching positions; now three-fourths of its applicants have been placed as physicists, chemists, office managers, sanitary experts, exhibit secretaries, and the like. The temporary positions used to outnumber the permanent placements; at present the reverse is true. Of the women placed, four times as many as formerly get salaries ranging above eighteen hundred dollars a year—

Not only the Labor Department has established a special women's division with a woman at its head, but the Ordnance Office of the War Department has opened in its Industrial Service Section a woman's division, putting Miss Mary Van Kleeck in charge.

But still our government lags behind our Allies in mobilizing woman's power of initiative and her organizing faculty. The Woman's Committee of the Council of National Defense, appointed soon after the outbreak of war, still has no administrative power. As one member of the Committee says, 'We are not allowed to do anything without the consent of the Council of National Defense. There is no appropriation for the Woman's Committee. We are furnished with headquarters, stationery, some printing and two stenographers, but nothing more. It is essential that we raise money to carry on the other expenses. The great trouble is that now, as always, men want women to do the work while they do the overseeing.'

HARRIOT STANTON BLATCH

Daily Mail, 29 October 1917

Splendid American women

1,000,000 MOBILISED
Walking down Madison-avenue (one of New York's famous highways) a few days ago I was attracted to a large house, no. 257, by the continual coming and going of women in khaki.

Up and down the brown stone steps they hurried, obviously intent upon earnest business, and my thoughts were transported to England, and to our members of the Women's Ambulance, Women's Legion, and Women's Volunteer Reserve, wearing a similar trim military uniform of khaki, and moving with the same alertness and smartness that comes of drill and discipline.

Over the doorway the Stars and Stripes hung, brilliant in the hot morning sunshine, and engraved on the portals were the enlightening words: 'Headquarters of the Women's League of National Service.'

The three thousand odd miles intervening between the battlefields of Europe and the United States have been bridged by this common war, which is just as real to the women here as it is to the women of England; for they, too, are giving their sons and sweethearts, and they, too, have come forward to assist in the winning of the war by relieving men for the battlefields, by caring for the troops at home and over seas, and by offering their willing services to the industries of the country.

All these things they are doing through the Women's League of National Service and the various existing organisations, over a hundred of which use the league as a clearing house to co-ordinate their war-time efforts. The league itself, in addition to its central organisation in New York, has State and local branches and working detachments in every part of the United States, and is perfectly organised.

Speaking of organisations, it is very gratifying to us women of England to know that our American sisters turned to the Motherland for the basis of their plan of mobilisation, and that our own V.A.D. has been the foundation on which their wonderful work has been constructed.

Our limitations too have been recognised and have served as a timely warning, for it is insisted that women shall enrol for and perform only those services for which they are fitted. They are adamant in their policy of utilising the trained mind in the direction in which it has been trained, and do not encourage or countenance the expert typist or telephonist to undertake motor driving, or vice versa.

This has brought about a high standard of efficiency. It entirely eliminates the dissipation of feminine energies which was unfortunately so apparent in our own country during the first two years of the war.

G. Ivy Sanders

An Irrepressible Crew: The Smith College Relief Unit

I met Wallace Speers yesterday & he offered to take a few uncensored bits of mail directly home to you, so I seize the opportunity of penning you a line & telling you what it is really like here. In the first place it is frightfully depressing in Paris – the streets are filled with blessés – we've got to the point where we feel as if we had no right to have all our arms and legs. Then in the second place everybody who knows anything on the inside says that the situation is very very critical – & I heard one Red Cross official say that he considered France & England were beaten – everybody seems to feel that we came in too late. Did you know that there was a regular crisis this spring in March? I hadn't realized it – they say the soldiers refused to fight – some had to be shot down – & they were so discouraged they said to let Germany have the north of France – they would keep the south – if they could only stop fighting. Everybody seems to consider the situation absolutely grave & as serious as possible. I find people are rather down on America – for not coming in before & for feeding Germany through neutrals & I heard one man say that America would never get any fighting in this war, it was too late & it would be over & that now our lines were just sitting behind the French. You'll be interested to know that our troops are *all* landing at St. Nazaire – there is a big Red Cross station there & military hospital. From there they are transported (in cattle cars) directly to the front which runs from Bar-le-Duc &

Dijon down to Champêtre with a big hospital. They are behind the French lines & of course is only a little way. Isn't it remarkable that it takes the whole *world* to beat Germany & even then it can't be done?

Catherine Baker Hooper

An Irrepressible Crew: The Smith College Relief Unit

December 17, 1917

I have been particularly begging for books. This starvation for books has gripped me in such a way that I have been fairly haunted by it. I never knew what it could be before to have absolutely no access to even one book. It's a lack and a hunger that needs to be met as much as that of the body. Think of children going through these formative years with none of the joys, none of the instruction, experience of knowledge that books can give, and in addition, of course, none of the inspiration and uplift that all the world and especially these poor people need so badly at this time; an outlook that has some light and some breadth and distance; thoughts that will lift them out of the conditions of their present life and the influence of living in small windowless stables, crowded lean-tos and cellars, with the constant coming and going of soldiers billeted upon them, and the ever-present uncertainty as to what the future will bring to them and their homes, especially to their kin who are somewhere in Germany or at the front: all this is to my mind more necessary than food for their bodies.

When I first saw the light in the eyes of the first children to whom I loaned books, children who had seen nothing for three years, I resolved then and there that I should beg, borrow or steal to satisfy this craving to some extent. My influence may be debatable, but the influence of the books is not. My influence may stop when I leave, but the books will be with them for years to come. So I started out with about 50 books, lending them to a few of the most intelligent and the cleanest. The demand has been tremendous, so at present I am in Paris adding to the supply. When I get back I shall have something over 400 books to lend. Even that will be merely a drop in the bucket for our 16 villages, but it is something. I have spent hours in second-hand book shops, for many books I want to get are out of print. I have been getting the best French advice possible as to the proper books to get. I have been getting introductions to the big book firms that I may get special prices. I have been getting French papers to advertise, a little French girl to appeal to her friends, a church to appeal to its Sunday school, and the head of a 'comme il faut' private school to appeal to his pupils, etc., and I hope in time to get what I want. One can reach children of 16 villages comparatively little during a week, but the books can be loaned for a week at a time and a whole family can profit by it.

ALICE LEAVENS

Minerva Quarterly Bulletin, Summer 1985

Women Veterans of the Great War: Service with the U.S. Signal Corps

The United States was an isolated country – we cared very little about the rest of the world before the war broke out. I was in Glenwood Springs, Colorado, on vacation when, on August 14, 1914, I picked up the morning paper and read: 'German troops invade Belgium'. For some reason that is a vivid memory though, at the time, I had no idea I would be involved in that war. As time passed and country after country became engulfed, people in the United States became 'world conscious'. Finally, with the sinking of the Lusitania, there was a wave of 'war mania'.

The first call was in November 1917. General Pershing had requested the 'enlisting' (note the use of that word) of American women to operate the Army switchboards in France.

One qualification, that they speak fluent French so as to be able to serve as interpreters, posed a serious problem. The first four units, composed mainly of French-speaking college women, were hurriedly trained as operators and sailed for France in March and April, 1918. As the A.E.F. telephone system expanded, there was a call for additional operators with, hopefully, some knowledge of French. Since I met those qualifications, I was in the Fifth Unit. We were told that we had officers' rating and officers' pay for their own uniforms. We had to have $500 before they'd take us. There were 223 women in the six units that went overseas.

I didn't mind anything so much as the black sateen bloomers we had to wear as part of our uniforms. They were the ugliest things! We had winter uniforms, and in mid-August, our unit had to march from the Prince George Hotel on 38th St. down to the Hudson dock and it was hotter'n – oh dear! The orders of the day, despite the heat, were long woolen underwear, bloomers and ankle-length skirts. And we were subject to all military regulations plus an additional ten prescribing the code of conduct for young women.

It was years later that I learned the ship I had sailed to France on, the *Aquitania*, was menaced on August 5th, by a German submarine that had somehow eluded the harbor patrol with our ship as its target. We were carrying 7000 men and 200 officers. It was one of the few ships without convoy, and as we left New York Harbor in the twilight, there was real emotional tension as we sailed past the Statue of Liberty, because for some there would be no returning and we were answering her call.

Docking at Liverpool, we were greeted by a swarm of small boys begging pennies while a band played 'The Long, Long Trail'. I gazed out at the rows and rows of chimney pots and realized we had completed the first phase of our momentous journey.

In Paris I was at the Hotel Ferras, headquarters for the Signal Corps women. Big Bertha *(the famous German long-range gun)* had been shelling the city when the first units arrived in March and

April and I was told they used the fifteen minute intervals between shellings to dash from the hotel to the Elysee Palace, where the American exchange was located—

After we were married, my husband wrote for my victory medal, as he was always proud of my service. They wrote back that I wasn't entitled to it, and that was the first time that I knew I wasn't in the army. I may be the only S.C. woman who was actually sworn in twice! First by the Adjutant General of Montana, and then by Mr Green of the phone company, I can see him so well, standing there saying: 'I have orders from the Army to swear you into the Army. Hold up your hands.'

MERLE EGAN-ANDERSON

I was working for Michigan Bell Telephone Company at Marine City, Michigan, in 1918, when General of the Army John J. Pershing's request for experienced telephone operators came through our company's channels for service in the U.S. Signal Corps in France. I wanted to travel, see some of the world and experience new adventures. War propaganda, especially that of accusing the Germans of massacring innocent Belgians, coupled with Kaiser Wilhelm's ambitions to Germanize Europe and President Wilson's pronouncements to make the world safe for democracy, had fired my imagination and thinking. Being of French descent, I felt some personal and patriotic interest in the conflict; patriotism was a virtue in those days and not carried on the sleeve of one's coat.

When I was told by the Detroit office of the Michigan Bell that I would be accepted for the position of telephone operator for the Signal Corps, I was instructed to be sworn in by a Justice of the Peace or Notary Public in Marine City, under Army regulations and articles of War, and to await telegraphic orders. In a few days, a telegram arrived that I was to proceed to New York — I remained in New York for two weeks, receiving training, including physical defense, and was fitted for a uniform—We sailed from Hoboken on the S/S *Olympic* — When we left Southampton for Le Havre, we were ferried by a British troop ship. It was a night crossing, as was the custom in war, and a rough one—

There were about thirty operators of the U.S. Signal Corps at Chaumont *(their general HQ)* — [We] worked in shifts between 8.00 a.m. and 9.00 p.m. — We were subject to U.S. Army rules and regulations, discipline was severe, and we were subject to court-martial, the same as the Army personnel — in the final drive of the war I heard cannons booming at night, and saw the flashes accompanying the booms, and it all sounded like an electric storm.

While in Paris on leave, we met British and French military people and were taken to two night clubs names 'Heaven' and 'Hell'. Everyone was having fun and someone suggested American numbers to dance to. I was elected, and while at the piano, I said: 'Here I am playing the piano in "Hell". This I expected some day, but not so soon.'

A fast and effective communications system was of paramount importance in the war effort and I feel our telephone operators contributed immensely towards this end.

OLEDA JOURE-CHRISTIDES

I Saw Them Die

An American Girl in France

Dr Le B.'s hands, encased in rubber gloves, were swift and sure. He always worked with a cigarette hanging limply from the corner of his mouth. It was part of my job to keep lighting fresh ones for him. At first when the ashes fell into an open wound over which he was working, I asked him frantically what I should do about it. He went on calmly, muttering: *'N'importe ça. C'est stérile.'*

It did not matter, the ashes were sterile. I have since been amused at the thought of so many men journeying through life sublimely unconscious of the fact that some part or another of their anatomy had once served as Dr Le B.'s ash-tray.

Have been working in the various wards and am rapidly becoming a real nurse. At least there is practically nothing I have not done in the last few weeks. I have taken care of, individually and collectively, hundreds of French, British, Algerians, Arabs, Zouaves, Senegalese, a number of Americans, and also many Germans.

The Germans are wounded prisoners, and, on the whole, thoroughly unpleasant. Especially the officers, who have been purposely mixed in with the enlisted men to give them a much-needed taste of democracy.

Some of the officers are members of the Kaiser's crack Prussian Guard Division, and bitterly resent the ignominy of capture. They are given the same consideration as our own men and the same care, but they are sulky and arrogant and give orders in a manner that makes our blood boil. We cannot help disliking them. They are the perfect picture of what one imagines an enemy to be: Insolent, cocky, and rude.

SHIRLEY MILLARD

Autobiography: Journey from the North (vol. 1)

The Texan was exactly my age. Possibly he was inquisitive about a young woman who did not know that she was badly dressed, had never been trained to entertain a caller, and might at any moment insult him. He began coming to the farm three or four times a week. He talked to me about Texas, his father, the military school he was sent to when he was five, fence-riding, the Mexican expedition and, when I provoked him, about the English.

I had had no idea that the rest of the world did not humbly admire, and if not love at least fear us. I was astonished to hear him talk about our limited ideas, out-of-date traditions, laziness.

'But what can you possibly know about our traditions?' I exclaimed. 'Or our civilization.'

'Only that it's on its way out. Your traditions, whatever they are, won't be any use to you after the war, your people are tired, they don't want to work, we shall beat you to the trade of the world before you know what's happening.'

'How long have you been in England?' I asked.

'Four weeks, ma'am.'

'You have fine instincts.'

One day, when he had come up against the Wing Commander, he said with some sharpness that an Englishman's idea of co-operation is to decide what he intends to do, and leave the other fellow to think of a way to conform.

'But why,' I said, 'should you imagine you know what to do in a war that has been going on for three years while you Americans have been lending money at interest and writing pompous Notes?'

He looked at me for a moment. 'You have the tongue of a rattlesnake.'

STORM JAMESON

The Times, 2 January 1918

Message to the Queen

'*A WORD OF CHEER*'

The following telegram has been received by the Queen from Dr. Anna Howard Shaw, chairman of the Women's Committee of the Council of National Defence of America:

December 29, 1917

The Women's Committee of the Council of National Defence,

representing every loyal woman in America, is anxious that, at this crisis in the world war, your Majesty should be assured, and through your Majesty every woman in Great Britain, that during the past two years of the war their sisters in America have watched with admiration and perfect confidence the fortitude, the unfaltering purpose, and unflagging effort of the women of the United Kingdom to further the cause which they had at heart, and for which their men have been facing death in the field.

Now that the United States of America has joined hands with Britain, France, and Italy, in this last and greatest of all crusades, we, the true daughters of American democracy, feel that a New Year should not open without a word of cheer, of trust, and of complete and thorough cooperation to those who have suffered and nobly endured trials and sorrows which must now be our own lot. We are proud to be associated with them. We say unhesitatingly that we shall persevere with them to the end. We ask your Majesty to tell our sisters across the seas that, no matter what the cost, America will be loyal to her pact, and that none will manifest their loyalty more thoroughly in word and deed than the women of this country.

The Queen has sent the following reply:

York Cottage, Sandringham,
January 1, 1918

I have received with much satisfaction and pleasure the friendly message you have addressed to me from the Women's Committee of the Council of National Defence.

Please convey to the sisterhood of your great country the warm thanks of the women of the British Empire for their inspiring words of encouragement and assurance.

The horrors of war have taught us to know one another better, and have strengthened the ties of kinship and mutual sympathy by uniting the women of the English-speaking races heart and soul in the struggle for liberty and civilization.

Confident of the valuable help we women can give our gallant sailors and soldiers, I pray God's richest blessing on our efforts.

MARY R.

Lady's Pictorial, 24 August 1918

It is a strange feeling to be in America, and to see her going through, and to see her surmounting the same difficulties that the women of England had to go through. To be in America is like being in England during the first year of war. As our women had, so the women here had to get over the prejudice against short skirts, army uniforms and so forth — and like our own Women's Volunteer Reserve, they are making their stand and making their way in the thoughts and minds of people, as a necessary factor in determining the end of this war. Above all, the American woman has enthusiasm, and an enthusiasm which never flags once it starts.

BERTHA BENNET BURLEIGH

The Queen, 19 October 1918

The United States and the War

This summer has seen various interesting, though no longer startling, developments in the political and industrial position of women in the United States. New York, for example, facing a shortage of policemen due to the draft, has begun to appoint women as patrolmen, with the right to wear a modified police uniform and to wield a revolver and night-stick. In California, a woman, for the first time in the country's history, has been made United States District Attorney. In two or three of the Western

States women have casually announced their candidacy for the United States Senate, and have proceeded to organise very efficient campaigns. One day saw five young women accepted as United States marines, although their work is to be clerical and the favourite rallying cry of the marines, 'First to fight!' is not yet for them.

ANNE O'HAGAN

The Sword of Deborah

Title of a book about the British women's
auxiliary forces in France
by F. Tennyson Jesse

Service with the Army

The Status of the WAAC: Camp Followers

One of the problems that confronted the authorities, when they
decided to send women, other than hospital personnel, to a
theatre of war was their legal position. Anyone engaged
exclusively in the care of the sick and wounded was protected by
the Geneva Convention of 1906. This protection extended to
members of voluntary aid detachments and therefore covered not
only military nurses but all other women hitherto employed.
Obviously it would not cover women replacing combatant soldiers, as members of the Women's Army Auxiliary Corps were to
do. It was therefore doubly necessary to consider their exact
status. Men needed for similar work would have been enlisted. To
enlist women seemed to require an Act of Parliament, or at any
rate a Defence Regulation, even though the Interpretation Act of
1889 had ruled that, in the construction of every Act of Parliament,
masculine words include the feminine. If not enlisted and, in the
case of those of officer rank, commissioned, they would still be
under the Army Act on active service, since the Act included
among those subject to military law as soldiers 'all persons . . . who

are followers of or accompany His Majesty's troops or any portion thereof when employed on active service'. This definition, summarized in the term 'camp-follower', was applied to the women serving in France, though not to those in the United Kingdom, where civil law was available. Camp followers were deemed, in accordance with section 184 of the Army Act, to be under the command of the commanding officer of the corps or portion of a corps to which they were attached, they could be tried by court martial, but were not subject to punishment by the commanding officer, nor could they be dealt with for desertion or absence without leave.

Some form of contract was, however, considered necessary, so the recruit, on enrolment, was required to sign a paper whereby she agreed to serve for twelve months or the duration of the war, whichever was the greater period, to fulfil the rules, regulations and instructions laid down from time to time for the Corps, to work wherever the Army Council required, to obey all orders, to perform any work, and finally to be discharged at a week's notice (later extended to a month) if her services were no longer required, or without notice for misconduct or breach of conditions.

HELEN GWYNNE-VAUGHAN

The Sword of Deborah

Let me admit that when those in authority sent for me to go to France and see what certain sections of the women there were doing, I didn't want to go. I told them rather ungraciously that if they wanted the 'sunny-haired-lassies-in-khaki touch' they had better send somebody else. I am not, and never have been, a feminist or any other sort of an 'ist, never having been able to divide humanity into two different classes labelled 'men' and 'women.' Also, to tell the truth, the idea of going so far behind the lines did not appeal. For this there is the excuse that in England one grows so sick of the people who talk of 'going to the Front,' when they mean going to some safe château at a base for a personally conducted tour, or – Conscientious Objectors are the worst sinners in this latter class – when they are going to sit at canteens or paint huts a hundred miles or so behind the last line of trenches—

And there was another reason, both for my disinclination and my lack of interest. We in England grew so tired, in the early days of the war, of the fancy uniforms that burst out upon women. Every other girl one met had an attack of khakiitis, was spotted as the pard with badges and striped as the zebra. Almost simultaneously with this eruption came, for the other section of the feminine community, reaction from it. We others became rather self-consciously proud of our femininity, of being 'fluffy' – in much the same way that anti-suffragists used to be fluffy when they said they preferred to influence a man's vote, and that they thought more was done by charm.—

With official recognition of bodies such as the V.A.D.s and the even more epoch-making official founding of the W.A.A.C.s, the point of view of the un-uniformed changed. The thing was no longer a game at which women were making silly asses of themselves and pretending to be men; it had become regular, ordered, disciplined, and worthy of respect. In short, uniform was no longer fancy dress.

F. Tennyson Jesse

The Letters of Thomasina Atkins

October 30th, 1917

Dear Peachie,

I am glad you are away from home for a few days, for it gives me the opportunity to write about something that – perhaps – I ought to have discussed with you before I took the plunge. You know how difficult it is for me to keep anything to myself – that is anything which concerns myself – and really the boiler has all but busted this week. To 'cut the cackle, and come to the 'osses,' I have joined the Women's Army. Why? Well, the idea has been simmering in my brain-pan for some time. A certain poster – 'Urgently Wanted, 100,000 Women for Home and Foreign Service' – has been staring at me, and arguing with me like a revivalist parson until I could no longer find an excuse for *not* being one of the units in the required number.

I hate being out of work, and, as you know, touring the Provinces has long since lost its novelty for me, while London theatrical managers, though encouraging as to the future, are not exactly camping on my doorstep this season. I have had a pretty easy time so far, and a little hardship won't make me any less of an actress – (No remarks, please!) – so there you are. Well! to return to the W.A.A.C. My references have been taken up, the Medical Board has passed me A1, and now nothing remains but to get my kit together and to await marching orders to the hostel where I am to be vaccinated, inoculated, and generally prepared for France. Because of my proficiency in languages I was advised to sign for Class A, 'Ordinary Clerical Work,' which seems to embrace all manner of jobs not strictly associated with clerking.

Au revoir, dear; you will come back to find me putting away all my fancy fribbles, and seriously contemplating practical duds, including the ribbed worsted stockings which my æsthetic soul has always abominated.

Fondly (from now),
　　Thomasina

November 13th 1917

I was quite bewildered last night from being trotted from place to place, and after we had been fed, I was so tired that I felt I could have slept standing – but when it came to lying down, it was a different matter. It was a night of 'cat naps'; the beds are very hard and the pillow is straw. My hot-water bottle was a joy

303

– my weaning from luxury is evidently going to take time. We wash in the basement, in tin basins – cold water. We feed in the mess hall in the house at the corner of the street. It used to be a concert hall. The stage is the officers' mess, and they have a tablecloth. Our tables are bare deal, and the *couvert* is primitive. The food is uninteresting, and the temptation to go out into the town and find some real *hot* tea is great.

There are hundreds of girls here, mostly of the factory and the domestic-servant class. Such priceless accents! And oh! such odd faces – just like a Phil May panorama. There is a draft going out to France to-morrow, and another on Saturday. I am to be inoculated to-morrow, and if I get over it without any trouble, I shall be sent over very soon. Well! the sooner the quicker, as we say. Here there is nothing to do but to 'fall in' for meals, and that gives us time to realise that we are distinctly cold, lonely, and a bit hungry—

This is a distrait sort of a letter, but I am more than a bit 'wuzzy' this morning. We get up at 6.45; roll-call at 7.45; then fall in and march to the mess hall. At night we have supper at seven: last night, soup and bread and bread pudding – not at all bad. Nothing to do after supper except to attend roll-call at 8.30; lights out 10.30.

We sleep in rooms, six girls in mine counting me. The other five are quite nice girls, so I am able to manicure my nails and rub cold cream on my face without being made to feel either superior or eccentric.

More to-morrow,
Fondest love,
Thomasina

Recollections of Life as a WAAC Private

I always wished I had been born a boy & never more so than at this period. I really wanted to be a soldier, so when I saw a poster

304

asking girls to enlist in the Women's Army Auxilliary *(sic)* Corps I straight away volunteered. After passing a medical I was told to wait for my call-up. This was arranged for the sixth of January 1918 & I found myself in married quarters in Aldershot. When first called on parade, whilst still in civvies, one of our number – a very prim lady – turned up with an open umbrella. She said she had never gone out in the rain without an umbrella.

The barracks were very spartan & food poor & there was very little of it. We were subject to all of a soldier's discipline, but had none of the privelidges *(sic)* of a soldier. We were drilled and marched and drilled again and for a change had to listen to boring lectures. A sargeant of the Coldstream Guards was awarded the doubtful honour of teaching us to march.

I don't suppose he really wanted that position, but he really inspired us with his 'Put some swank into it, girls', and soon he had us smart as a regiment of guards and was quite proud of us.

—Our weekly pay in the army was ten shillings and out of that we had to buy brushes for shoes, brushes for buttons & cap badges, all our underclothes including even corset, and we had to obtain, by hook or by crook, three sets of everything. We were issued with a hat, a chin-strap, one pair of stockings, a great coat, a pair of shoes, a coat dress and overalls. When any article needed renewing we had to pay for them and a pair of shoes cost ten shillings (our wages for the week) so we could never have a treat. We had the usual buttons and badges and had to buy Brasso and a button stick and boot polish. *She then transferred to Pirbright Camp as an army cook.*

All the cooks were on a rota. There were pastry cooks, meat cooks, vegetable cooks, fats & scraps cooks & fatigues. These tasks didn't fall regularly, but according to one's standing with that N.C.O. I was never able to pretend liking for some one I despised so I got my share of the rough jobs such as donning wooden clogs and scrubbing the cookhouse floor with caustic soda.

—Out of bounds was three miles away and one was not allowed to speak to a soldier within bounds. This was a very serious offence and repitition (*sic*) of it could get a girl dismissed from the service for unsatisfactory conduct.

So if a girl became acquainted with a nice soldier she had to run three miles, say 'Hello' and run back again. There were some very nice boys among the Irish guards but we could never trust a Coldstream Guard. They would threaten to throw us into the Brookwood Canal if they couldn't have their way with us & they seemed to have only one thought in mind. What did it matter to them if a girl lost her character and ended up in the workhouse with a baby?

We did, however, have a certain amount of fun if it was only in breaking rules and getting away with it. There were trenches all around the huts & we quickly learnt the geography of these. They were excellent hiding places and some of the more daring girls would take a chance & meet boy friends there. We who remained in the hut at night kept watch for them and when an officer made a spot check to see if any girl was missing, we would say that the girl had gone to the toilet & one of us would nip out quickly with a warning signal. The officer always came round again after a ten minute interval and of course every girl was present.

At one period during the summer of 1918 the huts were unbearably hot at night — we privates were very annoyed to find a large cool tent had been erected for the officers. We thought this most unfair, so we held a conference and asked for volunteers to let it down. We counted the ropes & pegs and allotted one girl to each. If alarmed we were to disperse quickly each to a different trench — Of course we had to reconnoitre to make sure the tent was unoccupied and one night we met at the tent & at a given signal got the ropes off the pegs & let the whole thing down & fled, getting back to our huts, via the trenches as soon as possible. There was a big inquiry the next day with a special parade, but the girls who took part in the escapade were never discovered. One trait stood out amongst us girls & that was loyalty to each other.

During one period while we were stationed in this camp we had no bread and army biscuits were distributed. It was impossible to break these and I lost two teeth trying to consume one, so we chipped out the centres leaving a frame into which we inserted a photograph. We also wrote on them, 'Man shall not live by bread alone'—

About this time the name 'Women's Army Auxilliary Corps' was changed to 'Queen Mary's Army Auxilliary Corps'. So Waacs became Quimaacs which seemed an impossible word & was rarely used except by using the full written title.

OLIVE MAY TAYLOR

Petit Parisien, 14 January 1918

In a few months, thanks to the bold initiative of our Allies, and their surprising forethought, the Women's Army is rendering each day ever increasing services. An unheard-of revolution in manners and customs has been accomplished without any shock or disruption, for the change had been in conformity with logic. At this critical hour, when we find that all effectives and all the efforts of all available men and women are indispensable for victory, is it too late for us to follow the example of our allies?

WAAC: A Woman's Story of the War

'Cuddle-Pups'

It was Gwen who introduced a delightful specimen to me. A subaltern in the A.S.C., aged about twenty-six. He was about the most precious thing I met during the war. In the horse transport, commonly called H.T., he had only recently come out. He showed me with pride his various properties. Among them was a solid leather suit-case, concave underneath, with a contraption of leather straps to buckle it to the cantle of the saddle. Then he opened it.

It was lined in pale blue silk and fitted with every article necessary for the toilet – silver-backed hair-brushes and combs, little crystal jars with silver screw tops, silver-topped bottles which looked suspiciously like scent bottles, razors and shaving-brushes and tubes of shaving paste and toothpaste, a large folding mirror with a small one alongside it – the latter a magnifier – and many other things.

'So handy, isn't it?' he said, ogling me. 'Look in the glass, dear, and you'll see a lovely lady. One just straps it on behind one's saddle, and then no matter where one finds oneself one has everything at hand. Look – this is to boil one's shaving water,' and he pulled out a little silver vessel.

Before I had known him a quarter of an hour he had told me that his mother was an honourable, who his father was, where he had been at school, the college at Oxford where he had completed his education, that he had formerly been in the Guards, and other information about himself and his past life. I heard afterwards that his beautiful suit-case was discovered by his Company Commander and confiscated. Still, I dare say he would have fought well enough had the occasion arisen or had he found himself in a tight place. Some of those cuddle-pups who seemed so effeminate and futile fought like tigers, I was told more than once.

A<small>NONYMOUS</small>

WRNS: A Naval Organisation for Women & the Women's Royal (Auxiliary) Air Force

From the beginning, the W.R.N.S. recruited through the Ministry of National Service which used the Labour Exchanges for providing Selection Boards at which our Recruiting Officers used to attend together with those of the W.A.A.C. and later the W.R.A.F. We needed very few women compared with the others as our total numbers never exceeded 7,000, even when we were still staffing Naval Air Stations.

In order to select our officers carefully we set up a very formal Selection Board, and women wishing to join the ranks had to fill in a very full qualification form and also to supply references—We got some funny answers to our questions, such as:

Question: 'Why do you wish to join the W.R.N.S.?'
Answer: 'Because the hat is so becoming.'
Question: 'What experience have you had to qualify you to become an officer?'
Answer: 'I am a good disciplinarian, having lived in South Africa and having had blacks under me.'
Question: 'What have you done in the way of administration?'
Answer: 'I have run my brother's house with two servants.'
Question: 'What war work have you done?'
Answer: 'None. I have never had to work for my living.'
Question: 'Then why do you want to begin now?'
Answer: 'Because I think that Naval men are so refined.'

It was sometimes very difficult not to turn and rend the women who gave such answers but what was the good? If they had reached this stage of the war, without getting more common sense, nothing one could have said would have made any impression—

The official intimation from the Air Ministry to the Admiralty that they had been considering the establishment of a 'Women's Air Force Service' was dated 1st February, 1918, and we were soon in the thick of correspondence between the Admiralty, Ministry of National Service and Ministry of Air, about recruiting for Air Stations and the transfer in the future.

There was a pleasant feeling of friendly intercourse between all the officers of the women's services, and the Admiralty did not tie us up too tight with red tape, so that we were free to discuss our work with all others who were concerned—

The delays in getting the W.R.A.F. safely launched could be attributed to a certain extent to the fact that its parent body the R.A.F. was of such recent birth, the Royal Naval Air Service and the Royal Flying Corps having only lately been amalgamated. But there were also personal factors involved as the individuals who were responsible for getting the Service organised seemed to be unable to pull together so that the difficulty of getting the women enrolled, paid and kitted up became exaggerated and this affected everyone else concerned as well as the W.R.A.F.—

The Navy supported us splendidly and took great pride in the Wrens, but the situation was delicate now and then as there had to be a rule by which no rating in uniform might go out with a naval officer; a ridiculous situation arose when some relative or friend of a naval officer had entered the W.R.N.S. and very naturally wanted to go out with him. We had to institute a pass which could be obtained to allow of this, and it was rather funny when some girl helping at Headquarters had to obtain this in order to go out with her father. It was really a necessary rule, as the customs of the Navy had to be maintained and ranks and ratings do not usually mix freely when off duty, but in our case the provision of a special pass got over the difficulty and saved the off-duty time of the ratings as changing into plain-clothes was wasteful of time.

Little things of this sort, although they may seem absurd now, in 1914–19 made or marred the good name of a Women's Service when uniformed women were still a novelty. It is, almost invariably, the women who are criticised if any cause for gossip or scandal shows, and people who were not in the thick of it all, as we were, cannot have any idea of what some women had to face in the way of condemnation, some of which was attributed to enemy propaganda.

The fear of what might be looked on as unsuitable behaviour was always at the back of our minds but, so far as my experience went, there was very little cause for it. The V.A.D.s had a very clean sheet and also the W.R.N.S. So much so that the V.A.D.s were nicknamed 'the Starched Brigade' and the Wrens 'the Prigs and the Prudes' or 'the Perfect Ladies' which we took as a compliment in both cases.

In the W.R.N.S. we had a very few cases of pregnancy and of V.D. In the former we discharged the women on benevolent grounds but saw them safely through the process of child-bearing; in the latter we ensured treatment for them but did not discharge as our Medical Directors and I agreed that we should do more to maintain a moral code by humane treatment than by punishment, and the response certainly justified this belief.

KATHARINE FURSE

Commission of Inquiry

Honour of W.A.A.C.

Complete Vindication

The honour of the Women's Army Auxiliary Corps, assailed by ignorant and irresponsible persons, has been completely vindicated by the Commission of Inquiry sent to France by the Ministry of Labour. The Commission, consisting of Mrs. Deane Streatfeild (chairman), Miss Violet Markham, Miss Carlin (Dock and General Workers Union), Miss Varley (Workers' Union), and Miss Ritson (Women's Friendly Society of Scotland), find that the vague charges of immoral conduct brought against members of the corps are slanderous and rest on no foundation in fact.

GROUNDLESS CHARGES

As a result of our inquiry we can find no justification of any kind for the vague accusations of immoral conduct on a large scale which have been circulated about the W.A.A.C. The chief difficulty of our task has lain in the very vague nature of the damaging charges we were requested to investigate. It is common knowledge that fantastic tales have passed from mouth to mouth of the numbers of W.A.A.C. women returned to England for misconduct of the gravest character. These stories are best refuted by the following official returns, which prove that not only are the statements untrue, but that up to the present the number of undesirable women who have found their way into the corps has been very small.

The first detachment of the W.A.A.C. arrived in France towards the end of March, 1917. The strength of the corps in France on March 12, 1918, was stated to us as being 6,023 women. We have examined the medical records both in England and France, and find that of this number twenty-one pregnancy cases (or about. 3 per cent.) have been reported since the arrival of the corps in France, and twelve cases of venereal disease (or about. 2 per cent.). As regards the first category, two were married women, and it appears that the bulk of the cases were pregnant before coming to France. As regards the second category, it appears that several cases were of old standing. In addition to the above, nineteen women have been returned to England on disciplinary grounds, and ten for inefficiency. Fifty-nine women have been discharged on medical grounds, including the twelve cases mentioned above, and twenty-one on compassionate grounds (i.e. family reasons). From July 1, 1917, to March 11, 1918 (nine months), the following offences have been recorded: Fines, 17; confined to camp, 41; restriction of privileges, 23; admonitions, 7; total, 88.

The employment of women for the first time in history as an organised corps of workers in close connection with the Army has been a new, and in some respects a revolutionary, experiment. Such an organisation involves the revaluation of many long-standing conventions, and this fact in itself is apt to excite comment. We feel that the large majority of the girls who have come forward in an hour of crisis and difficulty to share the work of the men in the field have upheld the honour of their sex and of their country in a spirit which should win for them the regard and gratitude of the nation.

ORIGIN OF RUMOURS

We must draw the attention to the fact that at the outset the advent of the W.A.A.C. created undoubtedly considerable surprise and some dismay among the serious-minded French population. French customs and traditions of family decorum are far removed from the general social ideas which in these latter times regulate the intercourse of young men and young women of British origin. Comradeship between the sexes, which is a commonplace in the one country, is unknown in the other. This freedom of social intercourse generally recognised in England is not rendered more comprehensible to a race with domestic customs wholly different from our own by the fact that the men and women concerned are both wearing uniform. The splendid traditions of the French army have not so far included the services of a body of women workers definitely enrolled as an auxiliary branch. It is very natural, therefore, that a section of our Allies viewed with considerable perplexity a situation so different from any with which they are personally familiar, and that at times the position was open to misconstruction in their eyes.

We were glad to understand that with the lapse of time the French point of view about the W.A.A.C. has been considerably modified, and that the work of British women in France is by degrees winning growing appreciation from them. It is interesting to note in this connection that we were told of a distinguished

French Senator who had inspected the W.A.A.C. in one area with a view to the possible establishment of a French corps of women organised on similar lines. The Senator in question expressed himself in eulogistic terms as to the work which was being carried on by the W.A.A.C., and had under consideration the extension of the principle to his own countrywomen.

It is further clear from the evidence we received, that these rumours have also obtained currency at home owing to letters addressed by soldiers on active service to their relations in England. In the opinion of witnesses qualified to judge, motives of varying character have probably influenced correspondence of this type. Our attention was frequently drawn to the point that certain men dislodged from noncombatant tasks in the bases by the substitution of women had in some cases shown jealousy and hostility towards the W.A.A.C. It was suggested to us that many of the rumours may have sprung from this source, and we were impressed with the consensus of opinion on this point.

Nursing and Bloody Madness

Unknown Warriors

Passchendaele 1917

Monday, July 30th, midnight. Brandhoek.
Cars came for us at 5 p.m. and here we are. By the time you get
this it will be history for better or for worse. By 6 a.m. our part
will have begun and everything is organised and ready up to the
brim. That we have 15 Theatre Sisters tells its own tale. We
have 33 Sisters altogether, and they are all tucked into their
bell-tents with hankies tied on to the ropes of the first ones to
be called when the first case comes in.

We have had a Gas Drill to-night from an Irish M.O. from up
the Line. It is a beastly job and rather complicated, and has to be
done in six seconds to be any good; we all take about six minutes!
The signal to put on box helmets is the C.O.'s whistle and a loud
banging on the Hospital gong (an iron rail hanging on a sort of gal-
lows). The din is marvellous. Some Grandmothers (15-inch guns)
on each side of us are splitting the air and rocking the huts, and
everything except the Field Gun drumfire, which hasn't begun
yet, is joining in. Fritz is sending his over too, with an ugly whang.
The illumination is brighter than any lightning: dazzling and

beautiful. Their new blinding gas is known as mustard-oil gas; it burns your eyes – sounds jolly, doesn't it? – and comes over in shells. I wonder how many hundreds or thousands have got only four more hours to live, and know it?

The first day we came up here we met some prisoners just taken, being marched down. I hope there'll be hundreds to-morrow. Good night.

4.15 a.m.

The All-together began at 5 minutes to 4. We crept out on to the duckboards and saw. It was more wonderful and stupendous than horrible. There was the glare before daylight of the searchlights, star-shells and gunflashes, and the cracking, splitting and thundering of the guns of all calibres at once. The S.O.S. call has come for three of the Sisters, but I think no cases are here yet. No mines have gone up yet.

6.30 a.m.

We have just begun taking in the first cases. An officer died soon after admission, between 4 and 5 a.m.

The Air people began streaming over at daylight adding their whirring and droning to the din. The mines have been going off since 5 like earthquakes. Lots of high explosive has been coming over, but nothing so far into this Camp. The uproar is almost stupefying. I'm going now to see how they are getting on in the Preparation and Resuscitation Hut.

Same day, 11 p.m.

We have been working in the roar of battle every minute since I last wrote, and it has been rather too exciting. I've not had time to hear any details from any of our poor abdominals, but the news has been good till this evening: thousands of prisoners – and Ypres choked with captured guns and ammunition, and some few miles (?) of advance. This evening they tell of heavy counter-attacks and some of our advance lost.—

We have a lot of Germans in – all abdominals. Everything has been going at full pitch – with the 12 Teams in the Theatre only breaking off for hasty meals – the Dressing Hut, the Preparation Ward and Resuscitation and the four huge Acute Wards, which fill up from the Theatre; the Officers' Ward, the Moribund and the German Ward. That, and the Preparation and the Theatre are the worst places. Soon after 10 o'clock this morning he began putting over high explosive. Everyone had to put on tin-hats and carry on. He kept it up all the morning with vicious screams. They burst on two sides of us, not 50 yards away – no direct hits on to us but streams of shrapnel, which were quite hot when you picked them up. No one was hurt, which was lucky, and they came everywhere, even through our Canvas Huts in our quarters. Luckily we were so frantically busy that it was easier to pay less attention to it. The patients who were well enough to realise that they were not still on the field called it 'a dirty trick.' They were not gas shells, thank Heaven. Bursting shells are an ugly sight – black or yellow smoke and streams of jagged steel flying violently in all directions.

It doesn't look as if we should ever sleep again. Apparently gunners and soldiers never do: it is difficult to see who can in this area. Our monster shells cutting through the air are the dizzy limit. There was a moment in the morning when the C.O. and I thought he meant to do us in, but they stopped about one o'clock. And there was a moment about tea-time when I thought the work was going to heap up and get the upper hand of us, but the C.O. stopped admitting for an hour and sent them on lower down, which saved the situation. It is going to be a tight fit. Of course, a good many die, but a great many seem to be going to do. We get them one hour after injury, which is our *raison d'être* for being here.

General S., the Director of Medical Services 5th Army, came round about 2 p.m. I took him round and he signed chits for lots of things we want from the B.R.C.S. He was annoyed about the shelling.

It is pouring with rain, alas, and they are brought in sopping.

317

Post just going. Soaking hopeless rain, holding up the advance; the worst luck that could happen. Poor Sir Douglas Haig. It has been so every time. Everything is a swamp and a pond, and tents leaking and dropping. Water in some of the Wards is half-way up the legs of the beds.

I got to bed between 2 and 7 and slept like blazes. This morning they really don't look so bad – for abdominals. Only 23 deaths. Some are sitting up smoking cigarettes and sorting their treasure bags. The noise has almost ceased, so those exhausted sopping gunners must be getting a sleep.

11.30 p.m.

Just finished my last round. Soaking rain all day still going on, complete hold-up of British Army. Absolute silence of our guns and only an occasional reminder from Fritz. Pétain and his crack Corps have done very well. Our success has varied; one Corps went too far and got caught in the back. The abdominals coming in are very bad to-day – both Boche and British. The work thickens as the wards fill up and new wards have to be opened. We are to take Chests and Femurs too, as soon as No. 44 and the Austr. C.C.S.'s open, which are alongside getting ready. The staffing of the wards for Night Duty both of Sisters and Orderlies is the problem, even with my 33. Some of these are first-class. It is getting very ghastly; the men all look so appalling when they are brought in, and so many die. I don't see how the 'break-the-news' letters are going to be written, because the moment for sitting down literally never comes from 7 a.m. to midnight. It is a good thing we are all fresh and fit.

Wednesday, August 1st, 12.15 midnight.

It has been a pretty frightful day – 44 funerals yesterday and about as many to-day. After 24 hours of peace the battle seems to have broken out again; the din is so terrific I can hardly sit in this chair. Our monsters are thundering over our heads from the giants

318

behind us, and some of theirs are coming this way. Must go and look round.

Thursday, August 2nd, 11.45 p.m. The uproar went on all night – no one slept much. It made one realise how far up we are to have streams of shells crossing over our heads. The rain continues – all night and all day since the Push began on Monday. Can God be on our side, everyone is asking – when His (alleged!) Department always intervenes in favour of the enemy at all our best moments.

The men are brought in with mud over their eyes and mouths, and 126 have died in 3½ days. In spite of the awful conditions, a remarkable percentage, especially of the first ones who came in early and dry, are doing brilliantly.

The 5th Army Commander, Gen. Sir Hubert Gough, and some of his Staff paid us a long visit this morning. He was taken round everything by the Colonel and Capt. B. and me, and was very charming. The weather was doing its worst and he congratulated us on carrying on on such a scale in such difficult circumstances. The Advanced Abdominal Centre Scheme is on its trial and they were all agreed that the results fully justified the plan. He was awfully nice to everybody, and most interested, and did a lot of the usual thanking for the Sisters' work. We stood in the rain and mud with streams trickling off our Brass Hats and Sou'westers down our backs, and he asked anxiously how we stuck it all, and I assured him we were all right. The Colonel told him about the shelling and said the Sisters enjoyed it! (Glad he thought so!) He sent a special message to me afterwards, through the Colonel.

Then the D.M.S. came all round (I didn't happen to see him) and was very pleased with the results. He has never been known to praise or thank anybody, but he had his appreciation and thanks to all ranks for 'very good work under trying conditions' put in Orders to-night. So we are all walking about with swelled heads. They were all immensely struck by the uncomplaining fortitude of the men. Gough talked like a father to them.

One boy of 18 said, 'Will you write to Mother? Give her my love. Say I'm all right; she's an invalid – mind you write her a comfortin' letter.' An oldish man wanted to be lifted up in the bed; when we'd done it, he murmured, 'What would we do without women in the world!' And they don't expect to find women up here.

Yesterday morning Capt. C., V.C. and Bar. D.S.O., M.C., R.A.M.C., was brought in – badly hit in the tummy and arm and had been going about for two days with a scalp wound till he got this. Half the Regiment have been to see him – he is loved by everybody. He was quickly X-rayed, operated on, shrapnel found, holes sewn up, salined and put to bed. He is just on the borderland still; better this afternoon and perhaps going to do, but not so well to-night. He tries hard to live; he was going to be married.

Sunday, August 5th, 11.30 p.m.

Capt. C. died yesterday; four of us went to his funeral to-day; and a lot of the M.O.'s; two of them wheeled the stretcher and lowered him. His horse was led in front and then the pipers and masses of kilted officers followed. Our Padre with his one arm, Father E. H., C.R., looked like a Prophet towering over everybody and saying it all without book. After the Blessing one Piper came to the graveside (which was a large pit full of dead soldiers sewn up in canvas) and played a lament. Then his Colonel, who particularly loved him, stood and saluted him in his grave. It was fine, but horribly choky.

K. E. LUARD

The 'Bloody' Madness of Young Girls

Letter to her publisher: undated but *Les Flanchards* was published in 1917

Dear Sir,

I have only a few more chapters of 'Les Flanchards' to write. Thank you for asking for another series. I will do it willingly.

May I criticise the 'bloody' madness of young women and girls who would do better to stay at home with their children, their brothers, or their parents, than be in operating theatres where, according to a doctor of and a friend of ours, they love to 'paddle around in blood' and where they see and hear things which are not meant to be seen and heard by young girls. Not to mention marrying Negroes or schemers who take advantage of the situation, while conversely elderly crafty women trick naive wounded soldiers. All for the fun of it of course.

I know of households turned upside down, where the husband serving at the front is distressed to learn that his house and children are left alone, and parents driven mad to see their daughters become strange creatures, neither women nor girls.

To make myself understand and to give you an idea of *this new hospital mentality*, I'm telling you something which is certainly not for the young female readers of 'Excelsior'.

A seventeen-year-old girl, rebelling against her family, is no longer prepared merely to serve meals to the wounded or to read to them. She wants to look after them completely, to go to the 'Peupliers' (the Red Cross clinical training school) to care for the seriously wounded, to wash them from head to foot!!!

Her rebellion is encouraged by slightly older friends (her best friend is 22) from the same kind of background as herself, strictly brought up on the old values – until the war. The young seventeen-year-old has a soldier brother who has been wounded and tended, to his great confusion and concern, by friends of his sister whom he had met as such, or at a ball; well, the way one meets well-educated young girls. While convalescent, coming from the hospital where he was cared for by the 22-year-old, he is horrified at the idea of his little sister doing the kind of things he cannot accept young girls should do. He tells her this and during their discussion he says among other things, 'I don't want you to be involved in a world which will deflower you.'

What does the young girl of seventeen understand? What does she repeat to the older friend who cared for her brother? Anyway, this is the letter the young man receives from his nurse (22 years old, of correct demeanour, excellent education, daughter of an admirable professor at the Sorbonne). I copy a passage which will, I think, astonish you!

'I am very surprised by the comments you made to Simone about her vocation. What business is it of yours? After all, even admitting that your sister might lose her virginity, it's not you who will have your eyes opened'!!!

I quote you this sample because I have it in front of me, but there are many others of the same kind. Hospitals are in the process of creating a type of young creature who will be hateful once the war is over. (And even during the war!!)

Yours sincerely,

GYP

A Diary Without Dates

It takes all sorts to make a hospital.

For instance, the Visitors . . .

There is the lady who comes in to tea and wants to be introduced to everyone as though it was a school-treat.

She jokes about the cake, its scarcity or its quantity, and makes a lot of 'fun' about two lumps of sugar.

When she is at her best the table assumes a perfect and listening silence – not the silence of the critic, but the silence of the absorbed child treasuring every item of talk for future use. After she goes the joy of her will last them all the evening.

There is the lady who comes in to tea and, sitting down at the only unlaid table, cries, 'Nurse! I have no knife or plate or cup; and I prefer a glass of boiling water to tea. And would you mind sewing this button on my glove?'

There is the lady who comes in and asks the table at large: 'I wonder if any one knows General Biggens? I once met him . . .'

Or: 'You've been in Gallipoli? Did you run across my young

322

cousin, a lieutenant in the . . . ? Well, he was only there two days or so, I suppose . . .' exactly as though she was talking about Cairo in the season.

To-day there was the Limit.

She sat two paces away from where I sit to pour out tea. Her face was kind, but inquisitive, with that brown liver-look round the eyes and a large rakish hat. She comes often, having heard of him through the *padre*, to see a Canadian whom she doesn't know and who doesn't want to see her.

From two places away I heard her voice piping up: 'Nurse, excuse my asking, but is your cap a regulation one, like all the others?'

I looked up, and all the tea I was pouring poured over the edge. Mr. Pettitt and Captain Matthew, between us, looked down at their plates.

I put my hand to my cap. 'Is anything wrong? It ought to be like the others.'

She leant towards me, nodding and smiling with *bonhomie*, and said flatteringly, 'It's so prettily put on, I thought it was different.'

And then (horror): 'Don't you think nurse puts her cap on well?' she asked Captain Matthew, who, looking harder than ever at his plate and reddening to the ears, mumbled something which did not particularly commit him since it couldn't be heard.

The usual delighted silence began to creep round the table, and I tried wildly to divert her attention before our end became a stage and the rest of the table an audience.

'I think it's so nice to see you sitting down with them all,' she cooed; 'it's so cosy for them.'

'Is your cup empty?' I said furiously, and held out my hand for it. But it wasn't, of course, she couldn't even do that for me.

She shook hands with me when she went away and said she hoped to come again. And she will.

There was once a lady who asked me very loudly whether I 'saw many horrible sights,' and 'did the V.A.D.'s have to go to the funerals?'

And another who cried out with emotion when she saw the first officer limp in to Mess, 'And can some of them *walk*, then?' Perhaps she thought they came in to tea on stretchers, with field-bandages on. She quivered all over, too, as she looked from one to the other, and I feel sure she went home and broke down, crying, 'What an experience . . . the actual wounds!'

ENID BAGNOLD

A Door is Open: Autobiography

A Volunteer Nurse in Berlin

For the first time I saw the misery which the madness of war has brought upon the people. Had I ever really thought about it before? Slowly I realised that my life until then had only been led in the narrow circle around me. Yes, I had given and helped wherever I could, but I had never been conscious of how many people were sacrificed on the whims and errors of those in power. I had great difficulty in carrying out my duties without crying or running from this immense misery. My work was very hard and I fell exhausted into bed in the evenings. Because time was so short we often ate our meals standing up and in the first weeks my feet swelled so severely that I had to wrap them in wet towels at night. There were far too few carers there. One sister and her assistants had to look after thirty badly wounded men.

I had been working for about six weeks when one day the chief doctor came to me and asked me if I would feel up to the position of sister, working independently with one assistant. I said no. But he impressed upon me the lack of sisters — Finally I said I would do it, but it was a long time before I lost my fear. I spent the whole time thinking I had missed something or done something wrong, thinking that I had harmed the patients instead of helping them, and even in my dreams I handled the instruments fearfully. The first time I attended an operation I nearly fainted when I was given a sawn-off leg to put in the corner. It took all my strength to pull myself together, but I can still feel the weight of that leg in my hands today.

TILLA DURIEUX

Not So Quiet: Stepdaughters of War

I have schooled myself to stop fainting at the sight of blood. I have schooled myself not to vomit at the smell of wounds and stale blood, but view these sad bodies with professional calm I shall never be able to. I may be helping to alleviate the sufferings of wretched men, but common sense rises up and insists that the necessity should never have arisen. I become savage at the futility. A war to end war, my mother writes. Never. In twenty years it will repeat itself. And twenty years after that. Again and again, as long as we breed women like my mother and Mrs. Evans-Mawnington. And we are breeding them—

Oh, come with me, Mother and Mrs. Evans-Mawnington. Let me show you the exhibits straight from the battlefield. This will be something original to tell your committees, while they knit their endless miles of khaki scarves—something to spout from the platform at your recruiting meetings. Come with me. Stand just there.

Here we have the convoy gliding into the station now, slowly, so slowly. In a minute it will disgorge its sorry cargo. My ambulance doors are open, waiting to receive. See, the train has stopped. Through the occasionally drawn blinds you will observe the trays slotted into the sides of the train. Look closely, Mother and Mrs. Evans-Mawnington, and you shall see what you shall see. Those trays each contain something that was once a whole man . . . the heroes who have done their bit for King and country . . . the heroes who marched blithely through the streets of London Town singing 'Tipperary,' while you cheered and waved your flags hysterically. They are not singing now, you will

325

observe. Shut your ears, Mother and Mrs. Evans-Mawnington, lest their groans and heart-rending cries linger as long in your memory as in the memory of the daughter you sent out to help win the War.

See the stretcher-bearers lifting the trays one by one, slotting them deftly into my ambulance. Out of the way quickly, Mother and Mrs. Evans-Mawnington – lift your silken skirts aside . . . a man is spewing blood, the moving has upset him, finished him – He will die on the way to hospital if he doesn't die before the ambulance is loaded. I know . . . All this is old history to me. Sorry this has happened. It isn't pretty to see a hero spewing up his life's blood in public, is it? Much more romantic to see him in the picture papers being awarded the V.C., even if he is minus a limb or two. A most unfortunate occurrence!

That man strapped down? That raving, blaspheming creature screaming filthy words you don't know the meaning of . . . words your daughter uses in everyday conversation, a habit she has contracted from vulgar contact of this kind. Oh, merely gone mad, Mother and Mrs. Evans-Mawnington. He may have seen a headless body running on and on, with blood spurting from the trunk. The crackle of the frost-stiff dead men packing the duckboards watertight may have gradually undermined his reason. There are many things the sitters tell me on your long night rides that could have done this.

No, not shell-shock. The shell-shock cases take it more quietly, as a rule, unless they are suddenly startled. Let me find you an example. Ah, the man they are bringing out now. The one staring straight ahead at nothing . . . twitching, twitching, twitching, each limb working in a different direction, like a Jumping Jack worked by a jerking string. Look at him, both of you. Bloody awful, isn't it, Mother and Mrs. Evans-Mawnington? That's shell-shock. If you dropped your handbag on the platform, he would start to rave as madly as the other. What? You won't try the experiment? You can't watch him? Why not? *Why not?* I have to, every night. Why the hell can't you do it for once? Damn your eyes.

Forgive me, Mother and Mrs Evans-Mawnington. That was not the kind of language a nicely-brought-up young lady from Wimbledon Common uses. I forget myself. We will begin again.

See the man they are fitting into the bottom slot. He is coughing badly. No, not pneumonia. Not tuberculosis. Nothing so picturesque. Gently, gently, stretcher-bearers — he is about done. He is coughing up clots of pinky-green filth. Only his lungs, Mother and Mrs. Evans-Mawnington. He is coughing well to-night. That is gas. You've heard of gas, haven't you? It burns and shrivels the lungs to . . . to the mess you see on the ambulance floor there. He's about the age of Bertie, Mother. Not unlike Bertie, either, with his gentle brown eyes and fair curly hair. Bertie would look up pleadingly like that in between coughing up his lungs . . . The son you have so generously given to the War. The son you are so eager to send out to the trenches before Roy Evans-Mawnington, in case Mrs. Evans-Mawnington scores over you at the next recruiting meeting . . . 'I have given my only son.'

Cough, cough, little fair-haired boy. Perhaps somewhere your mother is thinking of you . . . boasting of the life she has so nobly given . . . the life you thought was your own, but which is hers to squander as she thinks fit. 'My boy is not a slacker, thank God.' Cough away, little boy, cough away. What does it matter, providing your mother doesn't have to face the shame of her son's cowardice?

These are sitters. The man they are hoisting up beside me, and the two who sit in the ambulance. Blighty cases . . . broken arms and trench feet . . . mere trifles. The smell? Disgusting, isn't it? Sweaty socks and feet swollen to twice their size . . . purple, blue, red . . . big black blisters filled with yellow matter. Quite a colour-scheme, isn't it? Have I made you vomit? I must again ask pardon. My conversation is daily growing less refined. Spew and vomit and sweat . . . I had forgotten these words are not used in the best drawing-rooms on Wimbledon Common.

But I am wasting time. I must go in a minute. I am nearly loaded. The stretcher they are putting on one side? Oh, a most ordinary exhibit, . . . the groaning man to whom the smallest jolt is red hell . . . a mere bellyful of shrapnel. They are holding him over till the next journey. He is not as urgent as the helpless thing there, that trunk without arms and legs, the remnants of a human being, incapable even of pleading to be put out of his misery because his jaw has been half shot away . . . No, don't meet his eyes, they are too alive. Something of their malevolence might remain with you all the rest of your days . . . those sock-filled, committee-crowded days of yours.

Gaze on the heroes who have so nobly upheld your traditions, Mother and Mrs. Evans-Mawnington. Take a good look at them. . . . The heroes you will sentimentalise over until peace is declared, and allow to starve for ever and ever, amen, afterwards. Don't go. Spare a glance for my last stretcher, . . . that gibbering, unbelievable, unbandaged thing, a wagging lump of raw flesh on a neck, that was a face a short time ago, Mother and Mrs. Evans-Mawnington. Now it might be anything . . . a lump of liver, raw bleeding liver, that's what it resembles more than anything else, doesn't it? We can't tell its age, but the whimpering moan sounds young, somehow. Like the fretful whimpers of a sick little child . . . a tortured little child . . . puzzled whimpers. Who is he? For all you know, Mrs. Evans-Mawnington, he is your Roy. He might be anyone at all, so why not your Roy? One shapeless lump of raw liver is like another shapeless lump of raw liver. What do you say? Why don't they cover him up with bandages? How the hell do I know? I have often wondered myself, . . . but they don't. Why do you turn away? That's only liquid fire. You've heard of liquid fire? Oh, yes. I remember your letter . . . *'I hear we've started to use liquid fire, too. That will teach those Germans. I hope we use lots and lots of it.'* Yes, you wrote that. You were glad some new fiendish torture had been invented by the chemists who are running this war. You were delighted to think some German mother's son was going to have the skin stripped from his poor face by liquid fire . . . Just as some equally patriotic German mother rejoiced when she first heard the sons of Englishwomen were to

328

be burnt and tortured by the very newest war gadget out of the laboratory.

Don't go, Mother and Mrs. Evans-Mawnington . . . don't go. I am loaded, but there are over thirty ambulances not filled up. Walk down the line. Don't go, unless you want me to excuse you while you retch your insides out as I so often do. There are stretchers and stretchers you haven't seen yet . . . Men with hopeless dying eyes who don't want to die . . . men with hopeless living eyes who don't want to live. Wait, wait, I have so much, so much to show you before you return to your committees and your recruiting meetings, before you add to your bag of recruits — those young recruits you enroll so proudly with your patriotic speeches, your red, white, and blue rosettes, your white feathers, your insults, your lies . . . any bloody lie to secure a fresh victim.

What? You cannot stick it any longer? You are going? I didn't think you'd stay. But I've got to stay, haven't I? . . . I've got to stay. You've got me out here, and you'll keep me out here. You've got me haloed. I am one of the Splendid Young Women who are winning the War . . .

'Loaded. Six stretchers and three sitters!'

I am away. I slow up at the station gate. The sergeant is waiting with his pencil and list.

I repeat, 'Six stretchers and three sitters.'

'Number Eight.'

He ticks off my ambulance. I pass out of the yard.

HELEN ZENNA SMITH

The Forbidden Zone

Conspiracy

It is all carefully arranged. Everything is arranged. It is arranged that men should be broken and that they should be mended. Just as you send your clothes to the laundry and mend them

329

when they come back, so we send our men to the trenches and mend them when they come back again. You send your socks and your shirts again and again to the laundry, and you sew up the tears and clip the ravelled edges again and again just as many times as they will stand it. And then you throw them away. And we send our men to the war again and again, just as long as they will stand it; just until they are dead, and then we throw them into the ground.

It is all arranged. Ten kilometres from here along the road is the place where men are wounded. This is the place where they are mended. We have all the things here for mending, the tables and the needles, and the thread and the knives and the scissors, and many curious things that you never use for your clothes.

We bring our men up along the dusty road where the bushes grow on either side and the green trees. They come by in the mornings in companies, marching with strong legs, with firm steps. They carry their knapsacks easily. Their knapsacks and their guns and their greatcoats are not heavy for them. They wear their caps jauntily, tilted to one side. Their faces are ruddy and their eyes bright. They smile and call out with strong voices. They throw kisses to the girls in the fields.

We send our men up the broken road between bushes of barbed wire and they come back to us, one by one, two by two in ambulances, lying on stretchers. They lie on their backs on the stretchers and are pulled out of the ambulances as loaves of bread are pulled out of the oven. The stretchers slide out of the mouths of the ambulances with the men on them. The men cannot move. They are carried into a shed, unclean bundles, very heavy, covered with brown blankets.

We receive these bundles. We pull off a blanket. We observe that this is a man. He makes feeble whining sounds like an animal. He lies still; he smells bad; he smells like a corpse; he can only move his tongue; he tries to moisten his lips with his tongue.

This is the place where he is to be mended. We lift him on to a table. We peel off his clothes, his coat and his shirt and his trousers and his boots. We handle his clothes that are stiff with blood. We cut off his shirt with large scissors. We stare at the obscene sight of his innocent wounds. He allows us to do this. He is helpless to stop us. We wash off the dry blood round the edges of his wounds. He suffers us to do as we like with him. He says no word except that he is thirsty and we do not give him to drink.

We confer together over his body and he hears us. We discuss his different parts in terms that he does not understand, but he listens while we make calculations with his heart beats and the pumping breath of his lungs.

We conspire against his right to die. We experiment with his bones, his muscles, his sinews, his blood. We dig into the yawning mouths of his wounds. Helpless openings, they let us into the secret places of his body. We plunge deep into his body. We make discoveries within his body. To the shame of the havoc of his limbs we add the insult of our curiosity and the curse of our purpose, the purpose to remake him. We lay odds on his chances of escape, and we combat with death, his Saviour.

It is our business to do this. He knows and he allows us to do it. He finds himself in the operating room. He lays himself out. He bares himself to our knives. His mind is annihilated. He pours out his blood unconscious. His red blood is spilled and pours over the table on to the floor while he sleeps.

After this, while he is still asleep, we carry him into another place and put him to bed. He awakes bewildered as children do, expecting, perhaps, to find himself at home with his mother leaning over him, and he moans a little and then lies still again. He is helpless, so we do for him what he cannot do for himself, and he is grateful. He accepts his helplessness. He is obedient. We feed him, and he eats. We fatten him up, and he allows himself to be fattened. Day after day he lies there and we watch him. All day and all night he is watched. Every day his wounds are uncovered and cleaned, scraped and washed and bound up again. His body does not belong to him. It belongs to us for the moment, not for long. He knows why we tend it so carefully. He knows what we are fattening and cleaning it up for; and while we handle it he smiles.

He is only one among thousands. They are all the same. They all let us do with them what we like. They all smile as if they were grateful. When we hurt them they try not to cry out, not wishing to hurt our feelings. And often they apologise for dying. They would not die and disappoint us if they could help it. Indeed, in their helplessness they do the best they can to help us get them ready to go back again.

MARY BORDEN

Piety, Pacifism and
Turkish Women

Pall Mall Gazette, 16 March 1917

Sung Down

Perth (Australia) Monday
Miss Adela Pankhurst attempted to-day at the Midland Junction,
a strong Labour Centre, to deliver a lecture directed against Mr
Lloyd George and Mr Hughes. The audience sang her down with
'Rule Britannia' and 'Australia Will Be There'.

Daily Telegraph, 10 August 1917

Female Pacifists' Parade

Miss Sylvia Pankhurst and several supporters paraded outside
the House of Commons last night hawking copies of 'The
Workers Dreadnought'. Instead of contents boards they carried
linen bannerettes inscribed 'War is Murder', 'Give us back our
Brothers', 'Give us back our Sons', 'The Men in the Trenches
Long for Peace', and 'Stop this Capitalist War.' A good deal of
angry comment was occasioned by the parade, and in one

instance at least physical force was used in an attempt to destroy an offending banner—Some Canadian soldiers were moved to forcible language by the 'Soldiers in the trenches Long for Peace' legend, and shouted, 'It's a lie!', while another, addressing a policeman, asked if it was not possible to stop such a disgraceful display. 'I've come nearly four thousand miles to fight for this country,' he said with heat, 'and here, outside the Houses of Parliament, I find this sort of thing going on.'

Le Petit Journal, March 1917

A Second Jeanne d'Arc

In a remote corner of Anjou lives a young peasant girl, Claire Ferchaud, whose name as a seer of visions has spread throughout France — twenty-one years of age, destitute of vanity, respected by the neighbours, and of exemplary piety.

The clergy of the district, while sympathetic, prefer to express no opinion regarding the authenticity of the reported manifestations. The girl herself is quite illiterate, but her spoken and written *(by somebody else, presumably, if she was illiterate)* accounts of what the voices she has heard said to her would, as one priest remarked, have been remarkable coming from a theologian or a professor of canonical law.

She herself is very modest, disliking all the publicity now surrounding her, and saying that the current idea that it is she who will save France is exaggerated. All she asks is that people should pray for her rather than play the part of curious spectators. Still, the fact remains that there are in the little chapel near her parents' farm the photographs of over 30,000 poilus which they have left or sent asking for her prayers for their safety, and that many thousand pilgrims have travelled many leagues to kneel at the same altar where Claire Ferchaud knelt and heard spiritual voices.

Turkey's Time of Crisis

The shortage of bread is a great cause for complaint among the women. The Turkish Government, at the instigation of the Germans, early in the present year introduced a rationing system, but the wealthy Turks declined to submit to it, and the elaborate organisation set up speedily collapsed. The apathy of the Turks angers the foreign observer. Only once have they been roused from their apathy, and that was when the thousands of wounded poured into Constantinople from the Dardanelles. The sight of their dying men-folk caused several hundred women to march to the War Office to call on the Government to give them back their husbands and their sons.

In Turkey, as in other belligerent countries, the war has opened up new avenues of employment to women. The Greeks and Armenians formerly employed at the post and telephone offices have been dismissed and their places taken by Turkish women and girls. The war has hastened rather than checked the emancipation of Turkish women. All the young women wear veils of the flimsiest description, and in the tramcars they always draw them up from their faces. An incident which illustrates the strength of the 'new woman' movement in Turkey occurred quite recently. The following notice was issued by the police department:

The adoption of new forms of apparel has become a public scandal in Constantinople. All Mohammedan women are given two days in which to lengthen their skirts, discard corsets, and substitute thick for flimsy veils.

Two days passed, and the following notice appeared:

We regret that through the interference of certain old women a subordinate of the police department has attempted to regulate the costumes which Mohammedan women wear. The police department regrets this blunder and cancels the previous order.

The 'police subordinate' who blundered was an invention of the department, anxious to find an excuse to capitulate to the storm which the original order provoked. The wives of Turkish aristocrats, Ministers and high Government officials threatened to hold up the Red Crescent nursing work in Turkey, the telephone girls threatened to strike, the post-office girls to leave the post-office, unless the offending order was cancelled; and before two days had passed Turkish women, determined to be Westernised, had won. The incident provoked an outburst of indignation on the part of the women against the German authorities in Turkey, who were accused, probably wrongly, with wanting to keep Turkish women in a backward condition.

'Crossing the Bar'

My War Experiences in Two Continents

As the hot weather advanced it was hoped to move Miss Macnaughtan to the country. Her friends showered invitations on 'dear Sally' to come and convalesce with them, but the plans fell through. It became increasingly clear that the traveller was about to embark on that last journey from which there is no return, and, indeed, towards the end her sufferings were so great that those who loved her best could only pray that she might not have long to wait. She passed away in the afternoon of Monday, July 24th, 1916.

A few days later the body of Sarah Broom Macnaughtan was laid to rest in the plot of ground reserved for her kinsfolk in the churchyard at Chart Sutton, in Kent. It is very quiet there up on the hill, the great Weald stretches away to the south, and fruit-trees surround the Hallowed Acre. But even as they laid earth to earth and dust to dust in this peaceful spot the booming of the guns in Flanders broke the quiet of the sunny afternoon, and reminded the little funeral party that they were indeed burying one whose life had been sacrificed in the Great War.

Surely those who pass through the old churchyard will pause by the grave, with its beautiful grey cross, and the children growing up in the parish will come there sometimes, and will read and remember the simple inscription on it:

'In the Great War, by Word and Deed, at Home and Abroad, She served her Country even unto Death.'

Postscript to Sarah Macnaughtan's war diaries
edited by her niece
MRS LIONEL SALMON

With a Woman's Unit In Serbia, Salonika and Sebastopol

The Passing of Mrs. Harley

In December 1916, after the great work of the advance was over, Mrs. Harley resigned the command of the transport unit of the Scottish Women's Hospitals. She severed her connection with our Association and went to do relief work in the town of Monastir, for she felt that it was in this manner that she could best give her services. This town had been retaken in the Franco-Serbian advance of November 1916, and was still in the hands of the Allies—

It was the call of the children that touched Mrs. Harley, and early in January 1917 she and her daughter Edith had gone to Monastir laden with stores to start a feeding-centre for the hungry ones. British Headquarters were very much against her going there, and thought it was much too dangerous a mission, nevertheless she quickly got a successful scheme started. She lived in a little Turkish house, and though there was but little furniture in it, it was at all events quite intact, and was a little palace compared with the tent that had been her home for nearly two years. There were even a few red plush-covered chairs that must have hailed from Vienna, and with these, a camp-bed and a Primus stove, an old Serbian orderly as cook-general, and plenty of work, she was absolutely happy.

Bombardments took place, but as they were usually at the same hour each day, the people knew when to retreat to the cellars, and working hours could therefore be arranged. In a very short time Mrs. Harley got her scheme well organized.

On the afternoon of March 7th, after a busy day's work, there was tea and biscuits in the little Turkish house, and Mrs. Harley and a few friends were gathered there to enjoy this great luxury. Mrs. Harley was sitting by the window and was as usual bright and happy and talking of new schemes. Although it was not the time of the usual bombardment, a shell burst close at hand, and, as the custom was, everyone at once lay prone on the floor until the bombardment should cease. Looking up, Edith noticed that her mother was still sitting in her chair by the window, and entreated her to come and lie down on the floor for safety. There was no answer. She was already dead. The wound, which was a small one in the centre of the forehead, did not disfigure her beautiful face, and it was caused by a small fragment of shrapnel. She was taken to the military hospital, but there was nothing to be done. It was as though she had been translated; one second alive, happy, full of energy, the next, without pain, warning, or even a cry of apprehension, she was no longer one of us.

The funeral was arranged by the British Commander-in-Chief—The music was provided by the Serbian Royal Guards and by British and French bands. The coffin was carried on a light bier, escorted by British soldiers and preceded by the Serbian Royal Guards and French soldiers carrying huge laurel wreaths. We walked from the Curassi Road, where the procession was formed, some three-quarters of a mile to Zeitenlik Cemetery. It was a bitterly cold day, and the wind rushed across the bare hills and swirled down the exposed road. The tranquil Funeral March of Chopin and the restless, anxious Dead March in Saul were played alternately, the sound coming in a curious panting way carried by the puffs of wind. Florence and Edith Harley, Miss Palin and I, walked immediately after the bier. Behind us walked a long column of the most distinguished officers in Macedonia—

then came the Scottish Women's Hospital staff, members of the other hospitals, soldiers of all the Allied armies, and literally thousands of civilians. It was all most beautifully arranged, and was carried out with much dignity and with full military honours.

I. E. Emslie Hutton, MD

Dr. Elsie Inglis

The storm had spent itself, and the moon was riding high in a cloudless heaven, when others waiting in Edinburgh on the 26th learnt the news that she too had passed through the storm and shadows, and had crossed the bar—

Her people brought her back to the city of her fathers, and to the hearts who had sent her forth, and carried her on the wings of their strong confidence—

The Madonna lilies, the lilies of France and of the fields, were placed around her. Over her hung the torn banners of Scotland's history. The Scottish women had wrapped their country's flag around them in one of their hard-pressed flights. On her coffin, as she lay looking to the East in high St. Giles', were placed the flags of Great Britain and Serbia.

She had worn 'the faded ribbons' of the orders bestowed on her by France, Russia, and Serbia. It has often been asked at home and abroad why she had received no decorations at the hands of her Sovereign. It is not an easy question to answer.

On November the 29th, Dr. Inglis was buried, amid marks of respect and recognition which make that passing stand alone in the history of the last rites of any of her fellow-citizens. Great was the company gathered within the church. The chancel was filled by her family and relatives – her Suffrage colleagues, representatives from all the societies, the officials of the hospitals and hostels she had founded at home, the units whom she had led and by whose aid she had done great things abroad. Last and first of all true-hearted mourners the people of Serbia represented by

340

their Minister and members of the Legation. The chief of the Scottish Command was present, and by his orders military honours were paid to this happy warrior of the Red Cross.

The service had for its keynote the Hallelujah Chorus, which was played as the procession left St. Giles'—

The buglers of the Royal Scots sounded 'the Reveille to the waking morn,' and the coffin with the Allied flags was placed on the gun carriage. Women were in the majority of the massed crowd that awaited the last passing. 'Why did they no gie her the V.C.?' asked the shawl-draped women holding the bairns of her care: these and many another of her fellow-citizens lined the route and followed on foot the long road across the city—

LADY FRANCES BALFOUR

Manchester Guardian, 24 December 1917

Memorial Service to Elizabeth Garrett Anderson

The memorial service at Christ Church, Endell Street, on Sat a.m. to the late Mrs Garrett Anderson, the first English woman doctor, was a moving tribute to her work for the world. Two significant features marked off the service.

First, women took a considerable part in it. In place of the ordinary choir a number of women medical students led the singing, others acted as sideswomen, while a woman played the organ. Then again, the note of the service was not one of grief, but of thanksgiving and joy in the memory of a noble career. Instead of the customary funeral march, the service ended with 'Hark! the herald angels sing,' followed by a carol.

1918

On the Home Fronts war weariness had for the majority become the order of the day. In Britain a limited number of women – aged thirty with household qualifications – finally obtained the right to vote, while a wider franchise was won in the key American state of New York.

On the Western Front in March General Ludendorff launched the last great German offensive, knowing that unless he could bring the French and British armies to their knees before massive American reinforcements arrived, his country would lose the war. Field-Marshal Haig rallied his battered troops with a 'Backs to the Wall' message (which in the chaos few heard), while the Allied Commander-in-Chief General Foch remained buoyantly optimistic. Both men had learned a few lessons from the disasters of Verdun, the Somme *et al.*, and though advance German units again reached the River Marne they were soon retreating.

By August the Allies were on the offensive and the 'Black Day' of the German army occurred. Thereafter the Central Powers collapsed like dominoes. In September the Bulgarians, pushed steadily back on the Salonika front, signed an armistice; in October German sailors mutinied at Kiel and there were food riots in many cities; in Palestine the Turks surrendered to General Allenby; by early November riots and Socialist uprisings were occurring throughout Germany and Austria-Hungary withdrew from the fray.

At the eleventh hour of the eleventh day of the eleventh month the German armistice came into effect. All was awesomely quiet on the Western Front.

Votes for Women!

Manchester Guardian, 2 May 1917

The Ladies' Grille

That Ministerial Jack-of-all-Trades the First Commissioner of Works, in the intervals of refurnishing ducal mansions to suit new Government Departments and carving allotments out of the grounds of Holyrood Palace, may shortly be empowered to remove the Ladies' Grille from the House of Commons. Members who discussed the project yesterday were quite ready to admit that it will hardly be possible when women are enfranchised to pen a portion of the electorate behind a harem-like lattice screen in the Legislature. But in mitigation of a device that amazes everyone who sees it for the first time, except perhaps a Turk, it should be remembered that its institution was in the nature of a legitimate reprisal. In the brave days of the eighteenth century women not only watched the proceedings of Parliament, but gossiped merrily with members while debates were in progress. This was, indeed, a recognised evening amusement among the 'quality,' and Lady Mary Wortley Montagu records that when on one occasion the Commons decided that they would have 'no unnecessary auditors' the Duchess of Queensberry headed a resolute party of titled ladies who besieged the House and on being told by the Chancellor that 'By God, they should not come in' replied that 'By God, they would come in, despite the Chancellor and the whole House,' and having thumped, kicked, and rapped the door for a while with such violence that the speakers inside were scarce heard, they finally, and by subterfuge, forced an entrance. For an even wilder example of this sort of conduct they were excluded in 1778 for fifty years, though now and then a few were allowed to peer through a ventilator in the roof from which they could see the Speaker's legs and the tops of the heads of a few members. On this arrangement the present grille, proposed in 1835, was regarded as a dangerous advance. Lord Brougham remarked that ladies, though he liked to see them in their proper places, would be better employed in almost any way than in attending Parliamentary debates, and the Marquis of Lansdowne backed him vigorously in this view. It is a refreshing measure of our access of sanity about woman's part as a citizen that the grille should to-day be by common consent declared an indignity and an absurdity.

The Cause

Victory in the House of Commons

For all their certainty, however, the women who thronged the Ladies' Gallery on 19th June, when the House was to take the committee stage of Clause IV (the Women's Suffrage clause), were desperately excited. Often as some of them had sat there before, to hear their cause mocked at, or obstructed, or outvoted in the Chamber below, the scene was still painfully impressive. Through the bars of the absurd little cage in which they were penned they saw chiefly the tops of the heads of the legislators, but the atmosphere of excitement which pervaded the House was noticeable even so. Members trooped in in unwonted num-bers, and more than filled the benches. A dense crowd stood below the Bar, and overflowed into the side galleries. All the well-known friends and enemies were in their places, and there was that irrepressible buzz of sound which arises when the attention of the assembly is really aroused.

The debate went its way, noticeable chiefly for the great number of favourable speakers, and the hopeless tone of the opponents. They spoke, some of them, with all the passion which accrues to the convictions of a lifetime; those who still stood out against the change sincerely believed that it would spell ruin to the State, and disaster to the homes of the country, and spoke, therefore, from their consciences and their hearts. But they were very few. The tide had really turned, and when the time for the division came there were found to be but 55 opponents in the whole House, while 385, seven times their number, went into the other Lobby. This vote was larger than even the most optimistic had expected. It was victory without reserve.

RAY STRACHEY

The Cause

Victory: House of Lords: 8–10 January 1918

Lord Curzon wound up the debate on the afternoon of the 10th of January, and as he rose to speak there was a hush of excitement. One of the policemen at the door, friendly as the police always were to the women, went along the passage to the committee-room, where a number of them were gathered, and put his head round the door. 'Lord Curzon is up, ladies,' he announced, 'but 'e won't do you no 'arm.' And so it was. For the President of the Anti-Suffrage League was forced to strike his colours. He said, indeed, that the passage of the Bill would be the ruin of the country; women were politically worthless, and the whole ideal of the Women's Movement was disastrous and wrong; he felt bound to say these things, for he believed them. But when

347

it came to action he could not give so certain a lead. The majority in the House of Commons had been too big, and if the Upper House rejected Women's Suffrage all that would happen would be that the Bill would return to them again with the clause re-inserted—For his part, he said, he could not take upon himself the responsibility of 'precipitating a conflict from which your Lordships would not emerge with credit,' and he would abstain from voting, one way or the other, upon the clause. With that dramatic and wholly unexpected announcement the discussion ended, and the voting began; and the suffragists, as they waited for the figures, knew that their fight was won. One hundred and thirty-four Peers voted for the clause, 71 against it, and 13 abstained. The Representation of the People Bill was through both Houses; and on 6th February it received the Royal Assent and became the law of the land. The fifty years' struggle was over, and the sex barrier was broken down.

RAY STRACHEY

Suffrage Victory

Frau Marie Stritt, president of the Deutscher Reichsverbund für Frauenstimmrecht, to Mary Sheepshanks, editor of _Jus Suffragii_

We greet the victory of Englishwoman as especially significant for the women of the whole world — Like the dawn of a newer, better day, hope arises for us women and for tortured humanity out of the night of unspeakable and immeasurable sufferings of the last few years.

The vote was 'given' to them in 1918 rather as a biscuit is given to a performing dog who has just done its tricks particularly well.

MRS C. S. PEEL

From the Women's Council of Uruguay to the National Union of Women Workers of Great Britain, May 1918

The news of the passing of the Bill giving the vote to a great number of Englishwomen has overwhelmed us with joy, the greater in that the triumph is the exclusive work of woman, who during this horrible war has found a means of showing what she can do and be in social and, moreover, in economic value.

—We, your distant sisters, pray that you will accept our enthusiastic acclamations. May all women everywhere obtain from their sisters that which with your noble perseverance you have won from the great English Parliament – the honour and pride of democracy.

Le Journal, 22 June 1917

Women Suffragist Views

'Yes, we are claiming full political rights for women. They have earned them through the heavy burdens, both social and economic, that they have borne during the war. History shows that throughout long, exacting wars women have replaced absent men. But the gains they have won by their courage and intelligence have been in vain, because they have never enjoyed civil rights. In the France of tomorrow, there will be continuing need for us women, for the good of all, otherwise the same thing will happen again.'

MARGUERITE DURAND

'While the war lasts, there seems little likelihood of the commission of universal suffrage amending the current electoral system. We should, however, like to see Parliament tackling the problem, not only to be sure of our success, but to rouse public opinion and make people understand the importance of the question for the future of our country.'

MARIA VÉRONE

'For the moment, we consider that we should confine ourselves to municipal votes and elections, but on the condition that this does not limit our civil rights, as the Commission has done by refusing to allow us to be delegates to the Senate. We shall, of course, be delighted if we are given more than we ask, but we shall limit our ambitions, because we know it is wise to proceed step by step. In any case, electoral reform must be effected before any post-war reorganisation. Women will be called upon to collaborate in this task, as they collaborated in war work.'

MADAME DE WITT SCHLUMBERGER

Letter to the Editor of the New York Times

July 23, 1917

Dear Sir:–

In discussing the case of the small group of women in Washington who have been 'picketing' the White House, the Times makes an error which is appearing in many newspapers. It is to the effect that in Great Britain when war was declared, Mrs. Pankhurst and her militant organization laid aside their work for suffrage and devoted themselves to the demands of the war, and as a result the House of Commons by a large majority has voted to grant woman suffrage. They advise the women of the United States to profit by this example.

Nothing could be further from the truth—

The great mobilization of women's work during the war has been under the auspices of the National Union of Women's

350

Suffrage Societies, which corresponds to our National Suffrage Association and was formed the same year, in 1869. Mrs. Henry Fawcett has been its President for a quarter of a century; it has hundreds of branches and tens of thousands of dues-paying members; its methods have been strictly constitutional and non-militant and it has always been the bulwark of the suffrage movement in Great Britain. At the beginning of the war its Board of Officers at once placed all its resources at the service of the Government; its large income, its various headquarters and its force of trained workers. It has established hospitals in various countries wholly staffed by women and furnished ambulances and sent hundreds of women doctors and nurses to the front. Several of these 'units' are called by the name of Mrs. Fawcett. This Association has continued to publish its paper, 'The Common Cause', held its annual conventions and kept its organization intact throughout the war. Under the auspices of this newspaper a large building was recently completed in one of the munition centers for the care of its thousands of women workers. The Union has looked after the families of the soldiers and also thousands of the Belgian refugees, women and children.

It is because of the activities of this National Union that the Government has been brought to the point of conferring the suffrage on women. Its first action, with seventeen of its affiliations, when the decision of the House of Commons to consider woman suffrage was announced, was to hold a public demonstration in London, participated in by representative women from seventy trades, professions and organizations and officers of the Women's Liberal Federation, National Union of Women Workers, British Women's Temperance Association and many others. Mrs. Fawcett presided, members of Parliament were among the speakers and all urged the Government to act without delay. This was followed by mass meetings in various cities. Later Lloyd George received Mrs. Fawcett and the largest delegation that ever appeared before a Prime Minister.

Mrs. Pankhurst was not present on any of these occasions—
There is no desire to minimize the great personal sacrifices of
herself and her associates, but the statement that the franchise was
finally granted as a reward to them for ceasing their militancy is so
widely at variance with the facts that it should not be accepted.

Very truly yours,

IDA HUSTED HARPER,
Editorial Chairman Leslie Suffrage Bureau

U.S. Suffrage: Summer 1918

The United States is the only English-speaking nation, if we
except the southern extremity of Africa, which has not enfranchised women. It has become a pariah amongst nations.

IDA HUSTED HARPER

New York Times, 6 November 1918

New York Women's First Election Day

Mrs Carrie Chapman Catt, leader of the National Suffrage party,
did not let voting interfere with her daily morning marketing but
cast a ballot at 8 a.m. between visits to the butcher and baker.
Voting and marketing, notwithstanding the fact she had to wait for
parcels at two stores and have her picture taken at the polls, took
exactly twenty minutes, of which two were devoted to voting.

What is coming to be known as the baby carriage vote was
heavy between ten and noon when the sun was out. Women said
they found policemen outside the polls very obliging about
watching the babies while they voted.

In Brooklyn a woman of 92 years, Mrs Henrietta Benjamin,
voted soon after 6 a.m. at the booth on Fulton Street. She was
glad to vote before she died — Some of the new voters found that
too much knowledge is a dangerous thing. One woman said, 'The

more I read about the different candidates the more disgusted I am with the idea of voting for any of them.'

Dr. Katharine B. Davis, who voted at 165 East Thirty-fourth Street in a florist shop said, 'It felt fine to vote. My sister, who went with me to the poll said, "I hope grandmother can see us here." You see grandmother was the first suffragist in our family.'

Daily News, 25 July 1917

A Woman Candidate

MISS MACADAMS, THE CANADIAN NURSE WHO IS CONTESTING A SEAT IN ALBERTA

FROM OUR SPECIAL CORRESPONDENT

Orpington, Kent, Tuesday.
At the Ontario military hospital here I have had a chat with the nursing sister, Lieutenant Roberta MacAdams, Canadian Army Medical Corps, who, at the invitation of a strong delegation, is standing as a candidate for the Alberta Legislature. For two seats there are 21 candidates, including several lieutenant-colonels, and the voters, 38,000 soldiers and 75 nurses from Alberta, will cast their votes early next month.

Miss MacAdams, who has been engaged in hospital work in this country for 18 months, is a tall, attractive woman, with a soft musical voice such as one hears in the North of Ireland, where her father was born. She has a wonderful record of public work in the province of Alberta. She had charge of the teaching of household arts in all the schools in Edmonton, spent a year in the Department of Agriculture, and organised classes for women in the agricultural school, and has given five years to social service.

Very modestly she discussed with me her platform, which does not concern women's interests alone. She claims to know the aspirations of the soldiers when the war is over, and realises that

353

on the work of reconstruction will depend the standard of living to which the men will return. Miss MacAdams holds that while men are likely to think in terms of money, women will think in terms of human life.

She is prosecuting her candidature by means of a circular letter and poster which are being sent to all the hospitals where soldiers from Alberta are being nursed and to all the units in which they are fighting.

'If the good wishes I have received will get me into Parliament,' she said, 'I am there.'

Lieutenant MacAdams was elected with a substantial vote.

The Times, 19 June 1918

A Suffragist's Taxes

The reappointed public examination of Miss Evelyn Jane Sharp was held in the Bankruptcy Court yesterday. The examination had been adjourned *sine die* when the debtor last appeared. She had declined to pay the petitioning creditor's debt or to give information about her affairs because she was unfranchised. The petitioning creditor was the Crown, claiming £57 for taxes. The debtor now answered questions by the Official Receiver. She said that the political condition of women had been materially altered. All her debts had been paid.

The Times, 14 October 1918

Medical Women and Income Tax

Sir,

During the war we have seen the War Office seeking to increase its supply of medical practitioners by utilizing the services of women doctors.

Women are employed as surgeons in the General Military Hospital, Endell-street (573 beds), in many other places in the United Kingdom, and abroad in Malta, Salonika, and Egypt. Their competence as physicians and surgeons has not been disputed. Their position in military hospitals is, however, an unsatisfactory one. They are required to do the work of commissioned officers without a commission or even an honorary commission which would entitle them to wear badges of rank.

At the Military Hospital, Endell-street, where the entire staff consists of women, the duties of the doctor in charge are those of a colonel, and the discipline of the hospital is vested in her. The other members of the medical staff are graded and paid as officers. They perform all the duties of commissioned officers, and while they succeed in maintaining satisfactory discipline in their wards their work would be greatly facilitated if they were entitled to wear the badge of rank which the men recognize as a mark of authority. Medical women serving the War Office do not desire commissions for their own aggrandisement or in order that they may use military titles, but that their work may be more efficient, and that they may be spared the necessity of enforcing their authority, by a conscious personal effort, on the men passing through their wards. In civilian life medical women have the same status as medical men. Attached to the R.A.M.C., they receive the same rate of pay, but their status is an inferior one.

The Income-tax Commissioners have taken advantage of the anomalous position of women working in military hospitals to deny them the Service rate of income-tax. When appealed to on the ground that they are engaged 'in service of a military or naval character in connexion with the present war, for which they are paid out of moneys provided by Parliament,' the Commissioners refused the appeal, on the ground that the work of medical women in a general military hospital, such as Endell-street, is 'not work of a military character.' It is hoped that, by giving publicity to these facts, the necessary amendments may be made in the Finance Act and the Army Act, and that the service which women doctors are proud to give their country may no longer be hampered by petty difficulties and inequalities.

Yours faithfully,

LOUISA GARRETT ANDERSON, M.D.LON

The Living Present

It is probable that after this war is over the women of the belligerent nations will be given the franchise by the weary men that are left, if they choose to insist upon it. They have shown the same bravery, endurance, self-sacrifice, resource, and grim determination as the men. In every war, it may be argued, women have displayed the same spirit and the same qualities, proving that they needed but the touchstone of opportunity to reveal the splendor of their endowment, but treated by man, as soon as peace was restored, as the same old inferior annex.

This is true enough, but the point of difference is that never, prior to the Great War, was such an enormous body of women awake after the lethargic submission of centuries, and clamoring for their rights. Never before have millions of women been supporting themselves; never before had they even contemplated organization and the direct political attack. Of course the women of Europe, exalted and worked half to death, have, with the exception of a few irrepressibles, put all idea of self-aggrandizement aside for the moment; but this idea had grown too big and too dominant to be dismissed for good and all, with last year's fashions and the memory of delicate *plats* prepared by chefs now serving valiantly within the lines. The big idea, the master desire, the obsession, if you like, is merely taking an enforced rest, and there is persistent speculation as to what the thinking and the energetic women of Europe will do when this war is over, and how far men will help or hinder them.

GERTRUDE ATHERTON

356

Women Still at War

Modern Troubadors

In Egypt

We gave a concert at the hospital in Cairo last night, and one night we went to Gara; there were 2000 men there, and we gave a most wonderful concert. A platform was erected for us in the open. We had two great big electric lights for illumination, and the men sat on the sand in a huge semicircle – wave upon wave of them – and the stars were all out overhead, and everything was very, very still, except for the music we were making. I sometimes have to remind myself that this is not all a dream.

We have been to Luxor. We had a day and a half there, and it was so wonderful. We saw Karnak and Luxor temples and the tombs of the Kings of Thebes, and did thirteen miles on donkeys. The next day we got up at 5.30 a.m., and did a twelve hours' train journey and got to Shusha, where we gave a concert the same night. At Shusha and Gara we rode camels, the most supercilious and cynical brutes. When they get up you think you are coming off; they oscillate their necks so that they can bite your calves if they feel that way, and look down their noses at you and open their mouths, exposing terrifying yellow teeth, and say, 'Wuff, wuff, wuff.'

LENA ASHWELL

Flanders and Other Fields

An End to Pervyse

In February 1918 we went over to London for the grand Gala Sunday Matinée at the Alhambra in Charing Cross Road. This had been arranged for us ('The Women of Pervyse') by the famous actress Eva Moore, under the patronage of the Belgian Ambassador. Many Society beauties were fluttering about in the aisles selling programmes, and the place was simply packed. The programme included many celebrated artistes: Eva Moore, Irene Vanbrugh, who recited 'England, My England' with tremendous feeling, Mark Hambourg, the well-known Liszt pianist, the comedian Joe Coyne, and Violet Loraine and Marie Lloyd, who both sang so wonderfully.

I was second on the bill – and after the West End Cinema Theatre Orchestra under the direction of M. Luna – and was in a highly nervous state by the time I reached the stage. However, I got through my talk about Pervyse without any mishaps, and was told that it was a great success.

After I had done my bit I was able to relax and listen to violin and cello solos, and to a pretty soprano, all elocution and evening dress, who announced:

> Down in the forest something stirred,
> It was only the note of a bird.

This kind of pathos was not exactly my cup of tea. I preferred G. H. Elliott's Plantation Songs. But the matinée brought in well over £1000, and after we had been duly invested with our Order of St John at an impressive ceremony the next day we returned to Pervyse with the knowledge that we were well placed to extend the work and improve our equipment.

Our dug-out had been enlarged and its concrete reinforced with iron railings salvaged from all over the village, and we had reached a peak of fame and fortune. It couldn't last, of course, and of course it didn't—

It happened on March the 17th, 1918, almost exactly a month after the triumphal matinée. The Germans were preparing a terrific bombardment, and something warned me that we should get up and put on our gas-masks. Remembering to manoeuvre round the trap-door, I roused Mairi and called Barker and Beaumont. Just as they came up from their funk-hole there was a tremendous explosion, and gas poured through the slit. We started to pull on our masks, but we were all coughing and choking so much that it seemed a bit pointless.

My head was swimming, and I felt horribly sick. The place was in complete darkness, and I could see little through the goggles of my mask. Just as I found my torch and switched it on I heard voices cursing and swearing in the lower dug-out, into which some would-be rescuers had fallen, through the trap-door. I managed to crawl over and wheeze out some instructions as to how to get out of this lower dug-out. One of the men had already located the ladder. I heard him coming, but had not the strength to get out of the way, and so got a splendid uppercut from his steel helmet.

I vaguely remember being carried to an ambulance. The driver was saying, 'For Christ's sake hurry'; he wanted to get out of Pervyse and its shells. That is my last memory of the village where I had spent three and a half fantastic years.

BARONESS DE T'SERCLAES (MRS ELSIE KNOCKER)

That Friend of Mine: A Memoir of Marguerite McArthur

April 7th, 1918

I am loving it all, and it is more absorbingly interesting than I could have imagined. There is a lot of keenness for classes in a variety of subjects (I have been asked to arrange for Hebrew, Greek, botany, mining, engineering amongst more ordinary ones!) and the library is a great draw. All one's ideas of the overwhelming popularity of sevenpennies vanish promptly. Of course many men never ask for anything but fiction, but a large percentage are keen on poetry, plays, essays, history, science, travel, and so on. Shall I tell you what I do on a typical day? It starts late with breakfast at the mess about 9.30 – then a visit to the central bookstore or to our H.Q. for letters and parcels – then up to the hut by a walk along the river.—We are a big party for lunch, and I help to hand plates and dishes, clear the table, etc. Then, about 2.15, comes my free time till tea at 4. But as it is my only time for preparing for classes, there's not much choice as to methods of spending it! All the same, I sometimes go to visit men in hospital, or for a walk in the woods springing out of the sandhills, where the trees throw blue and pink shadows on the dazzling sand; or up the road by the river, past the cemetery, with its serried rows of little wooden crosses, where nowadays a military funeral, coffin draped with the Union Jack, is a common sight. I went once with some relatives, and was tremendously moved and impressed by the reverent simplicity of the service, and by the sense of triumphant peace outweighing the sadness. The cemetery is beautifully placed, looking across to the sea and England, with firwoods behind, and the sound of the winds and waves playing over it. Well, I have wandered much from the point. After tea is my busiest time; more men are off duty, and they crowd round the library counter, which is (or should be!) a bureau of miscellaneous information—Unfortunately, the evening is the only possible time for classes, so when mine are on I have to hand over the library to someone else. At present we have French (three classes twice a week, taught by me, if you please!), Shakespeare reading circle (likewise mine), Latin, shorthand, mathematics. I am just going to embark on English literature, and hope soon to arrange for history and several other subjects. I have the most flourishing French classes – about 12 in each – very keen. I found out by chance that at one hospital, from which several orderlies come, they have meetings between classes, to prepare and recapitulate. I love the teaching, partly, I suppose, because I only get the keen people – if they are bored they simply go! Shakespeare, too, is flourishing. We have nearly finished 'Hamlet,' and have had some excellent discussions. We have also just started an education committee for the Base, and this week are beginning central classes for Russian, Spanish, Italian, German, Latin and French.

Library and classes keep me as busy as I can be till 8.30, then I close everything and make a dash for the town and supper at 9. After that I go home with the friend I live with, and there are book lists to make out, classes to think of and prepare, letters and mending to get through, the day's experiences to talk over, and our kind French Madame always wants a little chat. So it is 12 at earliest before we get to bed; and I don't usually remember anything else till it's time to get up!

The men are dears. We have talks on every subject under the sun, grave and gay. I think that's one of the things they like best about a librarian – that one of her jobs is to be there to be talked to! I haven't described the hut. It is a double one – canteen in one huge room, with a stage at one end – library in the other, in which the men read or write and play quiet games. Then there is a billiard room and a class room, and separate rest rooms for the relatives. And I think that's all my news.

JOSEPHINE KELLETT

The Last Ride

The hardest job in the convoy was admittedly that of the big lorry, for, early and late, it was first and last on the field. It took all the stretchers and blankets to the different hospitals, cleared up the quay after an early evacuation, brought stretchers and blankets up to the convoy, took the officers' kits to hospital and boats, and rationed the ambulance trains and barges.

—While the Vulcan went for a thorough overhauling, a Wyllis-Overland was sent in its place. It was old and worn, and the men in Boulogne had refused to drive it. The tyres were solid, all vestige of springs had long since vanished from the seat and the roof was covered with tin so that it bent and rattled like stage thunder. The gears were very worn, and as you got out, the lever never lost the opportunity of slipping into first gear. Consequently the lorry always tried to run over you when you cranked up unless you remembered this foible.

It was chain-driven, and once on the move was like a travelling thunder-clap, so that it was impossible to hear what anyone said even if they were sitting beside you. Lowson, who drove it first, called it 'Little Willie'.

May 9th dawned fine and clear. There was not a cloud in the sky except those little white puffs where the Archie shells were bursting round a visiting Hun at the outskirts of the town. There was a nip in the air still.

I loaded up with the usual stretchers and collected a stretcher-bearer who always came to help unload.

As we bumped over the level-crossing, I saw with surprise that there was no sentry (I always used to throw him a packet of ration cigarettes as I passed). 'Wonder where he is?' I yelled to the man beside me. 'First time he hasn't been there.' My companion shook his head; whether he had heard what I said or not above the noise of the lorry, I didn't know.

Work proceeded as usual and we were done at eleven o'clock. It was hot now, the white ship with its red crosses drew slowly away from the quay, the stretchers were thrown into the lorry. I looked at Little Willie, no one could take any pride in him. All the same, I had tried to smarten him up by tying back the untidy canvas top over the driver's seat. I cranked up and got in.

'Time for breakfast,' I shouted; the man smiled assent. I turned on the quay and drove off. The stretcher-bearers wore mufti, and were old, rather shambling and pathetic. I did not know that he had jumped in behind with the stretchers for a lift.

The level-crossing was just ahead. I had forgotten all about the missing sentry by this time. The sun was beating down fiercely and the air was shimmering with heat; perhaps I had made a mistake to turn back the canvas hood, however ragged it was.

I was just on the crossing now, and automatically looked into the opening. My blood froze. A train was coming – it was only a few feet away – Little Willie's thunder had drowned any outside noise.

My mind worked like lightning. Odd at the Court of Enquiry later they should suggest that I lost my head. I knew in a flash that there could be no real escape. It was just a question whether it would be better to be caught in the front or the rear. If the former, it meant reversing, and the reverse took up badly. I was only in second gear anyway, as the lines projected several inches above the sleepers. I pressed the accelerator.

'Oh, God, make Little Willie go quickly for once, please.'

There was a frightful crash as the train caught the back of the lorry, spinning it round so that it was facing the direction from which it had come. I was hurled into the air, to fall and be swept along by the train, my face on the ground. At last, after what seemed an eternity, it stopped and I was left in a crumpled heap. Oddly enough, my first thought was of the car. 'There will be a row,' I thought, 'though I've never had an accident before.' From where I lay, I could see it standing sulkily, apparently undamaged, and still erect.

I tried to move, but found it impossible, and how my legs were aching. I tried to move them, but it was no use. I put my hand to my head and drew it away sticky.

What was it? I looked at my hand. It was covered with blood. I began to feel panic that my back might be injured and that I would not be able to get about again. The stretcher-bearer behind had been killed instantly, but I did not know of this till some time later.

The French soldiers up in their battery had seen the whole thing happen and were down in a trice. One of them gave a cry and was on the ground beside me trying to lift me, calling me his *'petit chou'* and 'poor little pigeon', and presently, with the help of another soldier, he lifted me as carefully as he might a baby and carried me away from the train.

The pain was increasing and I began to wonder just where my legs were broken, as the pain seemed worse there. I gave a gasp as I felt something tighten and hurt horribly. They had taken off their bootlaces to make a tourniquet to stop the hæmorrhage. The men stood round and I watched them furtively wiping away the tears that rolled down their furrowed cheeks. One even put his arm up over his eyes like a child. I wondered vaguely why they were crying; it did not dawn on me that it had anything to do with *me*.

One evening, the fourth or fifth I think, Captain Cook came in and sat down in the shadow, looking very grave. It must have been one of the worst half-hours he ever spent. It is not a task that any man would relish to tell someone who is particularly fond of life that she has lost one leg and the other has only just been saved. I was speechless for some minutes; my mind refused to take it in. It was a long time before the full horror of the situation dawned on me. It may seem odd that I did not feel that I had lost my leg, but one never has that sensation even when on crutches; the nerves are too much alive.

Captain Cook stayed a long time and the evening drew on; still he sat there and talked to me quietly in the darkness. I wondered why I couldn't cry, but somehow it seemed to have nothing to do with me at all. I was not the girl who had lost a leg. It was merely someone else I was hearing about. 'Jolly bad luck on them,' I thought, 'rotten not to be able to run about any more.' I loved running.

In time I began to get about on crutches and the question next arose as to where I was to go and convalesce. The then strange but later all too familiar phrase was first heard: 'If only you were a man, of course it would be *so* easy.' It was no good protesting that I had always wished that I were one; that did not help matters at all. I came to the conclusion that there *were* too many women in England.

Finally, thanks to Georgina, Lady Dudley's kindness, I became an out-patient at one of her officers' hospitals at Brighton, but even then it was a nuisance being a girl; people would stare as if I were a weird creature from the Zoo. Men on crutches had, sadly enough, become a familiar sight, but a F.A.N.Y. was something quite new and an object to be photographed. On some days, I felt brazen, but on others I went out for about five minutes and returned, refusing to move for the rest of the day. A bath-chair was not so bad, sometimes we had races with others, but the old men who pushed them were rather gone at the knees and did not enjoy it as much as the patients. One day I fell getting out of my chair, forgetting the absent leg, and came down heavily on the asphalt. It was odd that one never felt the absence of the limb – my fall was a lesson to be remembered.

PAT BEAUCHAMP

A Woman at War

The Worst Job

The little canteen was almost full, as the canteens invariably were, and it was evening. I made my way across the floor to the piano, and struck up a few chords which I hoped would please. In another ten minutes every seat was crammed, and they called for song after song, piece after piece, with merciless rapidity. I gave them all I could. Sometimes it was 'Hullo, who's yer lady friend,' Grieg's 'Morning Song,' 'Take me back to dear old Blighty,' Handel's 'Largo,' until over an hour had passed, and the hands of the clock reminded us that Roll Call was at nine. There was a general move, and as they filed out, with a word of thanks, sometimes with the shyness of a schoolboy, into the darkness, and the horrors that waited them, I thanked God for the gift of memory, which had helped men, for a time, to forget. One of them lingered.

'Thank you, Miss, especially for the bit I asked for myself – it was a touch of Heaven after Hell.'

I did not answer for a moment, and then to my surprise, for it was a rare thing, his conversation turned on the war. He told me he was down for a few days at the Rest Camp, and asked how long women had been employed at the base.

He paused for a moment.

'There are worse jobs than fighting.'

'Worse jobs than fighting?'

'Yes, it sounds strange, but it's true.'

A look of inexpressible weariness came over his face.

'I've been digging up dead bodies – digging them up for their identification discs, so that we can send word home . . . The fellow I was working with dug up his own brother, and cried like a child . . . We must try and bring home to the people of England what war really is – we must try and make them realise what it means to dig up dead bodies . . . '

I could not look at him.

MAUDE ONIONS

366

A History of the Scottish Women's Hospital

Ostrovo, 26th February, 1918.

Dear Miss Kemp,

I cabled to you on Monday about the destruction of tents wrought by Sunday's hurricane, but from my cable you can hardly conceive the condition of affairs here.

To begin with, a week earlier, we had three days' snow, so that the previous Sunday was spent by the personnel in digging their tents out of the snow; then came a thaw and frost, and further thawing, and so on. There is still, indeed, some snow lying about.

Well, on Saturday night it began to rain, and the whole camp was muddy and damp, and tent pegs refused to hold. About 2 a.m. on Sunday began the hurricane; by 3 a.m. most of the Unit was up endeavouring to save the tents from collapsing. By 8 a.m. practically every tent in the place had collapsed, the only exceptions being the telephone tent (saved by the devoted exertions of its occupant), the dressing tent, Dr. Rose's and Matron's tents, and one tent in Ward V.A, all of which had poles standing and sides collapsed, and Ward I.A (twenty beds), which weathered the storm successfully and was proudly erect. The garage and our kitchen were unroofed, and the patients' kitchen suffered only slightly. The new store (made of flooring and tarpaulin) also came through successfully. The tent stores (groceries, linen, splints, etc.) were scattered abroad. The X-ray and dark-room tents were both in ribbons. Such a scene of desolation has to be seen to be realised.

The Unit presented an interesting spectacle also: most of them (including myself) were clad in pyjamas, with stockings drawn over the legs, and shoes and a greatcoat on, and hair streaming wherever the wind listed. But none of us cared!

The patients stuck to their beds till the tents collapsed on them, and even then had to be ordered up. Fortunately no one was hurt, save for a bruise or two.

There were no fires, though we had three narrow escapes.

Braziers and stoves were all watered, and great care was taken. Luckily there was no rain, and there was a moon. We counted these three facts our crowning 'marcies.' We have had fine, calm, sunny weather since, also, in which to cope with the situation!

It was obvious that the only thing to do was to evacuate all the patients, and all, except seventeen (convalescent workers or sick *bolnichars*), were dispatched by train. We sent them down in ambulances (no cars were damaged except for their mica windows, some of which were broken), and got them away by the 'Sanitary Train.'

DR DE GARIS

'Disgrace of the London Streets'

Daily Express, 26 September 1918

Growing Demand for Action

Throughout the country there is now a rising agitation on the question of the scandal of the London streets, in consequence of the 'Daily Express' campaign to root this social canker out.

General Macready can no longer ignore a public duty. The new Commissioner's reputation as guardian of the safety of London is at stake.

The following article by a Canadian woman journalist shows how deeply representatives of the Dominions Overseas are concerned, and suggests the establishment of night courts with women magistrates to deal with the street harpies:

WOMEN TO TRY WOMEN
Where there is a will there can be found a way.

Hundreds of Overseas troops will be glad when some means are taken to free London streets of the vast hordes of vampires who have been allowed to prey upon the soldier on leave, and in many cases to cause his downfall.

I did not read with gratification that plucky Little New

Zealand had sent her women half round the world to protect her men in London streets, nor that Canada is sending her splendid women across the danger zone of the seas to keep watch and ward over her heroic troops that they may escape from London streets with clean bodies.

Nor can I understand how any Englishman can feel proud as he reads these statements in the 'Daily Express.' For years all Overseas Britons in London have felt the most bitter resentment against the authorities, who have apparently valued so little the great sacrifice Overseas Britons have made for the cause of humanity in the great war.

When one thinks that most of the Overseas troops are volunteers who have given up everything, and travelled thousands of miles to serve, bringing arms, clothing, food, equipment, medical corps, hospitals, nurses, transport, Red Cross societies, Y.M.C.A., and other hostels for men on leave, to say nothing of the colossal sums of money poured forth by each dominion, one naturally feels that they might be considered safe in London.

Why is it that other large cities – New York, for instance – have no such exhibition of street pests? The reason is that the people would not tolerate it for a minute. It seems childish to say that the scandal cannot be handled.

Every woman is supposed to have a national registration card, and what is the use of such a system if the police know nothing of the people in their precincts?

Establish night courts for women with women magistrates. Give these women magistrates the power to try women summarily.

Give the women police the power to arrest on suspicion, and hold – as we do in Canada – as a vagrant with no visible means of support. Have the night courts at frequent intervals in soldiers' areas. Once within the court it would become a question of grading these women. The professionals should be sent to a restricted treatment, the criminal to prison, and the silly little flapper, if she were kept in the court overnight and taken to her home by a policewoman in the morning, would probably vanish from the night life of London streets

MRS. D.MAC ALISTER FITZSIMMONS
(SPECIAL CORRESPONDENT IN LONDON
TO THE MONTREAL HERALD)

The Times, 24 September 1918

London Street Women

Sir,

As an American, and, moreover, an American editor, may I be permitted to reply to 'An American Editor's Indictment' in *The Times* of September 24, wherein Mr. Bok, editor of the *Ladies' Home Journal*, of Philadelphia, protests against 'the apparently uncontrolled solicitation of our boys by women on the London streets,' by 'our boys' meaning American soldiers, whom he describes as 'clean-blooded and strong-limbed,' being sent over here 'only to be poisoned and wrecked in the London streets.'

Mr. Bok will, I hope, pardon me for saying that, in the section of the United States whence I come, this kind of talk would be termed 'hogwash.' The average American soldier who comes to London is no more 'clean-blooded and strong-limbed' than the average British boy, and his parents are no more solicitous for his moral welfare than British parents.

No American soldier accustomed to walk the streets of his own large cities after dark needs to be accompanied by a guardian in the streets of London at the present time. Furthermore, the appearance of the women and girls who hang about therein for the purpose of exploiting soldiers is such as to afford no temptation whatever to the aforesaid 'clean-blooded and strong-limbed.' The American soldier who would fall a prey to their toothless and bedraggled charms must be exceedingly anxious to be 'poisoned and wrecked'; so determined, indeed, that the most stringent police regulations would be powerless to protect or prevent him— candour compels me to say that, as far as I am able to judge by superficial observation, such as that necessarily given to the subject by the editor of the *Ladies' Home Journal* during his brief stay here, the streets in the vicinity of the Bellevue-Stratford Hotel, Philadelphia, were more filled with courtesans, covertly, if not openly, plying their trade, than any of the streets of London I have seen, and I have been here since the middle of July, and during that time have walked about London at all hours of the day and night. In his personal investigation, Mr. Bok was probably unaware that solicitation of the sort he denounces is never experienced in London unless invited by the male.

I am, Sir, yours sincerely,

WILLIAM C. EDGAR, EDITOR, THE *BELLMAN*, MINNEAPOLIS, MINN.,
U.S.A.

Christian Commonwealth, 16 October 1918

The State of London Streets

'I suppose you want to know what I think of all this correspondence on "The state of London Streets",' she said quickly. 'It's all so one-sided, so unjust to women. They talk as if men were innocent angels, helpless in the hands of wicked women — many of them have worked for the starvation wages women used to get, and they have found a way of earning as many pounds in a night as they used to earn shillings in a week. If there were no demand there would be no supply.' She went on to rail about poor social conditions, which, she insisted, were to blame for most evils. Then she got back to the burning question. 'It is strange that nearly all those who have taken part in the discussion, whether they defend the character of London or not, are agreed as to the general responsibility of women for all wrong doings. That equality of men and women which has made so much headway in the world of labour is unknown here. In the realm of morals we have not advanced beyond Adam who was tempted by Eve.'

INTERVIEW WITH WOMAN POLICE COMMANDER
MARGARET DAMER DAWSON

Daily Mail, 3 October 1918

Women Police

A force of women police is to be created for London, officially recognized, under the control of the Commissioner of Metropolitan Police, and subject to the same discipline as the men. This is another 'break through' by women of that long line of positions that were assumed only to be fitting for men.

Women are likely to be firm and efficient constables—Our urban life will be cleaner by the presence of the woman constable.

In the woman constable's dealing with the venal minor male offender against the law, she is likely to be less lenient than the policeman, and to be less inclined to 'look the other way'. Man is apt to be merciful with man – and woman. Woman is not to be cajoled. When a woman has a sense of duty, she is inflexible. There is some amusement in the prospect that those who hear the chimes o'midnight will have to be wary of women police. These would be ill days for Sir John Falstaff.

'Hostilities Will Cease at 11.00 November 11 aaa'

Armistice message tapped out by the
army telegraphist Maude Onions

Behind the Lines: One Woman's War 1914–18

Republic of Germany!
10.11.18

My dear Emmie,

I have seen the red flag! I think long before this reaches you, you will have seen it too. It began last Monday – we read in the evening papers that the sailors in Kiel had risen, disarmed their officers, hoisted the red flag on all the ships, and that the Government had given in to practically all their demands. Later we heard that the whole fleet was under secret orders to sail on a last desperate attack on the English fleet, and was actually under steam. On Tuesday and Wednesday, the other great ports, Lubech Bremen and Hamburg followed suit – on Thursday Munchen and with it all Bavaria. On Friday, I was on my way to lunch, and coming into one of the main streets saw a dense grey crowd coming towards me and at the head of it a great red flag. I must say I stood rooted, with my heart in my mouth. As you know I have waited for it for weeks, but when one first sees it, it takes one's breath away. They were a few hundred soldiers, in their 'field-grey', that corresponds to our Khaki, but their shoulder-straps, numbers, belts and arms had vanished.—We got to the Volkshaus, the head quarters of the Social Democratic Party – then they picketed the streets, stopped the trams and took away the numbers and weapons from all soldiers and officers and police. It was absolutely orderly – an officer resisted and fired a couple of shots, but they simply disarmed him and let him go. By the evening the town was placarded with huge announcements, that the 'Workmen and Soldiers' Council' had taken over the government of the town, and that the military and civil authorities had submitted to them. On Saturday morning (I have lived in the streets of late) I saw the Mayor run up the red flag over the town-hall, and an hour later, the shout of a special went through the town, and we read that the Kaiser had abdicated. It was as if a weight had fallen from the people – one only heard one expression 'Thank God – at last!' The Reichskanzler resigned at once, and the Social Democrat, Ebert was chosen. One can really only have every respect for the absolute order and system with which such enormous upheavals and changes have been carried out so far—

Good night – perhaps my next letter will be written in times of peace –

Your loving,

Ethel

CAROLINE ETHEL COOPER

An English Wife in Berlin

The End of the War

November 10, 1918

I must confess that I myself feel shocked and surprised at the universal rejoicing manifested at the abdication of the Kaiser. They could not be more jubilant if they had won the war. *Vox populi, vox dei!* He may deserve his fate, but it seems very hard and cruel to

375

throw stones at him at such a moment, when he must be enduring untold anguish and sorrow.

Amongst the aristocracy the grief at the breakdown of their country, more than at the personal fall of the Kaiser, is quite heart-rending to see. I have seen some of our friends, strong men, sit down and sob at the news, whilst others seemed to shrink to half their size and were struck dumb with pain. There are men and women who have played an inconspicuous part enough at ordinary times, often pushed aside as people of no importance, who are now the most faithful to their monarch. But history takes no heed of the tears of the individual, and they only fall to join and swell the broad stream shed by mankind within the last four years, and which, as we hope, is carrying us forward to some brighter goal.

November 11, 1918

Things seem to have calmed down a bit, and one only hears a little desultory shooting now and again. We feel that it is growing safe once more, and this morning Gebhard went off to our apartment, to spend the day there putting things in order again. Frau Mainzer and I determined to go out together to see what the world looked like after the deluge of the last two days, and whether there were any signs of the waters abating or not. I paid several visits, and we all congratulated one another at still being alive, but we are none of us very certain as to what the hour may bring forth. Our general impression is that the people are much too weak and starved to be really bloodthirsty unless goaded on by fanatics like Liebknecht and Rosa Luxemburg, and one cannot help admiring the disciplined and orderly way in which a revolution of such dimensions has been organized, with until now the least possible loss of life. Truly, a great storm is passing over the land, and princes are falling from their thrones like ripe fruit from a tree, but every one seems to be acting under the impulse of a divine law which is leading the German nation to a new phase of development.

Evelyn, Princess Blücher

376

A Woman at War

The First Silence

I like to look back to eight o'clock on the morning of November 11th, 1918, because it was then that I tapped out the official message to the armies in the field, which helped to bring peace to a war-weary world.

'Hostilities will cease at 11.00 November 11th aaa. Troops will stand fast at the line reached at that hour which will be reported to Army Headquarters aaa. Defensive precautions will be maintained aaa. There will be no intercourse of any description with the enemy aaa. Further instructions follow.'

In the little Signal Office at Boulogne nothing happened at eleven o'clock, nothing except a silence, and an involuntary glance at the clock. Outside, nothing happened. It was the first great silence of armistice. It was as though France had just heaved a vast sigh of relief. It was not until the afternoon that any signs of rejoicing became evident. Then, as I made my way down to the quay side, on the stroke of three, every siren and hooter was let loose, every church bell clanged out – a deafening roar. But not a sound, not a movement, came from the hundreds of human beings who thronged the streets. The stricken soul of France seemed to have lost even the desire to rejoice.

A deafening noise, the flags of the Blighty boat ran up, and for the first time for four weary years she sailed without an escort. Some of us tried to cheer, but voice failed. Then suddenly through the noise and din, the sobbing of a woman, a few yards away – '*Finis – finis – incroyable . . .*'

Almost unconsciously, I found myself in the little military cemetery behind the congested streets of the town, where our men were buried three deep, for land was dear in France, and where the graves had been so beautifully kept by the loving hands of a khaki girl. I could not distinguish the names, for the mist of tears.

As I turned to go from that scene of peace, I stumbled and almost fell over something on the ground, a broken piece of wood, that had sunk so deep that it was scarcely visible. I knelt down to examine it, and it was with difficulty that I was able to decipher the lettering. It was the grave of a German soldier.

Cautiously, afraid of being seen, I stooped and placed some flowers at the foot of the broken cross.

Somewhere, a woman was sorrowing.

MAUDE ONIONS

Memoir

Armistice Day in London

I think we must have known the war was nearly over. Anyway, on the morning of 11th November 1918 I was on the day shift and I know we weren't working very hard. At 11 o'clock we heard the maroons going off which was the signal it had ended! We all poured out of the 'cow-shed' and in two shakes of a lamb's tail there were people everywhere, stopping the traffic, clambering over the trams, hanging out of windows, waving flags. I remember seeing the French tricolour and the American 'Stars and Stripes' as well as Union Jacks. We 'choir' girls linked arms and started singing at the tops of our voices. I can't remember what we sang but we were soon leading a procession all the way down the Grays Inn Road towards Holborn.

In the evening a group of us went up West. I think it was raining but we didn't care. We ended up in Trafalgar Square which was an absolute sea of people. They'd lit bonfires between the lions at the base of Nelson's column but they weren't dangerous because the crowd was so well-behaved. The glow of the flames shone on people's faces and we sang 'Keep the Home Fires

Burning' which I think is a lovely tune, though it isn't popular any more. Then somebody would start 'Land of Hope and Glory', or 'It's a Long Way to Tipperary', or 'Hello, Hello, Who's your Lady Friend?' and the sound was like the waves crashing on to a beach.

Casualty Lists

Young people have since asked me what we felt about the terrible casualties. Lists were printed in local newspapers and pinned up on the notice boards outside town halls. They were divided into 'Killed' and 'Wounded', officers first, then the other ranks. Particularly during the Somme offensive and Passchendaele there were pages and pages of them and there was often somebody you'd been to school with, or from your street, and sometimes you'd see people breaking down as they scanned the notice boards. But most of us, I suppose, accepted the fearful loss of life as part of a war we had to win as soon as we could. It never entered my head that we wouldn't win. But perhaps, until the Armistice, the Germans felt like that, too.

ALICE CONNOR NÉE KEDGE

How We Lived Then

Armistice Day: A Woman Assistant Editor in Fleet Street

The news came through to us on the telephone about 10.30. We opened the windows, and could hear cheering, and immediately somewhere a wheezy old gramophone began to play 'God Save the King.' I longed to go out into the streets, but could not because there was a great deal to do, and whatever happens or does not happen papers have to go to press. I was looking through some proofs, and found it very difficult to correct mistakes because my eyes kept filling with tears. I thought of —, for whom

379

peace had come too late and —. Her telegram had come only the day before. Naturally there was rejoicing, and yet what pain there was underneath it! By the time my work was over it was 5 o'clock and pouring with rain. I had to walk all the way home through the crowds.

I went through the Temple, which was deserted, and up one of those little streets near Charing Cross, and there under an archway were two old women in prehistoric-looking bonnets and capes dancing stiffly and slowly to a barrel organ, the kind which has one leg and which you hardly ever see nowadays, played by a man so ancient that he looked as if he should have held a scythe rather than a hurdy-gurdy. In the Mall crowds had come to look at the German guns, and there were still people standing and gazing at Buckingham Palace. When at length I got home I found out that — had just come in. He had been called out, and spent the day in the police station, and had seen nothing and heard only the church bells. Next day I had a letter from M—. She said that at B— no one seemed to know what to do at first. 'A few people cheered in the Market Place, and then some soldiers from the hospital set the church bells ringing and then the fire bell. After that the fire bell never ceased. Ding dong, ding dong – it went on all day. When one ringer tired another began. I felt so sorry for the fireman and his wife, for in the middle of the tumult the news came that his son had been killed. One of the last shots fired killed him. In the evening we held a thanksgiving service. My boy had come through safely, but that made one only the more heart-broken for the grief of others.

Even though peace has come one cannot be glad because of all that has been during these horrible years.

That night in Trafalgar Square there was dancing, singing, flags were waved, confetti thrown. 'Have we won the war?' was roared, and an answering roar came 'Yes, we've won the war.'

MRS C. S. PEEL

Armistice Day

Armistice Day arrived & we could not control our joy at soon being released from the Army. A milk-man delivered milk to the cookhouse each day in a van. Some of us jumped on his van for a ride, he took us a few miles & then told us to walk back. We were lectured & told we should be thinking of those who had died & it wasn't a time for happiness. We told the officers that we were happy because our relatives & friends who had been spared so far would be coming home safely.

OLIVE MAY TAYLOR

'Johnnie' of Q.M.A.A.C.

Armistice Day in Rouen

Suddenly, the hillside echoed and re-echoed, as volley after volley was fired from the big gun on the ramparts. In the distance, the cathedral bells pealed and clanged out the glad news. Flags were run up to the masthead on every boat and steamer in the river, and the Allies' colours were unfurled everywhere.

After sundown the city was transformed. Was it the same place through which we had passed in the morning? Or was it a dream city? One connected the sights with scenes described in Aladdin only, here there were *hundreds* of wonderful lamps. Spanning the river the bridges seemed like magic constructions, fairy arches. The myriad coloured lights suspended from the arches of the Pont Corneille were reflected in the river. Along the Quai de Paris a band was making its way. Crowds followed and clambered up beside the bandsmen—

Opposite the *Theatres des Arts*, an Australian band was playing the National Anthems of the Allies. On the bonnet of the car on which they were seated, an Aussie, a Tommy, and a French soldier, were standing singing lustily. 'Come up, Jock,' they shouted to a Gordon in the crowd. 'Come up,' he echoed. 'Naw, no me! I winna come up unless ye play "Scots Wha Hae."' Jock's face was a study when they replied that the band did not know it.

'Whit I want tae ken,' he shouted, 'whit I want tae ken is, whaur wis ye brocht up?' They offered to play 'Auld Lang Syne,' and to that familiar tune Jock took his place beside his brothers in arms. Suddenly above the shouting and noise, the skirl of the bagpipes was heard. Jocks mobilised without a moment's delay, and fell in behind the piper. They swarmed around and after him, keeping step to 'Hielan' Laddie.' And in behind the Jocks, French soldiers in their picturesque blue uniform, wounded Belgians, Aussies in hospital suits, fell into step. Americans, Portuguese, and Chinese swelled the procession, and crowding behind them, came swarthy South African Scottish, in Atholl tartan, stalwart Canadian Highlanders and Indians. One thought of the Pied Piper, enticing the children through the streets of Hamelin. But up the *Rue Grand Pont*, grown-up children from the ends of the earth pranced and danced to the skirl of the bagpipes. French civilians joined in the procession and armed the soldiers up the streets. Little children crowded in between the ranks, or were hoisted shoulder high. 'Hey, mon! get haud o' a pickle o' they wee parley-voos or they'll be knocked doon an' tramped on!' The children beamed, and shrieked with delight, as, hand in hand with giant New Zealanders and Tommies, they skipped and danced their way into *Rue Jeanne d'Arc* and thence to the *Hotel de Ville*. Here the historic procession halted, and, in the shadow of the magnificent equestrian statue of Napoleon, Jocks and French girls, Aussies and Tommies, danced and capered to the piping.

I have heard France's National Anthem sung by soldiers on their way up the line; by little children in the streets, and vast audiences in the Opera House, led by a magnificent band; but surely to-night the spirit of *Rouget de Lisle* himself inspired the sons and daughters of France. Close by me, hat in hand, and stick held aloft, an aged man in peasant dress sobbed it out brokenly, while the tears coursed down his withered cheeks. Young boys in high-pitched trebles sang it loudly, their faces glowing with animation. Perched shoulder high, tiny children waved flags, and shouted between the verses, *'Vive la France.'* In their enthusiasm, soldiers forgot the girls clinging to them, and shaking themselves free, extended both arms and beat the air with their hands. Officers wearing numerous decorations, snatched their hats off and waved them on high, and, with the emotion characteristic of their race, sang the 'Marseillaise' as it never was sung before. Women wept: little children's eyes grew round with wonder, as they lisped the rousing words, while hoarse shouts rent the air, and old men crossed themselves. Tears and laughter went hand in hand.

A LETTER FROM ELIZABETH 'JOHNNIE' JOHNSTON
MEMOIR EDITED BY AGNES ANDERSON

Memoirs

The Death of 'Johnnie'

Christmas morning, 1918

Nora Hall and I had a sad experience. We were in the fine church of St. Ouen when a young R.A.M.C. corporal came hurriedly up to us and said that there had been an accident. Someone had fallen from the roof of the south aisle. We went with him to a little side door and on the paving was a W.A.A.C. His companion had covered her with his overcoat but she was past all help.

'What's best to do?' he said. We said we would stay with his companion if he would try to find Military Police. There always were plenty of them parading the main streets in pairs and they were easy to spot as they had red caps and M.P. arm badges. I also told him to try to stop an ambulance. Drivers, of course, had strict orders not to do anything that was not 'on their paper' but I felt sure most would answer such an emergency call. It was not long before he came with an ambulance on its way to No. 8 and empty. The driver said O.K. and we watched it set off. He did not ask us where we were stationed and we decided not to say anything about it.

Matron, of course, heard about it as she was taken to No. 8, and the office VADs wondered who 'the two sisters' were who had called the ambulance to the scene. Afterwards we heard her name was Johnson and that a friend wrote a book about 'Johnnie – a W.A.A.C.' but I never saw it, so know nothing about her.

CHARLOTTE MACKAY BROWN

Letters from Africa 1918–31

To Ingeborg Dinesen

Ngong (Kenya): 23 October 1918
—surely no one, not even the Kaiser himself, would have started on it if one had known what it would be like; yet it cannot be peace yet. It is as if they had set such mighty forces in movement that they can no longer control them, and it is as in Goethe's poem about the sorcerer's half-educated apprentice, who calls up the spirits and commands them to carry water, and is about to perish when the sorcerer comes and stops them with one word. But when will the sorcerer come and utter the word!

Ngong: 15 November 1918
—all that I can really comprehend is that the shooting has stopped and that no more dead or wounded will be brought in — Tonight there is a great torchlight procession with music in Nairobi — 5,000 black soldiers will march through the city with torches. They have good reason to rejoice, poor things; the war has taken a terrible toll on the native population — Out here the crazy Gorringe has got all the settlers to agree to celebrate with a

'Bonfire' up on the Ngong Hills — As it is a very awkward journey up there even in daytime I don't know how they will manage, especially as most of them are very old women. But the English have enough enthusiasm to overcome all obstacles where picnics are concerned—

Isak Dinesen (Karen Blixen)

Memoirs

Royal Red Cross Investiture

Guests took their seats, first come, first served. One late-comer was a very irate lady, trembling with rage at being escorted to a seat beneath the gallery: 'You'll hear about this!' She announced that a front seat should have been reserved for her and was told no seats had been reserved (I don't quite believe this by the look of the front row occupants). King George asked if I'd served abroad and where.

We then walked to Marlborough House, to be presented to Queen Alexandra, who was President of the Red Cross Society — We were met by the Queen's Private Secretary, Lord Stamfordham, in a dowdy-looking hall with crimson hangings – very ancient probably. She had a strong German accent and presented me with a booklet, the History of the Red Cross, and a certificate of thanks, signed by her.

Charlotte Mackay Brown

Peace and Bread in Time of War

When the news came to America of the opening hostilities which were the beginning of the European Conflict, the reactions against war, as such, was almost instantaneous throughout the country. This was most strikingly registered in the newspaper cartoons and comments which expressed astonishment that such an archaic institution should be revived in Europe.—

By the end of the war we were able to understand, although our group certainly did not endorse the statement of Cobden:

'I made up my mind during the Crimean War that if I ever lived in the time of another great war of similar kind between England and another great power, I would not as a public man open my mouth on the subject, so convinced am I that appeals to reason, conscience or interest have no force whatever on parties engaged in war, and that exhaustion on one or both sides can alone bring a contest of physical power to an end.'

JANE ADDAMS

Sunday Times, 29 June 1919

London's Peace Night
How the Capital Received the News

CHEERING CROWDS IN STREETS AND SQUARES
At 3.40 p.m. Londoners knew that peace with Germany was an accomplished fact.

A crash of maroons, and the air seemed charged with electricity, for to the great populace of the metropolis this was the signal of peace. Amidst tremendous tension people speedily realised the portentous nature of the news, and the first emotional episode having passed, there came unforgettable outbursts of joy.

The long shadow had been lifted, and once the people fully appreciated the significance of the news they had received they gave vent to deep-throated cheering and congratulations on the wholesale scale. Underlying all was a sense of gratitude to the dead and a feeling of sympathy for the bereaved, and the most marked note was a fervent one of whole-hearted thankfulness.

Cheer after cheer was raised everywhere and anywhere where little or large groups had gathered together.

There were full-voiced roars for the Army, for the Navy, and the Allies, whilst flags made a lightning appearance, and soon almost everyone had some emblem to mark the historic occasion.

There was no 'mafficking.' The note of rejoicing was too real for such scenes to take place, and yet it was convincing by its vigorous spontaneity. Women vied with men in demonstrating their long pent-up feelings, and then all combined in raising united pæans of thankfulness.

A NAVAL ENGAGEMENT

'Let's all go down the Strand' got a new interpretation, for a band of bluejackets, headed by a piper, paraded up and down the famous thoroughfare with an enormous Union Jack. 'Tipperary' was revived for so appropriate an occasion, whilst popular cries and answering cheers showed whether we were downhearted.

Flag-sellers and those who retailed souvenirs had a prosperous time, for they disposed of their wares with little difficulty. In Trafalgar Square there was a crowd estimated at 100,000 people, and here the rejoicings were of a particularly animated description. Yet good humour and orderliness prevailed everywhere, and the arms of the law had no very difficult task to preserve order.

Daily Express, 28 June 1919

At the Heart of England

The jazziest of gowns, a champagne dinner, crowded streets where we should smile into each other's eyes from sheer joy and excitement, a theatre where we should catch again the thrill of that wonderful armistice-day, and then to dance – all night and into the morning hours, because of the gladness of it all.

That was how we planned in January to celebrate the peace-day.

We from the little village among the hills said that nothing but London would satisfy us on that day; we wanted to be among the throngs in the capital, to hear the guns boom and the bells ring, to experience that wonderful uplifting emotion that sways a crowd, to shout and cheer with the others.

This was when the crocuses pushed their bright heads through the snow, before the problems of the new era began to take the place of the old anxieties, before there came the new wave of restlessness, before we wearied of the constant bickerings and arguments of the peace-makers.

And now it is here. The day for which the world suffered is slipping quietly on us. Across the waters they will sign the peace. Again we shall hang out our victory flags. But shall we ever again equal the mad enthusiasm of armistice-day? I doubt it. We have somewhat sobered during this last six months. Many have already abandoned the peace plans they previously made: its celebration will take a deeper, quieter turn.

NATURE'S SHRINE

Here in the cottage, the riotous town revelry we had planned has quietly receded from our imagination; our peace will be quietly celebrated among the hills. The village will fly its flags and banners, their colours vying with the wealth of blossom in cottage gardens; many will slip into the little grey church and place their posy before the war shrine; old anecdotes and reminiscences will be repeated; and all around will be the calm of field and sky.

We shall, perhaps, realise the significance of the greatest day in the world's history more fully here in the silence than among the crowds of the city.

Here, in the laden orchards and fruitful fields stretching away in undulating lines to the surrounding hills; here among the scented meadows and rose-dappled hedgerows one meets the great peace. This is the lovely land for which they fought, they died that alien hands should never mar this glorious countryside. It lives and blooms as they wished. Its beauty tells of their victory.

It will be well to spend the great day in the heart of rural England. Its memory will be a fitting one to range alongside that other unforgettable day with our men in France.

Hilda M. Love

Manchester Guardian, 30 June 1919

Paris certainly amused itself last night. There were flags and fireworks, music and dancing, and torchlight processions. Long before nightfall the streets were black with humanity. Military lorries paraded the Champs Elysées and the boulevards loaded with Poilus, American soldiers and their lady friends.

As the evening wore on the fun waxed fast and furious. Hundreds of impromptu dances were held on the pavements or in the roadway — On the Grands Boulevards the throng was so thick that one could not move at more than a snail's pace. Some of the revellers were in fancy dress of a rather ambitious character. Military headgear was worn by excited damsels, and feathered toques adorned the heads of stern warriors. A few bold masqueraders had clad themselves more or less completely in the clothes of the other sex. All the cafés which remained open for the occasion till 1 a.m. were packed to overflowing, and one was lucky if one did not drink confetti with one's hock or lemonade. At midnight when I left the boulevards, the inevitable guns were being dragged noisily through the press, and dancing and kiss-in-the-ring were still in full swing.

Diary

Yesterday, the Germans signed the Peace Treaty: Peace was signed, and I could not rejoice. Germany has been humiliated to the dust, her country is in a seething, chaotic, turbulent condition. What then are we to rejoice about? The real rejoicing came last Nov. 11th. when at last the guns ceased firing and the hideous massacre ceased. Then was the time to rejoice.

Peace celebrations now seem to me a silly farce. To say Germany has deserved all her trouble etc. etc., is nothing to do with it. I cannot feel we should rejoice. At dusk yesterday the fireworks started. I stood and watched them all round the horizon and first felt only like crying. But when I realized it was after all an historic night and that all over the world the same sort of thing was going on, I became fascinated and could not tear myself away. There was no cause to rejoice but I liked to feel it was a great day in history and that all the world was taking part. And I knew there were all 'Those Others' too, looking on those who had fought and died for it, and that they saw deeper than we did and knew really that they had not died in vain. All the frivolity and silliness is probably only reaction, but what a much nobler, finer England it seemed while the war was on. Do we already need another big trial to call out the good in us, or will it gradually assert itself as the world settles down a bit? And why does no one ever sympathise with Germany? Plenty of pity perhaps, magnanimous pity, but I come across no sympathy at all. Bad look out for us all if God were so unsympathetic!

VIOLA BAWTREE

Appendices

Acknowledgements and Sources

For their assistance with copyright information, tracing copyright holders and biographical data my very special thanks go to: Gaynor Coules, Dafydd Wyn Phillips, and Heather Rosenblatt of the Authors' Licensing & Collecting Society (ALCS), London; Dr Hanna Behrend in Berlin; and Ann Fitzgerald and Carol McPhee who went into Californian overdrive on my behalf. Similar thanks to my old friend Dr Madeleine Thirieau-Michaut for her Parisian hospitality; to David Doughan of the Fawcett Library, London, for a perennial enthusiasm above and beyond the call of duty; to my friends Anne and Jeremy Powell whose Palladour Books specialise in First World War material; to Ruth Glatzer for permission to reprint material from *Berliner Leben 1914–18* which she and her late husband edited; to Renate von Hadeln for responding to queries about *Deutsche Frauen Deutsche Treue*; and last but very much not least to the relatives of contributors who gave copyright permission and took the time and trouble to supply me with biographical information.

May I also thank SCAM (France), VG-Wort (Germany), the Society of Authors (London) and Copydan (Denmark) for their assistance; Annie Metz of the Bibliothèque Marguerite Durand, Paris; Karen Eberhart, archivist of Smith College, Massachusetts; Priscilla Todd, honorary secretary of the International Alliance of Women, Melbourne; Dr Lesley A. Hall, senior assistant archivist, Wellcome Institute, London; the assistant librarian, Mitchell Library, Glasgow.

The Department of Documents at the Imperial War Museum, London, holds the Women at Work archive, assiduously assembled by British women determined that their Great War efforts should not be forgotten. It is also the depository for personal memoirs, letters and diaries. May I express my gratitude to the Museum's Trustees and to the Department of Documents, where it is always a pleasure to work; and to the principal archivist, Manchester Central Library, for permission to include letters from their IWSA archive. Since my research period the John Rylands suffrage archive has been catalogued. The innumerable boxes of Great War newspaper cuttings which I sifted through in the belief that they had been collected by the NUWSS were, I have now been informed, assembled by the IWSA and post-war sent to Manchester to join an existing NUWSS deposit. I remain grateful to have been able to draw on this treasure trove, extracts from which are reproduced by courtesy of the director and university librarian of the John Rylands University Library, Manchester.

Permission to reprint copyright material is gratefully acknowledged. Unless otherwise stated the place of publication is London.

Jane Addams extracts from *Peace and Bread in Time of War* (Macmillan Co., New York, 1922)

Edith Airey extract by kind permission of the Trustees of the Imperial War Museum and her daughter Valerie Corden

Mary E. Alderton letter by kind permission of the Trustees of the Imperial War Museum

Agnes Anderson extract from *'Johnnie' of Q.M.A.A.C.* (Plymouth Press no date)

Merle Egan-Anderson extract from *Women Veterans of the Great War: Service with the U.S. Signal Corps* oral histories collected by Michelle Joure-Christides published by *Minerva Quarterly Bulletin* (Pasadena, Texas) summer 1985, edited by Joyce Marlow

Anonymous extracts from *The Letters of Thomasina Atkins* (Hodder & Stoughton, 1918)

Anonymous extract from *WAAC A Woman's Story of the War* (T. Werner Laurie Ltd, 1930)

Lena Ashwell extracts from *Modern Troubadors* (Gyldendal, Denmark, 1922)

Margot Asquith extracts from her *Autobiography* vol. 1 (first printed 1920; Penguin edition 1936) by kind permission of Priscilla Hodgson

Gertrude Atherton extract from *The Living Present* (Frederick A. Stokes Company, New York, 1917)

Enid Bagnold extract from *A Diary Without Dates* (William Heinemann Ltd, 1933) by kind permission of Comtesse Laurian d'Harcourt

Lady Frances Balfour extract from *Dr. Elsie Inglis* (Hodder & Stoughton, no date)

Miss M. T. Barclay extract by kind permission of the Trustees of the Imperial War Museum and her daughter Mrs M. M. Keetch

Viola Bawtree extract by kind permission of the Trustees of the Imperial War Museum and her nephew Bruce Gordon-Smith

Pat Beauchamp extracts from *Fanny Went to War* (George Routledge & Sons, 1940)

Miss B. Bennett extract by kind permission of the Trustees of the Imperial War Museum

Miss Bickmore extract by kind permission of the Trustees of the Imperial War Museum

Harriot Stanton Blatch extract from *Mobilizing Woman Power* (Women's Press, New York, 1918) by kind permission of Rhoda Barney Jenkins

Evelyn, Princess Blücher extracts from *An English Wife in Berlin* (Constable & Co., 1920)

Norah Bomford extract from 'Drafts' published in *Scars Upon My Heart: Women's Poetry and Verse of the First World War* selected by Catherine Reilly (Virago Press, 1981) by permission of Virago Press

Mary Borden extracts from *The Forbidden Zone* (Heinemann Ltd, 1929) by kind permission of Colonel J. A. Aylmer

Maria Botchkareva *Yashka: My Life as a Peasant, Exile and Soldier* as set down by Issac Don Levine (Constable & Co. Ltd, 1919)

Vera Brittain extracts from *Chronicle of Youth edited by Alan Bishop* (Victor Gollancz Ltd, 1981) by kind permission of her literary executors Paul Berry and Mark Bostridge and Victor Gollancz Ltd.

Florence Farmborough extract from *Nurse at the Russian Front* (Constable & Co., 1974) by permission of Constable Publishers

Millicent Garrett Fawcett extract from IWSA archive, Central Library, Manchester

Elizabeth Fernside extracts by kind permission of the Trustees of the Imperial War Museum

Richard Findlater extract from *Lilian Baylis: The Lady of the Old Vic* (Allen Lane, 1975) by permission of Angela Findlater and A. P. Watt Ltd

Katharine Furse extract from *Hearts and Pomegranates* (Peter Davies, 1940) by kind permission of Commander J. R. C. Furse, OBE

Elizabeth Gore extract from *The Better Fight: The Story of Dame Lilian Barker* (Geoffrey Bles, 1965)

GYP letter by kind permission of Bibiothèque Marguerite Durand and Mme Sybille Gaudry

Helen Gwynne-Vaughan extract from *Service with the Army* (Hutchinson, 1942)

Cicely Hamilton extract from *Senlis* (W. Collins Sons & Co. Ltd, 1917) by kind permission of Lady Patricia Bower

Ida Husted Harper extract from IWSA archive, Central Library, Manchester

Mrs M. Harrold extract by kind permission of the Trustees of the Imperial War Museum and her daughter Mrs R. Venting

Sybil Harry letter by kind permission of the Trustees of the Imperial War Museum

Anne Haverty extract from *Constance Markievicz: An Independent Life* (Pandora Press, 1988) by kind permission of the author

Katherine Hodges extracts by kind permission of the Trustees of the Imperial War Museum and Michael Hodges

Gertrude Holland extracts by kind permission of the Trustees of the Imperial War Museum

Catherine Baker Hooper extract from *An Irrepressible Crew: The Smith College Relief Unit* by kind permission of Smith College, Massachusetts

I. E. Emslie Hutton, MD extract from *With a Woman's Unit in Serbia, Salonika and Sebastopol* (Williams & Norgate Ltd, 1928)

Storm Jameson extract from *Autobiography* vol. 1 (Virago Press reprint, 1984) by kind permission of Peters, Fraser & Dunlop

F. Tennyson Jesse extract from *The Sword of Deborah* (William Heinemann, 1919)

Barbara Wootton extract from *In a World I Never Made* (George Allen & Unwin, 1967)

Miss M. C. Youngs extracts by kind permission of the Trustees of the Imperial War Museum and her daughter Mrs Webb

Every effort has been made to trace copyright owners. Inadvertent omissions will be rectified by contacting the publisher.

Notes on the Contributors

Jane Addams (1860–1935) Founded the Hull House Settlement, Chicago, 1889. Campaigned throughout her life for feminism, pacifism and the underprivileged. Shared the 1931 Nobel Peace Prize. Described both as 'the best loved' and 'the most dangerous' woman in America.

Edith Airey (1898–1972) After her spell as a land girl worked in a munitions factory. Postwar joined WRAF until it was disbanded. Married, not her Scottish poet, but a groom at 'the Hall', by whom she had two children. He never fully recovered from his experiences as a Japanese prisoner-of-war.

Mary E. Alderton No information other than that her beloved son was killed on the Somme.

Louisa Garrett Anderson, CBE, MD Lond (1873–1943) Daughter of Elizabeth Garrett Anderson, Britain's pioneer woman doctor. Qualified in 1897. Although Aunt Milly (Garrett Fawcett) led the nonmilitant NUWSS, Louisa was a militant. Among the first women to receive a CBE in 1917 when the British government finally introduced honours for women. Postwar semi-retired but returned to serve at her mother's hospital during the London Blitz.

Agnes Anderson Published the story of her late friend Elizabeth Johnston as *'Johnnie' of Q.M.A.A.C.* because 'she was a woman of rare qualities and remarkable gifts'. No other information.

Merle Egan-Anderson No information.

Lena Ashwell, OBE, FRAM (1872–1957) Spent several early years in

Canada. Trained at the Royal Academy of Music but became a well-known actress. Active feminist and suffragist. Successful second marriage to surgeon Sir Henry Simson. Lessee Kingsway Theatre, London. Her lasting monument was the inauguration of troops concerts but postwar she ran a cooperative theatre in East End of London, the Century Theatre in Bayswater and the Lena Ashwell Players touring company. Collapsed early 1930s and semi-retired. Autobiography *Myself a Player*.

Margot Asquith (1864–1945) Eleventh child of Sir Charles and Lady Tennant. Outspoken, outrageous, deeply religious, antifeminist. Member of 'the Souls', the late-Victorian intellectual smart set. In 1894 married the widowed Liberal politician Herbert Henry Asquith. Fiercely devoted to him, especially after his fall from office. Their son Anthony ('Puffin') Asquith became a film director.

Gertrude Atherton (1857–1948) Born in San Francisco into a wealthy family. In 1876 married George Atherton, had two children, but maternity and housewifery not her style. Her husband fortunately died 1887. Thereafter she travelled extensively and produced a book a year virtually until death in her beloved San Francisco. Also worked in Hollywood as scriptwriter for Samuel Goldwyn.

Enid Bagnold (1889–1958) Father an army major. Prewar moved in the Chelsea set: Gaudier-Breska, Walter Sickert, Katherine Mansfield, the notorious Frank Harris (whom she allowed to seduce her). Postwar married Sir Roderick Jones, chairman of Reuters. Wrote novels and plays including *National Velvet*, *Lottie Dundas*, *The Chalk Garden*, and a stylish autobiography.

Lady Frances Balfour (d. 1931) Daughter of the 8th Duke of Argyll. In 1879 married Eustace Balfour. Moderate suffragist.

Elizabeth Banks *Dîk: A Dog of Belgium* was published as a 1d pamphlet, proceeds to help Belgian children and Belgian dogs. The story is about Dîk and his mother Fidèle both being trained as battlefield dogs. They part but meet again, he still succouring Belgians, she Germans. 'How had Fidèle and he come to be enemies, serving in opposite armies?' is the final pacifist question. No information about the author.

Miss M. T. (Margaret Thompson) Barclay (1881–1963) Born in Edinburgh into a family of eleven children. Three sisters VADs, three brothers in army, one killed in Ypres. Professional nursing sister. Married 1919. Settled in London 1924. Worked in hospitals and general practice until 1938. Suffered from frostbite incurred during Serbian retreat but refused to speak of First World War service.

Viola Bawtree (1883–1973) Born into middle-class family in Sutton, Surrey, where she spent her unmarried life. Afflicted by deafness. Confided her feelings to her diaries. Will, her nephew says, be purring in heaven at the thought of being included in an anthology.

Pat Beauchamp Came from Carlisle. Prewar trained as a violinist, worked in a bank, encamped with the FANY. Postwar did not allow an amputated leg to curtail her activities. Helped reorganise the FANY, married, and was again on active service when *Fanny Went to War* was published in 1940.

Bertha Bennet Burleigh A (Mr) Bennet Burleigh was a well-known war correspondent, one of the few accredited to the Western Front by the press-phobic top brass. Bertha was, the editor presumes, a relation.

Miss B. Bennett No information.

Miss Bickmore No information.

Ethel M. Bilborough Married to an affluent member of Lloyds of London. Lived in Chislehurst, Kent.

Harriot Stanton Blatch (1856–1940) Daughter of the pioneer American suffragist Elizabeth Cady Stanton. In 1882 married an Englishman. Impressed by British militant suffrage tactics, on their settling in America founded the Women's Political Union (1907). Once the USA was at war she worked in Food Administration. Postwar battled for Equal Rights Amendment.

Evelyn, Princess Blücher Born Stapleton-Bretherton in Lancashire. In 1905 married Gebhardt Lebrecht, 4th Prince Blücher von Wahlstatt of Radun Silesia. Postwar they again lived in England, working for Anglo-German reconciliation. In 1931 he died in Bournemouth. In 1932 Evelyn edited a memoir of his illustrious family.

Norah Bomford Her poem 'Drafts' was originally published in *Poems of a Pantheist* in 1918. No other information.

Florence E. Booth No information.

Mary Borden (1886–1968) Born in Chicago. Daughter of millionaire William Borden, she was educated at home and Vassar. Met her first English husband in Lahore, in 1908. They had three daughters. A prewar suffragette, author and literary hostess in London, between 1914 and 18 she funded own hospital unit in France. *The Forbidden Zone* is based on this experience. She had an affair with Major-General Sir Edward Spears and married him 1918; one son; a stormy but enduring marriage. Lost her fortune in Wall Street crash; wrote some 20 books. In WW2 she raised French ambulance unit. Lived mainly in England and died in London.

Maria Botchkareva (1889– ?) Dreadful childhood. Married at thirteen to Afanasi Botchkarev. Ran away. Attempted suicide and to kill Afanasi (with an axe). Met Yakov. They lived together by civil agreement until he was arrested. She went with him to the frozen north, then lost touch. Wore men's clothes. Among the Russian women who enlisted in 1914. Went to the Front. Wounded. Captured by Germans; released when found to be female. After the women's 'Battalion of Death' collapsed, she escaped to the USA via Vladivostok. She became a temporary celebrity.

Vera Brittain (1893–1970) English provincial background. Ambitious, dedicated writer and feminist. Her fiancé, brother, close male friends all killed in the war. Deep friendship with the writer Winifred Holtby, who also died young. In 1925 married George Catlin, a 'semi-detached' equal-rights marriage. Partly due to her pacifism in the Second World War, her reputation was at a low ebb when she died, but *Testament of Youth* has since been re-acclaimed as a classic. Daughter Baroness Shirley Williams a prominent politician.

Charlotte Louise Mackay Brown, RRC (1890–1979) née Fitzgerald Dalton. Prewar active VAD. War years as a nurse in France. In 1946 married George Mackay Brown. Active local historian, lace maker, Women's British Legion, Women's Voluntary Service, Church Council, until her final illness. Born and died in Bedfordshire.

Muriel Dayrell-Browning (1879–1933) Escaped c. 1900 from English provincial life to go as a lady's companion to Smyrna. Then governess to the Kipling children. Sacked for being 'totally unsuitable' and 'torturing' Rudyard by listening so avidly to his stories. Proceeded to marry, bear two children, go out to Africa. Left her husband 1915, sent children to their grandmother, went on intelligence work. Daughter Vivien, who married Graham

Greene, says her mother was a remarkable woman born out of her time. She died after breaking a hip running for a bus.

Ada Calwell (1892–1987) Afrikaner born in Cape Colony. Married in July 1914 Dr Gault Calwell who had been MO on Robben Island caring for lepers, convicts and lunatics. After their adventures on SS *Galician* they settled in his native Ulster, in general practice in East Belfast. Two of their sons also doctors. Ada a keen tennis player and captain of the Irish Women's Bowling Team.

Miss E. Campbell After the Dardanelles went with a hospital ship to India. Stayed until 1919. Came to England and nursed in the Royal Air Force.

Carrie Chapman Catt (1859–1947) Teacher and journalist in Idaho. First husband died 1886; married George Catt, who died 1904. Became chairwoman National American Woman Suffrage Association, then president IWSA and in 1915 president of NAWSA. Brilliant organiser but criticised for expediency.

Michelle and Oleda Joure-Christides No information other than daughter and mother.

Mary Clarke No information.

Adela Stanton Coit Close colleague of Millicent Fawcett's. Treasurer of the IWSA.

Alice Connor née Kedge (1895–1994) The editor's mother-in-law. Born in London. Eldest of six surviving children. On a church outing to Margate decided it was her idea of heaven. Ran a boarding house there for fifty years. During the Second World War supervised a British Restaurant. Irish-born husband died comparatively young from First World War injuries.

Caroline Ethel Cooper (1871–1961) Born in Adelaide, Australia, well-established family. Travelled to Europe. Studied music in Leipzig. Stayed there throughout the war. Wrote regular letters to her sister. Later returned to Australia.

Lady Diana Cooper née Manners (1892–1986) Daughter of the 8th Duke of Rutland. Strong individualist and famed beauty. Nurse at Guy's Hospital, London. Lost most of her many men friends in 'the Dance of Death'. In 1919 married diplomat Duff Cooper (later Viscount Norwich). One son, John Julius Norwich. Postwar toured the world as star of Max Reinhardt's *The Miracle*.

Lady Courtney of Penwith (1847–1929) Catherine, always known as Kate, was the second of nine Potter daughters. Her father was a wealthy businessman, her mother a Liberal intellectual. She became a social worker in the East End of London and in 1883 married Liberal MP Leonard Courtney, a spokesman for women's suffrage. She was a friend of Millicent Fawcett and a staunch pacifist.

Celia Croft From Richmond, Yorkshire. A secretary at Buckingham Palace, she accompanied Queen Mary on a wartime visit to Scotland. Married C. G. Knollys. During the Second World War she worked in intelligence.

Eve Curie (b. 1904) Younger daughter of Pierre and Marie Curie, Nobel Prize winning discoverers of polodium and radium. Wrote a best-selling biography of her mother. Spent the Second World War in England working for de Gaulle and the Free French. In 1954 married Henri Labouisse, executive director of UNICEF. Travelled the world with him.

Mabel Potter Daggett (1871–1927) Born in Syracuse, New York, graduated BA Syracuse University, elected Phi Beta Kappa (for high intellectual achievement). In 1901 married John Daggett. Established herself as journalist with a vivid style and strong interest in social problems, particularly children's.

Margaret Damer Dawson (1875–1920) Upper-class background. Studied at the Royal Academy of Music. Prewar campaigned against white slavery and for animal rights. Ran an animal refuge at her home in Kent. Pioneer British policewoman. Dropped dead of heart attack.

Louise Delétang A Parisian seamstress who lived near the Place d'Italie and published her wartime journal. No other information.

Isak Dinesen (1885–1962) Danish by birth and upbringing but partly educated in England and France. Married Baron Bror Blixen Finecke 1914 in Kenya. Her best-known book *Out of Africa* published as Karen Blixen. Passionate affair with English aristocrat Denys Finch Hatton (whose cousin Lady Muriel Paget was co-director of the Anglo-Russian hospital in Petrograd). On Finch Hatton's tragic death and the failure of her Kenyan coffee farm, she returned to Denmark.

Catherine I. Dodd, MA No information but presumably a dietician.

Rheta Childe Dorr (1866–1948) Born in Omaha, Nebraska. Aged twelve heard Elizabeth Cady Stanton and Susan B. Anthony speak. Thereafter a strong feminist. In 1892 married John Pixley Dorr. Fought to establish herself as journalist and for a women's page in the New York *Evening Post*. Travelled extensively in

Europe. Helped Emmeline Pankhurst write *My Own Story*. In 1917–18 war correspondent for the New York *Evening Post*. Suffered a severe accident 1919, never fully recovered.

Marguerite Durand (1864–1936) Started working life as an actress; 1881–89 at Comédie Française. Entered political scene via husband Georges Laguerre. *Le Figaro* correspondent to feminist congress 1896. Founded feminist magazine *La Fronde* 1897. Keen driver. Tried to organise wartime group of women drivers. Left mass of archive material to the City of Paris. Feminist library named after her.

Tilla Durieux (1880–1971) Born Vienna. Stage name of Ottilie Godefroy, grande dame of the German theatre. Worked with Max Reinhardt and Erwin Piscator. As a committed anti-fascist, she left Germany in 1933 and did not return until 1952. Settled in West Berlin but was an honorary member of Deutsches Theater, East Berlin. Second marriage to publisher Paul Cassirer. Still acting in her ninetieth year.

Florence Farmborough (1887–1978) Went to Russia 1908 as a governess. Kept voluminous wartime diary – some 400,000 words. Returned to England 1918 but spent interwar years as a university lecturer in Spain. There throughout the Civil War. Back in England for WW2. Fellow of the Royal Geographical Society.

Dame Millicent Garrett Fawcett (1847–1929) Born into an early feminist network. In 1867 married a Cambridge professor, later Liberal politician, Henry Fawcett. He was blind and she acted as his 'eyes' until his death in 1884. Campaigned for Married Women's Property Act, then women's suffrage. Later criticised for being too genteel but battled for fifty years. Helped found Newnham College, Cambridge, of which her daughter Philippa was a brilliant graduate.

Elizabeth Fernside No information.

Richard Findlater (d. 1985) Literary editor and theatre critic. Edited *The Author* for many years. Published several books about the theatre.

Isabella O. Ford (d. 1924) Born into a Leeds Quaker family. Trade unionist. Secretary of Leeds Society of Working Women. Organised workers' concerts. Author of three novels.

Dame Katharine Furse, GBE, RRC (1875–1952) Daughter of the Victorian man of letters John Addington Symonds. In 1900 married the artist Charles Furse, who died 1904 as their second son was born. Supported by family and friends but also earned a living as a woodcarver. On inception of VAD 1909 she became co-commandant. Resigned 1917 in protest at confused administration. Appointed director of WRNS (both sons naval cadets). Postwar helped found World Association of Girl Scouts and Girl Guides.

Dr de Garis No information other than served with SWH.

Elizabeth Gore Wrote a biography of her aunt Dame Lilian Barker, who in 1916 was appointed 'Lady Superintendent' of the Woolwich Arsenal, which then employed less than 100 women. Within three months there were 22,000 women munition workers and by the end of the war some 97,000.

GYP (1849–1932) Nom de plume of Sybille Gabrielle Marie-Antoinette de Mirabeau, Comtesse de Janville, descendant of the French revolutionary Mirabeau. A prolific author – she published over 100 novels – beloved by generations of French girls for her tomboy heroines. A strong nationalist and anti-Semite.

Charlotte von Hadeln (1884–1959) Unclear how she came to edit *Deutsche Frauen Deutsche Treue* as according to her surviving family, who had never heard of the book, she was 'purely a housewife and a fierce monarchist, head of the Bund Königin Louise, patronised by Crown Princess Cecilie of Hohenzollern'. Her eldest son was killed in the Second World War.

Adela Hall (1894–c. 1985) Aunt of editor's friend. Interviewed shortly before her death. Still sprightly. Never married but had 'lots of jobs and lots of boyfriends'.

Cicely Hamilton (1872–1952) Born in London. Father an army officer. Educated at Malvern College and in Germany. Actress, playwright, author, feminist. *Diana of Dobson's* produced prewar by Lena Ashwell was a huge success. Later published many fiction and nonfiction books and campaigned for contraception and abortion rights.

Ida Husted Harper (1851–1931) American suffragist. Chairman California Suffrage Publicity Committee, then editorial chairman Leslie Suffrage Bureau, New York. Author of a three-volume biography of Susan B. Anthony.

Mrs M. Harrold née Britton (1897–1987) On leaving the Land Army she worked in sewing-machine shops. Became manageress of Singer's Manchester branch. Married and had two daughters. Later took up flower arranging, won many medals and was presented to the Queen Mother.

Sybil Harry No information.

Anne Haverty Born in Tipperary, graduate of Trinity College, Dublin. Worked as a journalist in London and Dublin, and now lives in the latter city. Her novel *One Day as a Tiger* won the Rooney Prize 1997 and was shortlisted for the Whitbread Award.

Katherine Hodges (1888–1982) Daughter of the actor and playwright Horace Hodges. On her return from Russia she went to France as an ambulance driver. Awarded the Russian Medal of St George and Order of St Stanislas, and the Croix de Guerre. Married the army officer Peter North, who became a well-known photographer. In the Second World War she drove ambulances through the London Blitz. Worked for the Red Cross until 1968. Retired to her native Sussex.

Gertrude Holland Alas, no information. Her handsomely bound diary, handwritten with attached cuttings and photographs, is fascinating. The rescued cat was named Hofstadt, Hofy for short, after the Belgian village in which Miss Holland nearly shot him. Ever enterprising, she asked a war photographer to take his picture. After this had been published in *Ladies Field*, postcards of a fluffy, well-fed Hofy sold in their thousands, proceeds to 'the flying field hospital'.

Catherine Baker Hooper (1889–1968) After working with the Smith College Relief Unit she became involved with the American Committee for Devastated France. Later she organised conducted tours to battlefields and cemeteries and set up her own travel agency. She lived in Montclair, New Jersey.

Isobel E. Emslie Hutton A doctor who served with SWH in Serbia, Salonika and Odessa. No other information.

Margaret Storm Jameson (1891–1986) Born in Whitby, Yorkshire. MA Leeds. Her brother was killed in the Royal Flying Corps. Her second marriage (1925) to First World War survivor Guy Chapman was 'deeply happy'. She published forty-five novels, innumerable articles and two splendid volumes of autobiography. An outspoken opponent of fascism, in 1939 she became the first woman president of the British section of PEN.

F. Tennyson Jesse (1889–1958) Great-niece of Alfred, Lord Tennyson. Journalist, novelist and playwright in collaboration with her husband H. M. Harwood. Later specialised in writing about murder trials. *A Pin to See the Peepshow* was her most successful novel and play.

Elizabeth 'Johnnie' Johnston (d. 1918) Born in Anstruther, Scotland, eldest of seven children. Deeply religious family. Prewar she worked in the local post office, trained as a telegraphist and learned to drive. In 1917 she went out to France as a WAAC driver and telegraphist. On Christmas morning 1918 she came off duty in Rouen and went to St Ouen church where she requested permission to climb up to the tower. How she came to fall is unknown. 'Johnnie' wanted to be a writer and the book published by Agnes Anderson consists mainly of her letters home. A charming personality bubbles through.

Josephine Kellett Published a memoir of Marguerite McArthur. This mainly consists of informative, entertaining letters. No other information.

Beatrice Sarah Kelsey (1887–1975) Educated at Coventry High School for Girls. She was a governess in England before going to Vienna in 1912. On return home she worked as a VAD and in military intelligence. In 1921 married Jean de Quidt, a Belgian civil servant. They lived in Brussels but in 1940 escaped to England, where they remained, her husband being appointed to the Belgian Embassy. They had one son.

A. E. (Archibald Edmund) Clark-Kennedy, MA, FRCP (1893–1985) First World War service in India, Mesopotamia and France. Physician to the London Hospital 1925–58, Dean of its Medical College 1937–53. Author of many medical books.

Ellen N. LaMotte *The Backwash of War*, an American's observations from a French hospital, had a curious history. Published in 1916, it was banned in England and France as 'damaging to morale'. The book sold well in the USA until 1917, when it was banned there too and not reprinted until 1934.

Alice Leavens (1882–1964) From Boston, Massachusetts. Worked as a kindergarten teacher. In 1920 married Davis B. Keniston, who became chief justice of Boston Municipal Court. One son.

Amy Lillington Among advance guard of women journalists. No other information.

Mrs D. B. G. Line née Dimmock Born in Bombay. Father in Indian medical service. Passed Responsons for Somerville College, Oxford, 1914 but unable to pay the fees. Did relief work for SSAFA (Soldiers, Sailors and Air Force Association) before going into intelligence. In 1917 married Captain James Line, who survived the war. Postwar lived in Cambridge.

410

Hilda Love Among advance guard of women journalists. No other information available.

Phyllis Lovell Came from Birkenhead. In 1914 she founded the Home Service Corps and started women police patrols on Merseyside. Throughout the war she edited the weekly *Home Service Corps Review* packed with comment and information.

K. E. Luard, RRC and Bar Professional nursing sister. Worked at No. 16 General Hospital before becoming sister-in-charge of Advanced Abdominal Station at Brandhoek. A devout Christian, she was involved with Women's Toc H Association.

Marguerite McArthur (1892–1919) Born in London but spent half her short life in Canada. Studied at Newnham College, Cambridge. Worked in intelligence before going to France, where she died in February 1919 from the Spanish flu which swept the world. Emerges from Kellett's memoir as a most attractive personality.

Mary Macarthur (1880–1921) Born in Glasgow. Exuded energy 'always at top speed'. Became secretary of the Women's Trade Union League 1903 and National Federation of Women Workers 1906. Her greatest achievement was the minimum-wage Trades Board Act (repealed by the Thatcher government). In 1911 married the Independent Labour MP Will Anderson. He died in 1919 in the flu epidemic, she, exhausted, two years later.

Barbara McLaren No information.

Eva Shaw McLaren née Inglis (1866–1945) Born in India, father senior civil servant. The family returned 1879 to Edinburgh, where she later founded a Working Men's Club in the Fountainbridge slums. In 1899 married the surgeon John Shaw McLaren. Splendid mother. Never batted an eyelid when her nine-year-old daughter said she'd invited her class (27 strong) to tea. Out to India again but home by 1914. Wartime fund raiser for sister Elsie's SWH. Postwar edited its history and raised money for Elsie Inglis Memorial Hospitals in Belgrade and Edinburgh (the latter taken over in 1947 by NHS and sold for a huge profit).

Sarah Macnaughtan (d. 1916) Prewar travelled all over the world. From 1898 onwards published a dozen novels. Also a talented musician and painter. Awarded Order of Leopold for services in Belgium. After her work there she went out to Armenia, where she collapsed. Somehow she managed to get back to England. Her wartime diaries are among the editor's favourites.

Mary R (1867–1953) Born in London at Kensington Palace, daughter of the Duke and Duchess of Teck. Engaged 1891 to the Duke of Clarence, who fortunately for her soon died. In 1893 married the Duke of York, who in 1910 ascended the throne as King George V. During the war the family name was changed from Saxe-Coburg-Gotha to Windsor. Both king and queen became a focus of patriotism. Her strong sense of duty and personal morality helped establish the image of the British royal family.

Shirley Millard A New Yorker determined to do her bit, she went to France with a Red Cross Relief Unit. On return home she married her childhood sweetheart.

Flora Murray, CBE, MD, B.SC, DPH Camb (1870–1923) Born in Dumfriesshire, Scotland. Father a naval commander. Graduated 1903 in medicine and surgery from Durham. Worked in hospitals in Dumfries and London. Became a GP in London and in 1911 founded a children's hospital. A suffragette like her close friend Louisa Garrett Anderson.

Asta Nielsen (1881–1972) Danish-born actress and film star who worked mostly in Germany. Best-known films *Hedda Gabler*, *Hamlet*, *Miss Julie*. In 1961 she published her autobiography *The Silent Muse*.

Anne O'Hagan Among advance guard of women journalists.

Maude Onions Served with 807 Unit WAAC signallers in France and wrote a good book about her experiences. No other information.

Emmeline Pankhurst née Goulden (1858–1928) Born in Manchester. In 1879 married the lawyer Richard Pankhurst. Campaigned for left-wing causes until his death in 1898. In 1903 she and daughter Christabel founded the WSPU, which coined the slogans 'Votes for Women' and 'Deeds not Words'. The WSPU moved 1906 from Manchester to London. Imprisonment, hunger-striking, forcible feeding, arson attacks followed. Her only son Harry, swamped by his remarkable mother and sisters, died young. She grew increasingly conservative but remains a major figure in the fight for women's rights.

Estelle Sylvia Pankhurst (1882–1960) Born in Manchester. Talented artist but devoted her life to Socialist and pacifist causes. Broke 1912 with mother and sister Christabel to found the WSPU East London Federation. In 1935 championed Emperor Haile Selassie after Abyssinia (Ethiopia) had been brutally invaded by

Mussolini. Ended her days under the Emperor's patronage in Addis Ababa.

Mrs. C. S. (Dorothy) Peel, OBE (1872–1934) Grew up in Monmouth, Wales. Journalist protégée of Arnold Bennett. Married her cousin Charles Peel. Combined career and motherhood. Appointed to the Ministry of Food 1917 for 'twelve nerve-racking months'. *How We Lived Then* is an invaluable social history. Published her autobiography *Life's Enchanted Cup* 1933.

Dr Marion Phillips (1881–1932) Socialist, trade unionist, public health campaigner. Secretary of the Women's Labour League, latterly the Labour Party's Chief Women's Officer. Sharp tongue. Much disliked by other Labour women, according to Beatrice Webb.

Frances Eleanor (Ellie) Rendel (d. 1942) Born into the interesting, affluent Rendel–Strachey network. Studied at Newnham College, Cambridge. Active in NUWSS, excellent public speaker, expected to enter politics. On her return from Russia in 1917 she went out to Serbia. Postwar qualified as doctor and became a GP in London.

S. Rhodes Author of a touching letter to Lieutenant, later Captain, Oscar Eckhard, who did survive the war. No other information.

Viscountess Rhondda (Margaret Haig Thomas) (d. 1958) Father Welsh coal owner, Liberal politician, first (and last) Viscount Rhondda. Brought up in Wales. Studied at Somerville College, Oxford. In 1908 married Sir Charles Mackworth but never used his name and divorced 1923. Excellent business woman. Founded the influential feminist magazine *Time and Tide* (with Cicely Hamilton and Rebecca West), 1928–1958 its proprietor and editor. Her autobiography *This Was My World* is unrevealing.

A. Maude Royden (d. 1956) Daughter of Sir Thomas Royden. Educated at Cheltenham Ladies' College and Lady Margaret Hall, Oxford. Dedicated Christian (Anglican). Brilliant speaker. First woman assistant preacher, City Temple, London. Lifelong campaigner for women's ordination. Curious *ménage à trois* with Rev G. W. Hudson Shaw and his mentally unstable wife. On her death in 1944 they married.

G. Ivy Sanders Among advance guard of women journalists.

Flora Sandes (1876–1956) A vicar's daughter. Always a tomboy. Originally went to Serbia as a nurse. Served with 1st Serbian Army

1915–18. Received their highest military award, Kara George Star. Married a Russian soldier. Postwar they lived in Paris, she a wardrobe mistress at the Folies Bergère. They went back to Belgrade and were there during the Second World War, in which her husband died. After the war she returned to England and spent her last years in Suffolk, where she grew up.

Louise Saumoneau (1875–1950) Genuine member of the working class. Arrested and imprisoned 1915 for distributing pacifist leaflets. Had little support from her comrades. Hardline Communist to the end of her life.

Marguerite de Witt Schlumberger (1843–1924) Granddaughter of the Protestant politician and author François Guizot. Moderate but dedicated suffragist. L'UFSF was founded 1909, she became its president 1913. Her opposition to wartime pacifism is understandable in that she had five sons and a son-in-law at the front.

Toni Sender (d. 1964) Born in the Rhineland into an orthodox Jewish family. From 1910 worked in Paris as a stenographer. Became a Socialist. Returned to Germany on the outbreak of war. Attended the Socialist Women's Congress. Back home distributed pacifist leaflets but continued to work for a metal firm. Left Germany after Hitler assumed power. Came to England, published her autobiography, but settled in the USA. Died in New York.

Baroness de T'Serclaes MM **(Elsie Knocker)** Born in Devonshire. Her parents died when she was a baby, and she was adopted by a public-school teacher and his wife. In 1906 she escaped into unhappy Knocker marriage, one child. Divorced. Trained as a nurse and became an enthusiastic motorcyclist. In 1916 married a Belgian, Baron de T'Serclaes (d. 1919). On her return to England 1918 she joined the WRAF. Enlisted in the WAAF in the Second World War and was soon put in charge of a famous Radar Group. Resigned 1942 when her only son was killed on a bombing mission.

Edith Shackleton Among advance guard of women journalists.

Evelyn Sharp (b. 1869) A Londoner, staunch feminist, noted journalist. Twice imprisoned for suffrage activities. 1915–23 staff writer on the Labour paper the *Daily Herald*. Had a long relationship with the journalist and women's suffrage campaigner Henry Nevinson. On the death of his wife in 1933 they married.

Anna Howard Shaw (1847–1919) Despite family opposition, qualified first as a Doctor of Divinity, then of Medicine. Ordained

1880 by the Methodist Church. Became a leading American suffragist. President of NAWSA 1904–15. Superb speaker but poor administrator. Stepped down for Carrie Chapman Catt.

Mary Sheepshanks (1872–1958) Born in Liverpool, eldest of seventeen children. Father a vicar, later Bishop of Norwich. Not a happy family. Principal 1897–1913 Morley College for Working Men and Women (started at the Old Vic by Lilian Baylis's aunt Emma Cons). Editor of *Jus Suffragii*. Dedicated pacifist. Postwar secretary of Women's International League. Later forgotten. Virtually blind and immobile, stoically committed suicide.

May Sinclair (1870–1946) Joined Women's Freedom League, WSPU breakaway group. Journalist, poet, author of twenty-four novels, expert on the Brontës. Rebecca West considered her *Journal of Impressions in Belgium* (1915), in which she praised her comrades but confessed to having been personally unable to cope, 'a gallant humiliated book'.

Helen Zenna Smith (1896–1985) pen name of Evadne Price. Born at sea – Indian Ocean. Actress, playwright, screenwriter, journalist, novelist, astrologer. Stage debut 1906 in *Peter Pan*, Sydney, Australia. Came to England 1914. During the war she worked on munitions and at the Air Ministry. Gave up acting 1923 and became a newspaper columnist. In the Second World War she was a feature writer for the *Daily Sketch*. Twice married. Wrote scores of novels, and plays with her second husband Ken Attiwell.

Dame Freya Stark (1893–1993) Childhood divided between England and Italy. Postwar became famed Middle Eastern traveller and writer. Retired to Italy.

Muriel St Clair Stobart (d. 1954) Father Sir Samuel Boulton. Grew up in Hertfordshire. An unhappy marriage to St Clair Stobart produced two sons. Remarried the barrister John Stobart Greenhalgh. Wrote plays and short stories. Founded the Women's Sick and Wounded Corps. Having ridden for 800 miles at the head of her column during the terrible Serbian retreat, wearing a floppy-brimmed hat that was a gift to war artists, she became temporarily famous as 'the lady on the Black Horse'. On her return home, weighed down with Serbian medals, she went on a lecture tour of Canada and the USA. A strong Christian and spiritualist.

Baroness Mary Stocks (1891–1975) Member of Rendel–Strachey clan. Ellie Rendel was her cousin. Educated at St Paul's Girls'

School and the London School of Economics. In 1913 married fellow academic J. L. Stocks. Lecturer at Kings College, London; LSE; Manchester University. Principal of Westfield College, London, 1939–51. Was created a life peeress 1966.

Gilbert Stone Edited *Women War Workers*. Postwar wrote histories of England and Wales.

Ray Strachey (1887–1940) Daughter of Mary Pearsall Smith and B. F. C. Costelloe. Studied at Newnham College, Cambridge and Bryn Mawr, USA. Married Lytton Strachey's brother Oliver. Combined career and motherhood. NUWSS Hon. Parliamentary Secretary and editor of *Common Cause*. Stood as an independent parliamentary candidate 1918, 1922 and 1923 but failed to be elected. Wrote a biography of Millicent Fawcett and an excellent account of the British women's movement, *The Cause*. Continued to campaign for women's rights.

Marie Stritt (1855–1928) Lived in Dresden and was President of Frauenstimmrechtsbund, the German suffrage society affiliated to the IWSA. Steered a middle course between Germany's main decorous society the Bund Deutscher Frauenvereine and the ultra feminist splinter groups. Known in England as 'the Mrs Fawcett of Germany'.

Helena Swanwick, MA, née **Sickert** (1864–1939) The most cosmopolitan of British suffragists. Born in Munich, Danish father, English mother. The painter Walter Sickert was her brother. Studied at Girton College, Cambridge. Married 1888 F. T. Swanwick, a lecturer at Manchester University. First editor of *Common Cause*. Dedicated pacifist. First president of the Women's International League, British section. Delegate to the League of Nations. Her autobiography *I Have Been Young* is most interesting. Committed suicide shortly after the Second World War broke out.

Olive May Taylor (1898–1988) Born into rural poverty in Lincolnshire wolds. Clever girl, managed to stay at school until fourteen. Then into service, munitions, the WAAC and postwar to London. Married early 1930s, two boys, but husband soon disappeared. She had a hard life but later enjoyed visits to Africa where a son was working, then remarried and returned to Lincolnshire. Loved writing. Chronicled her early rural life and also collected and performed Victorian and Edwardian monologues.

Blanche Thirieau (1880–1956) Grandmother of the editor's friend. Her husband survived the war. When first encountered in 1947 she was still running the family mattress and beds business. Utterly self-confident and the epitome of sang-froid. After the factory caught fire in 1930s, for example, she left *les pompiers* to do their job and went to see a Charlie Chaplin film.

Violet Thurston Trained at the London Hospital. To Belgium with the St John Ambulance Brigade. There when Brussels fell. Expelled by the Germans and crossed into Denmark. Heard that the Russians needed nurses and went out to Poland. On her return home, was appointed matron of a Belgium military hospital, then of the New Zealand General Hospital.

Dame Helen Gwynne-Vaughan, GBE, CBE (1879–1967) Educated at Cheltenham Ladies' College and King's College, London. 1909–1917 head of Botany Department, Birkbeck College – expert on fungi. Married 1911 Professor D. T. Gwynne Vaughan (d. 1915). First Controller WAAC 1917–18. Commandant WRAF 1918–19. Postwar professor of botany, London University. 1939–41 director of the Auxiliary Territorial Service (ATS), the Second World War successor to WAAC.

Maria Vérone (1874–1938) Born in Paris. Graduated 1907 as fifth female *avocat* (women were still not allowed to practise law in UK). First Frenchwoman to plead at the assizes. Activist Ligue Française du Droit des Femmes. Campaigned for children's rights. Twice married. Successful postwar career. Chevalier of the Legion of Honour 1936.

E. W. Walters No information.

Beatrice Webb (1858–1943) Eighth of nine Potter daughters, sister of Kate Courtney. Diary keeper from her teens. Trained herself as a social scientist and researcher. 'Passionate infatuation' with the politician Joseph Chamberlain but in 1892 married Sydney Webb. Founder members of the Fabian Society and the London School of Economics, they were pivotal figures in British left-wing political and intellectual life for fifty years. Beatrice chose not to have children.

Miss G. M. West Daughter of a vicar in Selsey, Gloucestershire. Worked as VAD cook before starting a canteen in an aircraft factory and enrolling as a munitions policewoman. Diaries most interesting. No other information.

Dame Rebecca West (1892–1983) Born Cicely Fairfield. Educated Edinburgh. Pen name taken from the strong-willed character in Ibsen's *Rosmersholm*. Early success as a journalist. Brilliant polemicist, staunch suffragist and feminist. Her affair with H. G. Wells produced a son b. 1914. In 1930 she married a banker, Henry Maxwell Andrews. Wrote novels and nonfiction and covered the Nuremberg War Trials. In 1959 created a Dame Commander of the British Empire.

Barbara Wootton, Baroness Wootton of Abinger (1897–1988) Born in Cambridge into an academic background. Educated at Perse High School for Girls and Girton College, Cambridge. Postwar economics lecturer at Girton, research officer at Trades Union Council, principal of Morley College and 1927–44 at London University. Well-known broadcaster from late 1920s and became a BBC governor. Among first life peers 1958. Deputy speaker of the House of Lords.

Miss M. C. Youngs In domestic service before joining LNER as a stewardess on the North Sea Ferries. Spent the rest of the war as a railway ticket collector in Ipswich, where she lived all her life. Married a ticket inspector, one daughter b. 1919.

No information on the contributors to *Women War Workers* edited by Gilbert Stone, nor *Deutsche Frauen Deutsche Treue* edited by Charlotte von Hadeln. The editor will be pleased to hear from any reader who knows of contributors she has been unable to trace.

WAVE ME GOODBYE

Anne Boston

**'Each story in *Wave me Goodbye* is a relic of the
Second World War'** – *Sunday Times*

'Wish me Luck as you Wave me Goodbye' went the
jaunty wartime song and that was what the brave-faced
women did as they bid their men fond farewell. This
collection of short stories written by women when war was
a way of life includes some of the finest writers of that
generation such as Rosamond Lehmann, Elizabeth Bowen,
Doris Lessing, Rose Macaulay, Stevie Smith and Elizabeth
Taylor. War had traditionally been seen as a masculine
occupation but these stories show how women were equal
if different participants. They reveal hardship, isolation, and
deprivation suffered by most women who also felt left
behind as their men moved on. By turn comical, stoical,
compassionate, angry and subversive these intensely
individual voices bring a human dimension to the
momentous events that reverberated around them and each
opens a window on to a hidden landscape of war.

MILLIONS LIKE US
British Women's Fiction of the Second World War

Jenny Hartley

'Expert guidance from a continuously alert commentator' – *TLS*

The Second World War saw women fully involved and experiencing work outside the home; the temporary nature of their new role was echoed in the fiction of the era, where the heroine's work remained a prelude to her return to domesticity. Their relative freedom is also reflected in wartime fiction that saw women fulfil a range of roles at one time – mother, worker, home-maker. From the blitz to secret surveillance, from film and radio to letter-writing, women wrote about it all and here Jenny Hartley offers a fascinating and enlightening criticism, discussing a range of authors including: Elizabeth Bowen, Olivia Manning, Rosamond Lehmann, Rose Macaulay and Stevie Smith.

Now you can order superb titles directly from Virago

☐ Wave Me Goodbye	Anne Boston	£7.99
☐ Millions Like Us	Jenny Hartley	£14.99
☐ Bombers and Mash	Raynes Minns	£10.99
☐ Blood Rites	Barbara Ehrenreich	£9.99
☐ The Things we do to Make it Home	Beverly Gologorsky	£9.99

Please allow for postage and packing: **Free UK delivery**.
Europe; add 25% of retail price; Rest of World; 45% of retail price.

To order any of the above or any other Virago titles, please call our credit card orderline or fill in this coupon and send/fax it to:

Virago, 250 Western Avenue, London, W3 6XZ, UK.
Fax 0181 324 5678   Telephone 0181 324 5516

☐ I enclose a UK bank cheque made payable to Virago for £ ....

☐ Please charge £.............. to my Access, Visa, Delta, Switch Card No.

☐☐☐☐☐☐☐☐☐☐☐☐☐☐☐☐☐☐☐

Expiry Date ☐☐☐☐   Switch Issue No.   ☐☐

NAME (Block letters please) ....

ADDRESS ....

....

....

Postcode ....Telephone ....

Signature ....